Kitaab At-Tawheed
"The Book of Tawheed"

Shaikh Imam Muhammad Abdul-Wahhaab

Translated by Sameh Strauch

Foreword & On Tawheed

All praise be to Allah (swt) `The Exalted, the *Rabb* of the worlds, and our Prophet, Muhammad (saas ) `Blessings and Peace be upon him', and upon all his family and companions.

When I embraced Islam in 1983, by the grace of Allah (swt), one of the first books which I was given to read was a translation of *Kitaab At-Tawheed* by the renowned scholar, Muhammad Ibn `Abdil Wahhaab: I understood very little of it and was driven to the conclusion that this was because I was new to Islam and therefore lacked knowledge. It was only later, when I was fortunate enough to study the book, *Taiseer Al-'Azeez Al-Hameed* in Arabic, that I realized that not even Arabic speakers try to understand *Kitaab At-Tawheed* without the benefit of an explanation.

It has therefore been in my mind for some time to try to provide English-speakers with an explanation of this great work, but unfortunately, other projects diverted me until now.

In compiling this explanation, I have relied mainly on *Al-Jadeed Fee Sharh Kitaab At-Tawheed* by Shaikh Muhammad Al-Qar'aawi, *Tafseer Ibn Katheer* and a number of books of Hadith.

I ask Allah (swt) that He accept this humble effort from me and make it of benefit to my brothers and sisters in Islam.

> " *Our Rabb! Punish us not if we forget or fall into error, our Rabb! Lay not on us a burden like that which You laid on those before us; our Rabb! Put not on us a burden greater than we have strength to bear. Pardon us and grant us forgiveness. Have mercy on us. You are our Protector; and give us victory over the disbelieving people" (Qur'an 2:286)*

On Tawheed

Allah (swt), says:

> " *And I created not the jinn and mankind except that they should worship me. I seek not any provision from them, nor do I ask that they should feed Me. Verily, Allah is the All-provider, Owner of Power - Most Strong"* (Qur'an 51:56)

Allah (swt), informs us that it is He (swt) Who created the jinn and mankind, and that the wisdom behind that creation was that they worship Him (swt), Alone and reject the worship of any other, and that He (swt) did not create them for any benefit for Himself, but in order that they should worship Him (swt); and He (swt) has undertaken to provide sustenance for them, and He (swt) is the Most Truthful in keeping His (swt) Promises and Able to fulfill them, for He (swt) is Strong.

Benefits Derived from This Verse

1. That the wisdom behind Allah's creation of the jinn and mankind is that they worship Him Alone.

2. Confirmation of the presence of the jinn.

3. Allah's complete independence from His creation.

4. That the source of all sustenance is Allah, but the slave is commanded to do all in his power to attain his needs.

5. Confirmation of two of Allah's names: *Ar-Razzaaq* (the All-provider), *Al-Mateen* (Owner of Power).

Relevance of This Verse to the Subject of *Tawheed*

That these Qur'anic verses show the wisdom behind the creation of the jinn and mankind is worship of Allah (swt), Alone and the rejection of all objects of worship besides Him.

..ooOOoo..

Allah (swt), says:

> " *And verily, We have sent among every community a Messenger [proclaiming]: "Worship Allah [Alone] and avoid the Taaghoot .[1] Then of them were some whom Allah guided, and of them were some upon whom the straying was justified. So travel through the land and see what was the end of those who denied [the truth]"* (Qur'an 16:36)

Allah (swt), informs us in these Qur'anic verses that He has sent to every community of mankind a Messenger (saas), who conveyed to them the Message and ordered them to believe in only One God – Allah (swt) and to reject all those false gods besides Him (swt). And the people who heard from these Messengers (saas) are divided into two groups: The first, those whom Allah (swt) guided to goodness and who responded positively to the guidance of the Messenger (saas) and abstained from all that was forbidden to them; the second group were forbidden from success and rejected the truth, and therefore they were losers, both in this world and the Hereafter. And whoever travels throughout the earth, seeking to learn from it, will see the evidence of Allah's Retribution upon some of those who stubbornly rejected the Guidance of Allah (swt) and His Messengers (saas), such as `Aad, Thamood [2] and Fir'aoun.[3]

Benefits Derived From This Verse

1. Evidence that mankind has not been neglected and left without guidance.

2. The universality of the Message to all nations, and the fact that the Message brought by each new Messenger abrogated that of the previous Messenger.

3. That the mission of the Messengers was to call the people to the worship of Allah and to reject all false deities.

4. That the Guidance of Success is through Allah, Alone.

5. That the fact that Allah has ordained something for a person does not necessitate His liking for it.

6. The desirability of travelling througout the earth, with the intention of taking heed of the

example of the communities of old, whom Allah has destroyed because of their disbelief.

Relevance of This Verse to the Subject of *Tawheed*

That these Qur'anic verses prove that worship of Allah (swt) is of no benefit if the worship of others besides Him is not rejected.

..ooOOoo..

Allah (swt), says:

> " *And your Rabb has decreed that you worship none but Him, and that you be dutiful to your parents. If one of them or both of them attain old age in your life, say not to them a word of disrespect [uff!], nor shout at them, but address them in terms of honour. And lower unto them the wing of submission and humility through mercy, and say: "My Rabb! Bestow on them Your Mercy as they did bring me up when I was a child.""* (Qur'an 17:23-24)

Allah (swt), commands all those obligated to obey Him to worship Him, Alone and to observe filial piety and devotion; and He affirms the right of parents upon their offspring immediately after mentioning His right upon His slaves. Then He describes some of the types of filial piety, especially when they become frail and elderly, such as not displaying annoyance with them and not raising one's voice or scolding them, speaking to them in tones of gentleness and kindness and supplicating Allah (swt) on their behalf - both while they are alive and after their death.

Benefits Derived from These Verses

1. The obligation of worshipping Allah (swt) Alone.

2. The obligation upon every Muslim of filial piety and devotion towards both his parents.

3. The communal responsibility of the whole Muslim society to ensure the rights of parents upon their offspring.

Relevance of These Verses to the Subject of *Tawheed*

That these Qur'anic verses prove the obligation of worshipping Allah (swt), Alone, without partners.

..ooOOoo..

Allah (swt), says:

> " *Worship Allah and join none with Him in worship, and do good to parents, kinfolk, orphans, the poor, the neighbour who is near of kin, the neighbour who is a stranger, the companion by your side, the wayfarer and those [slaves] whom your right hands possess. Verily, Allah does not love those who are proud and boastful"* (Qur'an 4:36)

Sincerity is the foundation upon which true religion is built and Allah (swt) has commenced this *Surah* by commanding sincerity in worship and rejection of all false deities and He has followed this up by mentioning the obligation of filial piety because they (our parents) are the means by which we are brought into the world; and He (swt) has not neglected the rights of the kinfolk for they are the most deserving of his (the Muslim's) benevolence and kindness. And in order that the rest of his brothers and sisters in Islam be not downhearted, Allah (swt) has enjoined upon him kindness to the orphans and poor, whether close relatives or not. Then Allah (swt) has made clear the rights of those close to him in this life, mentioning first the neighbour who has Islamic rights and familial rights over the Muslim, then the nearby resident who has rights of a neighbour only - and he is the *zimmi* .[4] Then Allah (swt) mentions the rights of the close relatives such as the wife, the travelling companion etc. And Islam has encouraged the Muslim to travel in the land with the intention of doing business and of taking heed of the punishment meted out to former peoples, and because of this Allah (swt) has obliged the Muslim to help the traveller who is in need of it - whether it be material or otherwise. He (swt), also affirms the obligation of fairness and justice in dealing with other Muslims; but Islam has not forgotten the slaves: In fact, Allah (swt) requires us to give them all their rights, to treat them with gentleness and mercy and to recognize their human rights. And because these deeds are righteous deeds, they bring about a fear of Allah (swt), and prevent the Muslim from becoming proud and self-absorbed because these two attributes would cause the reward of the deeds to be lost.

Benefits Derived From This Verse

1. The obligation of worshipping Allah (swt), Alone.

2. The obligation of filial piety and obedience - so long as it does not entail disobedience to Allah (swt) and His Prophet (saas) nor harm the one so ordered, for Allah's Messenger said: "Do not harm others nor reciprocate (when harm is done to you)." [5]

3. The legal obligation of maintaining close family ties according to the closeness of the relationship.

4. The duty of treating well the orphans in one's care, bringing them up and investing their wealth.

5. The virtue of kindness to the poor and needy - and the varieties of kindness are numerous.

6. The obligation of giving the neighbour his rights.

7. The exhortation to help all one's companions who request assistance, whether travelling companions, or resident.

8. The duty to help the lost wayfarer.

9. The obligation of kindness to the slaves.

10. The forbiddance of pride and vanity.

11. Affirmation of Allah's attribute of Love.

Relevance of This Verse to the Subject of *Tawheed*

That these verses prove the obligation of sincerity and purity of worship for Allah (swt) Alone, and the rejection of all other objects of worship.

Note:- The neighbour falls into three categories:

1. The first has three rights: (i) The right of a Muslim upon his brother, (ii) The right of kinship, (iii) the right of a neighbouring resident.

2. The second has two rights: (i) The right of a Muslim upon his brother, (ii) The right of a neighbouring resident.

3. The right of a neighbouring resident only - and he is the *zimmi*.

..ooOOoo..

Allah (swt), says:

" *Say [oh, Muhammad!]: "Come, I will recite what your Rabb has prohibited for you: Join not anything in worship with him; be good and dutiful to your parents; kill not your children because of poverty - We provide sustenance for you and for them; come not near to shameful sin [adultery, fornication etc.], whether committed openly or in secret, and kill not anyone whom Allah has forbidden except for a just cause [in accordance with Islamic Law]. This has He commanded you that you may understand"* (Qur'an 6:151)

Allah (swt), orders His Prophet Muhammad (saas) to call the people to come forth and listen to the Commands of Allah (swt), concerning what has been prohibited for them; and because it is the idolator who most often opposes all good deeds, Allah (swt) has begun by warning them to abstain from associating partners with Him, then He (swt) has mentioned many of the evil deeds which they are wanted to commit and forbade them from doing so. He (swt), orders them to be kind and dutiful to their parents and forbids them from killing their offspring, for such acts are evil and result in the cutting of the family tree - and He has mentioned poverty here because the fear of poverty was the most common reason for the killing of children in the days of ignorance. And the extra-judicial killing of any person is a great sin, whatever the reason. And because fear of poverty was the most common reason for the killing of one's young, Allah (swt) has undertaken the responsibility of sustaining them and their children; then He (swt), has prohibited all acts of disobedience - both open and secret. And because unlawful killing causes many problems in society, such as breakdown of law and order, social unrest, revenge killing, vigilantism, etc., Allah (swt) has laid great stress upon the prohibition of unlawful killing, by His saying: " *This has He commanded"* - that His slaves may understand and act in accordance with it.

Benefits Derived From This Verse

1. That *Shirk* [6] is the greatest of sins and that no other deed will be accepted by Allah (swt) if there is any association of partners involved in it; and because of its importance, Allah (swt) has mentioned it first.

2. The obligation of filial piety.

3. The prohibition of killing one's children - and this includes abortion if carried out after forty days from the start of the pregnancy. [7]

4. That Allah (swt) has undertaken the responsibility of providing for all mankind.

5. Attempting to prevent pregnancy due to fear of poverty is an act from the days of ignorance.

6. The forbiddance of committing shameful sins, such as adultery and fornication and all that leads up to them (flirting, dating, kissing, caressing etc.)

7. The prohibition of killing any person has been forbidden by Allah (swt), except by judicial means.

8. Allah (swt) has not defined here what is meant by judical means, but the Prophet (saas) has mentioned something about it in an authentic Hadith, concerning adultery after chastity, disbelief after belief and the taking of a life for a life.[8]

The Relevance of This Verse to the Subject of *Tawheed*

That the verse warns against *Shirk* in any shape or form.

..ooOOoo..

It is reported on the authority of Mu`aaz Ibn Jabal (ra ) `May Allah be pleased him', that he said: "I was riding behind the Prophet (saas) on a donkey when he said to me: "Oh, Mu`aaz! Do you know what is the right of Allah (swt) upon His slaves and what is the right of the slaves upon Allah (swt)?" I said: "Allah (swt) and His Messenger (saas) know best." He (saas) said: "The right of Allah (swt) upon His slaves is that they worship Him and do not associate anything with Him; and the right of the slaves upon Allah (swt) is that those who do not associate anything with Him will not be punished." I said: "Oh, Messenger of Allah (saas)! Shall I not inform the people (of this)?" He (saas) said: "Do not inform them, in case they rely upon it." (Narrated by Bukhari and Muslim)

Mu`aaz Ibn Jabal (ra ) informs us that one day he was riding behind the Prophet (saas ) on a donkey, and he (saas ) wished to favour him with the answers to certain important questions: In order to do this, he (saas ) chose to ask Mu`aaz some rhetorical questions to arouse his curiosity. Mu`aaz did not venture an opinion on a matter of which he had no knowledge, and so he replied that Allah (swt) and His Messenger (saas) know best. So the Prophet (saas) explained to him two important Truths: The obligation which Allah (swt) has placed upon His slaves, and the Bounty and Grace which He has made incumbent upon Himself. And because Mu`aaz cared so much about the welfare and happiness of the Muslims, he asked the Prophet's permission to inform them of this good news, but the Prophet (saas) refused his request for he feared that the Muslims might depend upon this promise and stop competing with each other in the performance of good deeds which wipe out their bad deeds and elevate them in status. However, eventually, Mu`aaz informed them of this, fearful of concealing anything of the Guidance from them although the reason for the Prophet's warning his people against depending upon these words is clear.

Benefits Derived From This Hadith

1. The legitimacy of riding behind another, if it does not overtax the riding beast.

2. The humility of the Prophet (saas) in sharing his donkey with another.

3. That the sweat of the donkey is not impure.

4. The virtue of Mu`aaz Ibn Jabal (ra).

5. That asking rhetorical questions is an Islamic way of teaching.

6. The forbiddance of a person venturing to discuss matters about which he has no knowledge.

7. That the first obligation of the slave towards Allah (swt) is to worship Him Alone.

8. That the one who dies believing and practising *Tawheed* is saved from the torment of the Hell-fire - so long as he does not commit any of the major sins which would cause him to be punished in the Fire.

9. Although it is mentioned in an authentic Hadith that the Prophet (saas) said: "Whoever concealed knowledge, Allah (swt) will make him wear a bridle of fire on the Day of Resurrection,"[9] there is no contradiction here, because the forbiddance of concealing knowledge in the above Hadith is general, while the first Hadith contains an exception to that forbiddance in special circumstances: For it permits one to conceal knowledge if there is a fear that revealing it will cause disorder or strife in the Muslim community.

Relevance of This Hadith to the Subject of *Tawheed*

That the Hadith proves that the right of Allah (swt) upon His slaves is that they worship Him, and do not associate any partners with Him.

The Virtue of *Tawheed* and What Sins It Removes

Allah (swt), says:

> " *It is those who believe and do not adulterate their faith [in Allah's Oneness] with zulm [wrongdoing, i.e. associating partners with Him], for them [only] is there safety and they are rightly-guided"* (Qur'an 6:82)

Allah (swt), informs us that whoever practised *Tawheed*, without confusing their faith with *Shirk*, verily, Allah (swt) has promised him safety from the Fire in the Hereafter, and He will guide him to the Straight Path in this life.

Benefits Derived From This Verse

1. That faith, when adulterated by *Shirk* has no value.

2. *Shirk* is referred to as *zulm* by Allah.

3. That whosoever does not confuse his belief with *Shirk* is promised safety from punishment in the Hereafter.

Relevance of This Verse to the Subject of *Tawheed*

That the verse proves that whoever dies practising *Tawheed*, having turned to Allah (swt) in repentance from any major sins he may have committed, will be saved from any punishment in the Fire; and whoever dies practising *Tawheed*, having committed major sins without having repented, will be saved from eternal damnation in the Fire (although he may be first punished therein, or forgiven as Allah (swt) Wills).

..ooOOoo..

It is reported on the authority of `Ubadah Ibn As-Saamit (ra) that he said: "Allah's Messenger (saas) said:

"Whoever testified that none is worthy of worship except Allah (ra), Alone, without partners, and that Muhammad is His slave and Messenger (saas) and that Eisa (as) is His slave and Messenger, and His Word which was bestowed upon Maryam, and a Spirit (created) from Him, and that Paradise and Hell are realities, Allah (swt) will admit him to Paradise, whatever his deeds might be." (Narrated by Bukhari)

This Hadith tells us that whoever pronounced the *shahadah*, [10] understanding its meaning and acting in accordance with it in his worship, affirming his belief in the status of Muhammad (saas) as Allah's slave and Messenger and likewise believing in Eisa's status as slave and Messenger of Allah (swt) and that he was created by Allah's Word: "Be!" from Maryam (may Allah's peace be upon both of them) and that He absolved her from the charges levelled against her by the iniquitous Jews, affirmed his belief in Paradise for the Believers and Hell for the disbelievers, and he who dying in this state of belief will enter Paradise, in spite of his deeds.

Benefits Derived From This Hadith

1. That the Muslim *shahadah* or testimony is the essence of the religion.

2. That the *shahadah* is not valid except from one who understands its meaning and acts accordingly.

3. The mentioning together of the Prophet's status as slave and Messenger is a refutation of those who make exaggerated claims for Him (saas).[11]

4. Affirmation of the status of Eisa (as) as Allah's slave and Messenger; and this is a rebuttal of the claims of godhood made for him by the Christians.

5. Affirmation of Allah's Attribute of speech.

6. That Eisa (as) was created from Maryam by His Word: "Be!" without a father; and this is a refutation of the claims of the Jews, who accused Maryam of the sin of fornication.

7. Affirmation of the resurrection of mankind on the Day of Judgement.

8. Confirmation of the existence of Paradise and Hell.

9. That the sinning Muslims will not dwell eternally in the Hell-fire.

Relevance of This Hadith to the Subject of *Tawheed*

That the Hadith proves that whoever dies, practising *Tawheed* will enter Paradise, whatever his deeds may have been.

..ooOOoo..

`Itban (ra) reported that the Prophet (saas) said:

> *"Indeed, Allah (swt) has forbidden from Hell the person who testifies that none is worthy of worship except Allah (swt), seeking nothing by it but Allah's Countenance."* (Narrated by Bukhari and Muslim)

This Hadith informs us that Allah (swt), will save from the punishment of the Hell-fire all those who confirm His Oneness and act in accordance with that, intending nothing thereby except to get close to Allah (swt), without *riyaa'* [12] and without *sum'ah*. [13]

Benefits Derived From This Hadith

1. That none who sincerely believe in the Oneness of Allah (swt) will enter the Hell-fire.

2. That words and deeds are of no value without the intention of getting closer to Allah (swt).

3. Confirmation of Allah's Attribute of a Face.

Relevance of This Hadith to the Subject of *Tawheed*

That the Hadith proves that whoever died, believing sincerely in the Oneness of Allah (swt) will be saved from the Hell-fire.

..ooOOoo..

It is reported on the authority of Abu Sa'eed Al-Khudri (ra) from the Messenger of Allah (saas) that he said: "Moosa said: "Oh, *Rabb*! Teach me something by which I may remember You and supplicate You." Allah (swt) Said: "Say, oh, Moosa: "*Laa ilaaha illAllah*." [14] Moosa Said: "Oh, *Rabb*! All of Your slaves say that." Allah (swt) said: "Oh, Moosa! Even were the seven heavens and all that they contain other than Me [15] and the seven earths as well all put in one side of a scale and *Laa ilaaha illAllah* put in the other, the latter would outweigh them." [16]

Our Prophet (saas) informs us that Allah's Messenger, Moosa (as) requested Allah (swt) to teach him a special act of worship by which he might worship Allah (swt) and praise Him and get closer to Him; and so Allah (swt) taught him the words of sincerity, which are: *Laa ilaahah illAllah*. But Moosa (as) asked Allah (swt) to teach him something else, because the *shahadah* was well-known to all the people, at which Allah (swt) told him that were this *shahadah*, to be weighed against the seven heavens and the seventh earths and all that is in them, it would outweigh them, for it is the essence of every religion and the foundation of every community.

Benefits Derived From This Hadith

1. That it is permissible to ask Allah (swt) for something specially for oneself.

2. That the Messengers (saas) know not except what Allah (swt) Inform them.

3. Confirmation of Allah's Attribute of Speech.

4. Evidence of the fact that the heavens contain inhabitants.

5. Proof that the seven earths are, like the seven heavens, inhabited.

6. Evidence of the difference between some deeds and others.

7. That the Hadith clearly demonstrates the greatness and virtue of *Laa ilaaha illAllah.*

Relevance of This Hadith to the Subject of *Tawheed*

That the Hadith proves that the words of *Tawheed*: *Laa ilaaha illAllah* are the best *zikr* and the weightiest in value.

..ooOOoo..

It is reported that Anas (ra) said: "I heard Allah's Messenger (saas) say: "Allah (swt), Said: "Oh, son of Adam (as)! Were you to come to Me with the world full of sins, and meet Me without associating any partner with me, I would come to you with a similar amount of forgiveness."[17]

Allah (swt), informs us in this Hadith *Qudsi*[18] that whoever dies, sincerely believing in the Oneness of Allah (swt), having rejected all manner of *Shirk*, Allah (swt) will replace all his bad deeds with good, even were his sins to fill the earth or to almost fill it.

Benefits Derived From This Hadith

1. Confirmation of Allah's Attribute of Speech.

2. Proof of the vastness of Allah's Generosity and Mercy.

3. That to die in a state of belief in the Oneness of Allah (swt) is a condition of obtaining Allah's Forgiveness; and this matter necessitates explanation:

a. Whoever died upon *Shirk Akbar,*[19] will dwell eternally in the Hell-fire.

b. Whoever died, rejecting both *Shirk Akbar* and *Shirk Asghar,*[20] will dwell eternally in Paradise.

c. Whoever died without committing *Shirk Akbar*, but was guilty of a small amount of *Shirk Asghar*, if his good deeds outweigh his sins, will enter Paradise.

d. Whoever died without committing *Shirk Akbar*, but was guilty of a small amount of *Shirk Asghar*, if his sins outweigh his good deeds, will enter the Fire, but will not remain therein forever.

Relevance of This Hadith to the Subject of *Tawheed*

That the Hadith proves that whoever died, without being guilty of any kind of *Shirk*, will enter Paradise, even if his sins were great enough to fill the earth.

Footnotes

1. Taaghoot: All that is worshipped or obeyed in disobedience to Allah (swt) and His Messenger (saas). There are many kinds of Taaghoot: Their leader is Iblees - Allah's curse be upon him - and all those who change the judgement of Allah (swt); and all those who judge by other than that which Allah (swt) has revealed; and all those who call to the worship of others besides Allah (swt); and all those who are worshipped besides Allah (swt) and they are pleased with that worship.

2. 'Aad and Thamood: Communities of old, whom Allah (swt) destroyed, because of their disbelef and rejection of the Messengers.

3. Fir'aoun: Pharoah.

4. Zimmi: A non-Muslim living under the protection of a Muslim State.

5. Narrated by Ahmad and Ibn Majah.

6. Shirk: Associating partners with Allah (swt).

7. This does not mean that abortion before forty days is legal, but that before forty days it is not considered murder, but is still forbidden, unless there is some life-threatening danger to the mother.

8. Narrated by Abu Dawood - The import of this Hadith being that it is not permissible to take the life of a Muslim except for three reasons: (i) Adultery, (ii) apostasy and (iii) murder.

9. Narrated by Abu Dawood.

10. Shahaadah: The declaration made by every Muslim: That none has the right to be worshipped but Allah (swt) and that Muhammad (saas) is His Messenger.

11. Such as the deviant Braillawis of the Indian Subcontinent who have elevated him e to the status of a deity - may Allah (swt) save us from such blasphemy!

12. Riyaa`: Lesser Shirk: Performing good deeds in order to be seen doing so.

13. Sum'ah: Performing good deeds in order to gain a good reputation.

14. Laa ilaaha illAllah: None is worthy of worship except Allah (swt).

15. This must not be understood to mean that Allah (swt) is contained in His creation, as Allah (swt) has confirmed in innumerable places in the Qur`aan that He is Above His creation.

16. Narrated by Ibn Hibbaan and Al-Haakim, who declared it authentic.

17. Narrated by At-Tirmizi, who declared it hasan (good).

18. Hadith Qudsi: A Hadith in which the Prophet (saas) says: "Allah (swt) said..."

19. Shirk Akbar: major Shirk.

20. Shirk Asghar: minor Shirk.

Kitaab At-Tawheed, Chapter: 1

Whoever Fulfilled the Requirements of Tawheed Will Enter Paradise Without a Reckoning

Allah (swt), says:

> " *Verily, Ibrahim was an Ummah [a leader, good and righteous] obedient to Allah, Haneefan [worshipping none but Allah], and he was not one of the polytheists"* (Qur'an 16:120)

Allah (swt), informs us in this verse that His Messenger, Ibrahim (as) was a leader in religion, a teacher of goodness, always humble and obedient to his *Rabb*; and that he rejected *Shirk*, in all its manifestations and devoted himself exclusively to the worship of Allah (swt), Alone, without falling into *Shirk*, either in word, deed or belief.

Benefits Derived From This Verse

1. That *Tawheed* is the basis of all religion.

2. The obligation to follow Ibrahim, by sincerely worshipping Allah, Alone.

3. It is an obligation upon the *daa'iyah*[1] to set a good example to the people in all that he does.

4. The unchanging nature of true worship as exemplified by the Prophets.

5. *Tawheed* is not acceptable without rejections of *Shirk*.

6. Rejection of the claim of Quraish in the days of ignorance that in practising their *Shirk*, they were following the religion of Ibrahim.

Relevance of This Verse to the Subject of *Tawheed*

That the verse proves that whoever exemplified these four attributes, has earned the right to Paradise, as did Ibrahim (as), without reckoning or punishment.

..ooOOoo..

Allah (swt), says:

> " *And those who live in awe for fear of their Rabb; And those who believe in the Signs of their Rabb, And those who join not anyone [in worship] as partners with their Rabb; And those who give that which they give [i.e. charity] with their hearts full of fear [whether their charity has been accepted or not], because they are sure to return to their Rabb"* (Qur'an 23:57-60)

In these verses, Allah (swt), describes the Believers by four of their attributes for which they deserve praise and commendation: They fear the punishment of their *Rabb*, they believe in the revealed Signs of Allah (swt) and His natural Signs (the planets, the stars, the seasons, the animals, the birds, the plants etc.) which prove the existence of Him (swt) and the truth of the Message of Muhammad (saas); and they are guided by these Signs and do not associate partners with Allah (swt), either openly, or secretly; and because of their strong faith, they fear that Allah (swt) will not accept their charity and good deeds; and Allah (swt) Testifies to their mutual rivalry in performing virtuous deeds, and He Informs us that they precede others in doing so.

The Benefits Derived From These Verses

1. The obligation to fear Allah.

2. The obligation of belief in the signs of Allah.

3. The forbiddance of *Shirk* in all its manifestations.

4. The concern of the Believers as to whether or not their deeds will be accepted.

5. The preferability of competing with others in the performance of good deeds.

Relevance of These Verses to the Subject of *Tawheed*

That the verses prove that whoever personifies these four attributes and purifies himself from *Shirk* which nullifies good deeds, will have the right to enter Paradise without a reckoning and without punishment because he has achieved the purest *Tawheed* and this is his reward.

..ooOOoo..

It is reported on the authority of Husain Ibn `Abdul-Rahmaan that he said: "I was with Sa'eed Ibn Jubair and he asked: "Who among you saw the shooting star last night?" I answered: "I saw it," and I explained to him that I had not been at prayer, because I had been stung (by a scorpion). He asked: "Then what did you do?" "I used a *ruqyah*,"[2] I replied. He said: "What made you do that?" I answered: "A Hadith I heard from Ash-Sh'abi." He asked: "What did he tell you?" I said: "He reported from Buraidah Al-Husayyib, who said that *ruqyah* is not permitted except in two cases: "*Al-'ain*[3] and stings." He said: "He who limits himself to what he has heard, has done well; but Ibn `Abbas (ra) reported to us that the Prophet (saas) said: "All the nations were made to pass before me, and I saw a Prophet (saas) with a small group, and a Prophet (saas) with only one or two men, and a Prophet (saas) with none. Then there was shown to me a large number of people which I thought to be my *Ummah*,[4] but it was said to me: "This is Moosa (as) and his people." Then I looked and saw a huge crowd at which it was said to me: "These are your people: Among them are seventy thousand who will enter Paradise without a reckoning or punishment." Then he (saas) got up and went to his house, and the people began to discuss who they might be: Some of them said: "Perhaps they are the Companions of the Messenger of Allah (saas); others said: "Perhaps they are the those who were born in Islam and have never associated any partners with Allah (swt). While they were talking thus, the Messenger of Allah (saas) came out and they informed him (about what they had been discussing). He (swt) said: "They are those who do not treat themselves with *ruqyah*, nor practise treatment by cauterization, nor believe in good or bad omens - but depend upon and trust in their *Rabb* (Alone)." `Ukkashah Ibn Mihsan (ra ) stood up and said: "Ask Allah (swt ) for me that I be one of them." He (swt ) said: "You are one of them." Then another man stood and said: "Ask Allah (swt ) that I (also) be one of them." He (saas ) said: "`Ukkashah has preceded you." (Narrated by Bukhari and Muslim)

Husain Ibn `Abdul-Rahman (ra) informs us of a discussion which took place between him and the *Tabi'i*,[5] Sa'eed Ibn Jubair, concerning the use of *ruqyah*, due to the fact that Husain had been stung by a scorpion, for which he resorted to a *ruqyah*, in accordance with the *Sunnah*.[6]

When Sa'eed asked him for a proof for that, he informed him of the Hadith of Ash-Sh'abi which permits the use of *ruqyah* for the treatment of *al-'ain* and stings. Sa'eed praised him for his adherence to the Hadith, but related to him a Hadith which advocates rejection of *ruqyah* - the Hadith of Ibn `Abbas (ra ) which also mentions cauterization and belief in omens, and requires us to have complete trust in Allah (swt ), and depend upon Him (swt ), Alone; and says that when `Ukkashah (ra) requested the Prophet (saas) to ask Allah (swt) to make him one of the seventy thousand who would enter Paradise without reckoning and without punishment, He (saas) informed him that he was one of them, but when another man made the same request, the Messenger of Allah (swt) gently, but firmly closed the door upon any further requests by saying: "`Ukkashah (ra) has preceded you."

Benefits Derived From This Hadith

1. That the *Salaf* [7] used to keep away from *riyaa*` and anything that might lead to it.

2. The obligation to ask for proof before accepting anything in the religion.

3. The permissibility of using *ruqyah* for *al-'ain* and stings, on condition that the *ruqyah* is of a kind endorsed by the *Shari'ah*[8] - from the Qur'an or the authentic supplications of the Prophet (saas) in the Arabic language.

4. The profound knowledge of the *Salaf.*

5. Acting in accordance with the Qur'an and the *Sunnah* takes precedence over all opinions.

6. The virtue of the *Salaf* and their good manners and politeness in passing on Islamic knowledge.

7. The disparity in the number of followers of one Prophet and another, and that some Prophets have no followers.

8. The number of followers a person may have is not necessarily an indication of the truth or falseness of the message.

9. The virtue of Moosa (as) and his people.

10. The excellence of the *Ummah* of Muhammad (saas) in comparison with other peoples.

11. The love of the Companions for all good deeds.

12. The permissibility of engaging in debate in religious matters.

13. Whoever possesses the four attributes mentioned in the Hadith, has perfected *Tawheed* and will enter Paradise.

14. The permissibility of asking virtuous persons to supplicate Allah (swt) on our behalf.

15. That there is no contradiction between the Hadith of Ash-Sh'abi - which permits *ruqyah* when the conditions for its acceptance are met - and the Hadith of Ibn `Abbas (ra) - which forbids *ruqyah* when those conditions are not met.

Relevance of This Hadith to the Subject of *Tawheed*

That the Hadith proves that whoever possessed the four attributes mentioned therein, has perfected *Tawheed* and will enter Paradise without reckoning or punishment.

Footnotes

1. Daa'iyah: One who invites people to Islam.

2. Ruqyah: To recite a part of the Qur'an (e.g. Qur'an Al-Faatihah), or to supplicate Allah (swt), using words prescribed by the Messenger of Allah (saas) in authentic Hadith, in order to obtain relief from illness.

3. Al-'ain: The evil eye.

4. Ummah: Community.

5. Taabi'i: A Muslim who met and reported from one or more of the Companions of the Prophet (saas).

6. Sunnah: Words and deeds of the Prophet (saas) and those of which he approved.

7. The Salaf: The pious, early generations of Muslims.

8. Shari'ah: Islamic Law.

Top | Prev | Next

Kitaab At-Tawheed, Chapter: 2

Fear of Shirk

Allah (swt), says:

> " *Verily, Allah forgives not that partners be set up with Him [in worship] but He forgives other than that to whom He pleases; and whoever sets up partners with Allah [in worship], he has indeed invented an enormous wrong"* (Qur'an 4:48)

Shirk is the most dangerous of all sins, the wickedest and the most severely punished because of the dishonour and denigration of the *Rabb*, Almighty, All-powerful, and the likening of Allah (swt) to His creation which it entails. Allah (swt) informs us in this verse that He will not forgive the one who commits *Shirk* and dies as a *Mushrik*,[1] but as for the one who dies believing in the Oneness of Allah (swt), although he may have committed some sins, Allah (swt) has promised him forgiveness in accordance with His Will. Then He explains why the *mushrik* will not be forgiven, saying that by his association of partners with Allah (swt), he has rejected Him and belied Him and committed a sin the like of which there is no other.

Benefits Derived From This Verse

1. That whoever dies being guilty of *Shirk Akbar*, will assuredly go to the Fire.

2. Whoever dies believing in the Oneness of Allah, although he may have committed major sins, may be forgiven if Allah, Most Glorified, Most High Wills.

3. In the verse is a reply to the *khawarij*,[2] who charged those guilty of major sins with disbelief, and to the *mu'tazilah*,[3] who believed that those guilty of major sins would spend eternity in the Fire.

4. Confirmation of the Divine Will which is one of His Attributes.

Relevance of This Verse to the Subject of *Tawheed*

That it proves that Allah Will not forgive those who are guilty of *Shirk* and this should be a warning to all.

..ooOOoo..

Allah (swt), says:

> " *And [remember] when Ibrahim said: "My Rabb! Make this city one of peace and security, and keep me and my sons away from worshipping idols"* (Qur'an 13:35)

Allah (swt), Most Glorified, Most High, informs us that Ibrahim (as) supplicated Allah (swt) to make

Makkah a place of safety and stability, because fear and chaos prevent people from performing their religious rituals. Then he followed this with another request to his *Rabb*: That He preserve him and his family from idol worship, for he knew the danger of that and he knew how easily people can be seduced by it.

Benefits Derived From This Verse

1. The virtue of Makkah over other cities.

2. Ibrahim's prayer for the security and stability of Makkah.

3. Evidence of the benefit of supplication.

4. That the original religion of all the Messengers is one: Belief in the Oneness of Allah.

5. The desirability of one's supplicating on behalf of his family.

6. The forbiddance of worshipping idols.

Relevance of This Verse to the Subject of *Tawheed*

That it proves that Ibrahim, with his strong faith, fears for himself and his family that they may be affected by *Shirk*; thus, the obligation upon us to fear *Shirk* is that much greater.

..ooOOoo..

It is reported that the Prophet (saas) said: "Of the things which I fear for my *Ummah*, the thing which I fear most is minor *Shirk*. Then he was asked about minor *Shirk*, and he said: "It is *ar-riyaa*."[4]

The Prophet (saas) informs us in this Hadith that he fears for us, and that what he fears most for us is minor *Shirk*. This shows how kind-hearted and compassionate the Prophet (saas) was towards his *Ummah*, and how concerned he was for their good: He knew the dangers of minor *Shirk*, how it can strongly manifest itself in the community, polluting the pure monotheism of the Muslims, especially since it can afflict them without them even knowing it. This is why the Prophet (saas) warned them to beware of it.

Benefits Derived From This Hadith

1. The care and concern shown by the Messenger of Allah (saas) for his *Ummah*.

2. The division of *Shirk* into two categories: Major and minor.

3. That *riyaa`* is considered *Shirk*.

4. The obligation of asking the people of knowledge about matters which confuse them.

Relevance of This Hadith to the Subject of *Tawheed*

That the Hadith proves that Allah's Messenger (saas) feared for his Companions that they might unwittingly fall into minor *Shirk*; this, in spite of their strong faith and understanding of Islam and *Tawheed*. Therefore, we, with our comparatively weak faith and little knowledge, are even more obligated to fear both major and minor *Shirk*.

..ooOOoo..

It is reported on the authority of Ibn Mas'ood (ra) that the Messenger of Allah (saas) said:

> *"Whoever died while supplicating another deity besides Allah (swt), will enter the Fire."* (Narrated by Bukhari)

The Prophet (saas) informs us in this Hadith that whoever adulterated that which should be purely for Allah (swt) (i.e. worship), by worshipping others besides Him, and died in this state, will have his abode in the Hell-fire.

Benefits Derived From This Hadith

1. Whoever died as a *Mushrik* will enter the Fire - If it was major *Shirk*, he will abide therein forever, but if it was minor *Shirk*, then Allah (swt) will punish him as much as He wishes, then he will be allowed to leave the Fire.

2. That a person will be judged upon his last act in this world.[5]

Relevance of This Hadith to the Subject of *Tawheed*

That the Hadith proves that whoever died calling upon a deity other than Allah (swt), will enter the Hell-fire, therefore it is incumbent upon us to fear *Shirk*.

..ooOOoo..

It is reported by Muslim, on the authority of Jabir (ra), that Allah's Messenger (saas) said:

> *"Whoever meets Allah (swt), without associating partners with Him, will enter Paradise; and whoever meets Him as one who associated anything with Him, will enter the Fire.*

The Prophet (saas) informs us in this Hadith that whoever died without associating partners with Allah (swt) - either in Rabbship or worship or in His Divine Names and Attributes is promised an abode in Paradise, while whoever died as a *Mushrik*, will abide in the Hell-fire.

Benefits Derived From This Hadith

1. Confirmation of the existence of Paradise and Hell.

2. That a person will be judged upon his last act in this world.

3. Whoever died believing in the Oneness of Allah (swt), will not dwell forever in the Hell-fire, but will find his eternal abode in Paradise.

4. Whoever died as a *Mushrik* must dwell eternally in the Hell-fire.

Relevance of the Hadith to the Subject of *Tawheed*

That the Hadith proves that whoever died as a *Mushrik* will enter the Fire, and the knowledge of this obliges us to fear *Shirk* in all its manifestations.

Footnotes

1. Mushrik: One who commits Shirk.

2. Khawaarij: A deviant sect, who claimed that committing major sins takes a person out of the fold of Islam.

3. Mu'tazilah: A deviant sect, who denied the Divine Attributes of Allah (swt), and claimed that those who committed major sins would dwell eternally in the Hell-fire.

4. Narrated by Imam Ahmad.

5. It is reported on the authority of 'Abdullah Ibn 'Amr (ra) that Allah's Messenger (saas) said: "...verily, he whose abode will be Paradise, his final deed will be of the deeds of the people of Paradise, whatever he did (previously), and verily, he who is destined for the Hell-fire, his final deed will be of the deeds of the people of the Hell-fire, whatever he did (previously)." (Narrated by Ahmad and At-Tirmizi, who said it is hasan-saheeh-ghareeb i.e. somewhere between the classifications of saheeh (authentic) and hasan (good), though narrated at some point(s) in its sanad by only one narrator.

Top | Prev | Next

Kitaab At-Tawheed, Chapter: 3

The Call to Testify That None is Worthy of Worship Except Allah

Allah (swt) says:

> " *Say (O Muhammad) : "This is my way; I invite unto Allah with sure knowledge, I and whosoever follows me. And Glorified and Exalted is Allah. And I am not of the Mushrikin."* (Qur'an 12:108)

Allah (swt) commands His Prophet (saas) in this verse to teach the people and make clear to them his Religion and his *Sunnah* and his way of life and that of those who follow the call to Allah's Religion, and practice *Tawheed*, and that by so doing, he and those who obey him and believe in him are following Divine Guidance and acting upon knowledge and clear evidence; and they exalt their Lord and glorify Him above any association of partners, in His Lordship, in worship and in His Divine Names and Attributes; and he (swt) is innocent of the polytheists and their *Shirk*.

Benefits Derived From This Verse

1. The obligation of sincerity and purity of faith, when calling to (the worship of) Allah.

2. The call should be based upon a foundation of truth and evidence.

3. The obligation to stay free from *Shirk* and its followers.

4. That deeds are not accepted unless they are in conformity with that which was brought by the Messenger of Allah.

5. The obligation to exalt Allah above all that is not becoming His Majesty.

Relevance of This Verse to the Subject of *Tawheed*

That it proves that the way of the Prophet (saas) and those who follow him is to call the people to the religion of Allah (swt), and this embodies the testimony that none is worthy of worship except Allah (swt).

..ooOOoo..

It is reported on the authority of Ibn `Abbas (ra ) that Allah's Messenger (saas ) said when he sent Mu`aaz (ra) to Yemen: "You are going to a people who are from the People of the Book: So the first thing to which you call them should be the testimony that none has the right to be worshipped except Allah (swt)." - And in another narration: "that they testify to the Oneness of Allah (swt)." - "And if they obey you in that, then inform them that Allah (swt) has made compulsory upon them five prayers every day and night. And if they obey you in that, then inform them that Allah (swt) has made incumbent upon them a charity (*Zakah*) which is to be taken from the rich among them and given to their poor. And if they obey you in that then be careful not to take the best of their wealth (as *Zakah*), and be careful of the supplication of those who have suffered injustice, for there is no obstacle between it and Allah (swt). (Narrated by Bukhari and Muslim)

The Prophet (saas) sent Mu`aaz Ibn Jabal (ra) as his representative to Yemen, and he advised him of what was required of him there, beginning with the call to worship Allah (swt), Alone, without partners, and that if they accepted that then he must inform them of the greatest obligations upon them after *Tawheed*, which are: prayer and *Zakah*; and that if they obeyed this, then it is incumbent upon him to maintain justice with them, and not to wrong them or cause suffering to them by taking the best of their property as *Zakah*, for that would constitute an injustice to them and might provoke them and cause them to invoke Allah (swt) upon him - and the invocation of the oppressed and the wronged is never rejected by Allah (swt).

Benefits Derived From This Hadith

1. That the first thing to which the *Du'ah*[1] must call is *Tawheed* - the Oneness of Allah (swt).

2. The obligation to call to Allah (swt) with wisdom, step-by-step, beginning with the most important, then the next most important, and so on.

3. The obligation of observing five daily prayers.

4. That *witr* prayer [2] is not obligatory.

5. The obligation upon those who have more than they need to fulfill their basic every-day needs to pay *Zakah*.

6. That *Zakah* is not paid to the unbeliever.[3]

7. That the *fuqaraah`* are legitimate recipients of *Zakah*.

8. The permissibility of paying *Zakah* to one category of recipients from amongst the permitted categories.

9. That it is not permissible to pay *Zakah* outside the country unless there is no one in need of *Zakah* within it.

10. It is not permissible to pay *Zakah* to the wealthy.

11. The forbiddance of taking *Zakah* from the best of the people's wealth.

12. The forbiddance of any kind of injustice.

13. That the invocation of the wronged is answered.

Relevance of the Hadith to the Subject of *Tawheed*

That it proves that the first thing with which the *da'iyah* must begin his message is the call to testify that none is worthy of worship except Allah (swt).

Important Note

(a) Although they are two of the five pillars of Islam, fasting and Hajj have not been mentioned in this Hadith; this is because at the time Allah's Prophet (saas) made this statement, those pillars which had been made obligatory upon the Muslims were *Tawheed* and belief in the Messengership of Muhammad (saas), prayer and *Zakah* - all of which were made incumbent from the beginning of Islam, while the time of fasting and Hajj had not come.

(b) It is mentioned in this Hadith the obligation to be careful of the supplication of those who have been wronged, because there is no obstacle between it and Allah (swt), and Allah (swt) has said in Qur'an:

" *Is not He [better than your gods] Who responds to the distressed one when he calls Him?"* (Qur'an 27:62)

And it is mentioned in another Hadith that the answer to the one who calls upon Allah (swt) is of three types:

That it is answered quickly, (ii) that some of his sins will be blotted out in accordance with the measure of the supplication, or (iii) that it will be stored up for him on the Day of Resurrection.[4] We may reconcile this Hadith with the above narration by saying that the latter concerns the one who is not oppressed or distressed, while the former concerns the supplication of one who suffers oppression or distress for it is answered even if after some time, and Allah (swt) alleviates his distress and bestows His Mercy upon him.

..ooOOoo..

It is reported on the authority of S'ad Ibn Sahl that he said: "Allah's Messenger (saas) said on the Day of (the Battle of) Khaibar: "Tomorrow I shall indeed give the flag to someone who loves Allah (swt) and His Messenger (saas) and is loved by Allah (swt) and His Messenger (saas): Allah (swt) will grant victory under his leadership. The people spent the night absorbed in discussing who might be given the flag. In the morning, they came eagerly to Allah's Messenger (saas), each of them hoping to be given the flag. Allah's Messenger (saas) asked: "Where is `Ali Ibn Abi Talib (ra)?" They replied: "He is suffering from an eye ailment." He was sent for and brought to the Prophet (saas) who spat in his eyes and prayed for him whereupon he was cured as if he had not been in pain before. Allah's Messenger (saas) then gave him the flag and said: "Advance with ease and gentleness until you arrive in their midst, then call them to Islam and inform them of their duties to Allah (swt) in Islam. By Allah (swt)! If He may guide through you a single man to Islam, it would be better for you than red camels."

Benefits Derived From This Hadith

1. Evidence of the virtue of `Ali Ibn Abi Talib (ra).

2. Confirmation of Allah's Divine Attribute of Love.

3. Evidence of the Prophet's miracle.

4. The love of the Companions for all that is good.

5. The questioning of the Imam about the individual members of his congregation and his concern for their welfare.

6. The obligation of belief in Divine Ordainment and Predestination, as shown by the Companions when the flag was given to the one who did not ask for it.

7. The obligation of the leader to behave in a good manner, with gentleness, but with firmness.

8. The obligation to begin with the call to Islam before engaging in battle for the benefit of those who have not heard the message.

9. The testimony of belief in the Oneness of Allah (swt) and the Messengership of His Prophet, Muhammad (saas) is not sufficient unless accompanied by deeds.

10. The permissibility of swearing in Allah's name concerning one's pronouncements as a means of emphasis.

11. The permissibility of invoking Allah's name without calling upon Him for a definite purpose.

12. The virtue of calling people to Allah (swt) and of teaching.

Relevance of the Hadith to the Subject of *Tawheed*

That it proves that the first thing with which the caller to Islam should begin and the first pillar of Islam is the *Shahaadatan.*[5]

Important Note

The position of the Imam with regard to the disbelievers, if they are from the People of the Book, is that he gives them three choices in this order: (i) To embrace Islam, (ii) to pay the *jizyah* or (iii) to fight.

As for the idol-worshipers, their choices are but two: (i) To embrace Islam or (ii) to fight.[6]

Footnotes

1. Du'ah: Plural of da'iyah (caller to Islam).

2. Witr prayer: Literally, odd prayer; so called because it consists of an odd number of raka'ahs (units) - one, three five etc. - it is performed any time after'ishaa` prayer, until fajr. Having said that it is not obligatory, it is strongly recommended, for the Prophet (saas) never abandoned it, even when travelling.

3. ...unless he is one of those whose heart is inclined to Islam, for Allah (swt), says: (Qur'an 9:60)

4. Narrated by At-Tirmizi.

5. The Shahaadatan: The two testimonies (i) that none is worthy of worship but Allah (swt) and (ii) that Muhammad is the Messenger of Allah (saas).

6. It is authentically reported that the Prophet (saas) said: "I was ordered to fight the people until they testify that none is worthy of worship except Allah (swt)." (Narrated by Bukhari) and it is reported that the Prophet (saas) wrote to Munzir Ibn Sawaa, who was the leader of the people of Hajr: "As for the Arabs do not accept anything from them except Islam or (to be killed by) the sword, and as for the People of the Book and the Majiians, accept from them the

jizyah." (Narrated by Al-Kalbi)

Top | Prev | Next

Kitaab At-Tawheed, Chapter: 4

Explanation of the Meaning of Tawheed and the Testimony: Laa ilaaha illallaah [1]

Allah (swt), says:

> " *Those whom they supplicate [created beings, such as Prophets, pious men, or angels],
> desiring means of access to their Rabb, as to which of them should be the nearest - they [the
> Prophets pious men etc.] hope for His Mercy and fear His punishment: Verily, the
> punishment of their Rabb is fearful"* (Qur'an 57:17)

Allah (swt) informs us in this verse that those whom the polytheists worship besides Allah (swt), the
Almighty, the All-powerful, such as the angels and the pious people, themselves try to get nearer to
Allah (swt) by obedience to Him, worshipping Him and carrying out His Commands, hoping for His
Mercy; and they abstain from those things which He has prohibited, in fear of His punishment because
every true Believer fears and dreads His punishment.

Benefits Derived From This Verse

1. The falseness of the worship of deities other than Allah, by the polytheists, since their
objects of worship themselves seek nearness to Allah and hope for His Mercy and fear His
punishment.

2. The piety of those who are worshipped does not validate the act of worshipping them.

3. Confirmation of Allah's Divine Attribute of Mercy.

4. The true Believer approaches Allah in a state between fear and hope, except at the time when
death approaches, then hope becomes stronger.

Relevance of the Verse to the Subject of the Chapter

That it proves that the meaning of *Tawheed* and the testimony *Laa ilaaha illallah* is the abandonment of
the deeds of the polytheists such as calling upon the Prophets and the Righteous and requesting their
intercession with Allah (swt); and the verbal recitation of the testimony is not sufficient if the worship
of all deities besides Allah (swt) is not rejected.

..ooOOoo..

Allah (swt), says:

> " *And [remember] when Ibraheem said to his father and his people: "Verily, I am innocent
> of what you worship, except Him Who originated me, and He will certainly guide
> me"* (Qur'an 43:26-27)

Allah (swt), informs us in this verse, that His Messenger and *Khaleel* [2], Ibraheem (as) told his father -
Aazar - and his people that he was totally blameless and guiltless of all of their deities except One: Allah

(swt), Who created him, and Who, Alone Can Grant him success, and by Whose Hand he may be benefitted or harmed.

Benefits Derived From These Verses

1. That the basis of the Religion taught by all the Prophets was one: *Tawheed.*

2. That speaking out in the cause of Truth is an essential attribute of all Messengers.

3. The obligation to condemn that which is detestable, even though it may be found in one's close relatives.

4. The obligation to declare oneself free (in word and deed) from the wickedness of *Shirk.*

5. Evidence that Ibraheem's people used to worship Allah, but associated partners with Him.

6. That the Guidance of Success comes only from Allah.

Relevance of These Verses to the Subject of *Tawheed*

That the verses prove that a person's *Tawheed* is not correct if he does not declare (by word and deed) his innocence of the worship of any deity besides Allah.

..ooOOoo..

Allah (swt), says:

" *They have taken their Ahbaar[3] and their Ruhbaan[4] to be Rabbs beside Allah, and the Messiah, the son of Maryam, though they were not commanded but to worship One God: There is none worthy of worship but He, glorified be He: [Far is He] above that which they associate [with Him]"* (Qur'an 9:31)

Allah (swt), informs us in this verse that the Jews and Christians have gone astray from the Straight Path, and have done what they were never commanded to do: They raised their scholars and men of religion to the status of gods, worshipping them beside Allah (swt); this, by obeying them, when they declared that which Allah (swt) has forbidden to be permissible, and when they declared what Allah (swt) has permitted to be forbidden, thus elevating them to the level of *Rabb*, since only the *Rabb*, Most High ordains what is permissible and what is forbidden. Indeed, the Christians, not content with this, began to worship Eisa (as), and considered him a son of Allah, though they were not ordered in the Tauraa and the Injeel except to worship Allah (swt), Alone: Far above that which they attribute to Him is He, the *Rabb* of the worlds.

Benefits Derived From This Verse

1. That obedience to other than Allah, in contradiction to Allah's Commands constitutes *Shirk.*

2. It is forbidden to obey one of Allah's creatures, if in so doing, one is disobedient to the Creator.

3. Deeds will not be considered righteous unless two conditions are met: (i) That the deeds are done purely for Allah, and (ii) that they conform to the teachings of the Messengers.

4. That the scholars of religion are not infallible.

5. Evidence that the Jews and Christians have gone astray from the correct precepts of their Religion: i.e. *Tawheed*.

6. The danger of misguided scholars to the *Ummah*.[5]

Relevance of This Verse to the Subject of *Tawheed*

That it proves that the meaning of *Tawheed*, and the testimony: *Laa ilaaha illallaah* entail confirming the Oneness of Allah by obedience to Him and to His Messenger, because whoever obeyed the Messenger has obeyed Allah.

..ooOOoo..

Allah (swt), says:

> " *And amongst mankind are those who take [for worship] others besides Allah, as equals [with Allah]: They love them as they should love Allah. And those who believe love Allah more [than anything else]. If only the wrongdoers could see, behold, they would see the punishment: That to Allah belongs all power, and Allah is Stern in punishment"* (Qur'an 2:165)

Allah (swt), informs us in this verse that some of mankind set up for themselves deities which they love more than they love Allah (swt), then He, Most Glorified explains that the Believers are stronger in their love for Allah (swt) than the polytheists because the Believers are pure and sincere in their love of Allah (swt), Alone, while the polytheists divide their love between Allah (swt) and their false gods; and whoever was sincere in loving Allah (swt), Alone, his love would be stronger than that of the polytheist who divides his love. Then Allah (swt), Most Glorified promises those who associate partners with Him that when they see the punishment which He has prepared especially for them on the Day of Resurrection, they will wish that they had not associated others with Allah (swt), either in love, or in anything else. Then they shall know, with certain knowledge that all power belongs to Allah (swt), and that Allah is Stern in enforcing His punishment.

Benefits Derived From This Verse

1. That love is a kind of worship.

2. Confirmation that the polytheists love Allah, but this will not benefit them so long as they are guilty of *Shirk*.

3. The negation of faith of those who commit *Shirk* by loving other deities besides Allah.

4. Confirmation of Allah's Divine Attribute of all-embracing Power.

Relevance of This Verse to the Subject of the Chapter

That it proves that the meaning of *Tawheed* and the testimony: *Laa ilaaha illallaah* is to confirm the Oneness of Allah in a foundation of love which entails purity and sincerity in all acts of worship for Allah, Alone.

..ooOOoo..

It is authentically reported that the Prophet (saas) said:

"Whoever said: "Laa ilaaha illallaah," and rejected all that is worshipped besides Allah (swt), (know that) Allah (swt) has forbidden the taking of his property and the spilling of his blood; and his account will be for Allah, the Almighty, the All-powerful." [6]

Whoever said: "*Laa ilaaha illallaah*," pronouncing it, understanding its meaning and acting upon all that it entails, and rejected all that is worshipped besides Allah (swt) (i.e. by his heart, his tongue and his actions), it is forbidden for the Muslims to take his property (except what the Law requires such as the payment of *zakah*), or to take his life, except as the Law requires (such as the punishment for adultery after chastity, or disbelief after belief or for murder); and his account will be for Allah (swt): That is, He will take charge of his account on the Day of Resurrection, and if he was truthful in his testimony, He will reward him, but if he was insincere in his testimony, He will punish him.

Benefits Derived From This Hadith

1. The virtue of Islam which protects the life and property of whosoever embraces it.

2. The obligation to desist from enmity towards the disbeliever, should he embrace Islam, even though he should do so during a battle until and unless it should be proved that his testimony was false.

3. That a person might say: "*Laa ilaaha illallaah*, without rejecting that which is worshipped besides Him."

4. That the conditions of acceptance of faith include pronouncing the *shahaadah*: *Laa ilaaha illallaah*, and rejecting all that is worshipped besides Him.

5. That judgement in this world is based on appearances.

6. The forbiddance of appropriating the property of the Muslim unless it is ordained by Islamic Law, such as *zakah,* or a legally imposed fine in compensation for that which he has destroyed (be it property or a life).

Relevance of the Hadith to the Subject of the Chapter

That it proves that the meaning of *Tawheed* and the explanation of the *shahaadah*: *Laa ilaaha illallaah* are not complete without a categorical rejection of all that is worshipped besides Allah (swt).

Important Note

The disbelieving polytheist has only two choices: (i) To embrace Islam or (ii) to be fought; but the People of the Book have three choices: (i) To embrace Islam, (ii) to pay the *jizyah*, or (iii) to fight (in that order).

Footnotes

1. Laa ilaaha Iilallah: None has the right to be worshipped except Allah (swt).

2. Khaleel: Friend; Ibraheem u is referred to by Allah (swt) as: Khaleelullaah, i.e. The Beloved of Allah (swt). The common translation of Khaleelullaah as the Friend of Allah (swt), is far from doing justice to this illustrious title, for according to scholars of Arabic language, the word khalla, from which the word khaleel is derived indicates a greater degree of love than is conveyed by the word friend.

3. Ahbar: (sing.= Habr) Religious scholars, according to At-Tabari.

4. Ruhban: (sing.= Rahib) Reciters of Scriptures and scholars of Religious Jurisprudence, according to At-Tabari.

5. Ummah: Community, i.e. the Muslim Community.

6. Narrated by Muslim.

Top | Prev | Next

Kitaab At-Tawheed, Chapter: 5

It is an Act of Shirk to Wear Rings or Threads
or the Like as a Means of Prevention or Lifting of Afflictions

Allah (swt), says:

> " *Say: "Tell me then, the things that you invoke besides Allah - if Allah intended some harm to me, could they remove His harm, or if He intended some mercy for me, could they withhold His Mercy?" Say: "Sufficient for me is Allah; in Him those who trust [the true Believers] must put their trust.""* (Qur'an 39:38)

In this verse, Allah (swt), Most Glorified, Most High commands His Prophet, Muhammad (saas) to reject those powerless, graven images worshipped by the polytheists, which can neither remove any harm which might befall a person by Allah's Decree, nor prevent any sustenance or blessings which might come to a person from Him. Then He commands him to place his trust in Allah (swt), for He is Sufficient to bring benefit or prevent harm for all who sincerely depend upon Him.

Benefits Derived From This Verse

1. The obligation to reject the abominable.

2. The falseness of idol-worship.

3. That the removal of harm and the bringing of benefits is only from Allah.

4. The obligation to trust in Allah and depend upon Him, free from dependence upon any other, and this does not conflict with the requirement to take whatever legal measures one can in order to achieve one's objectives.

Relevance of This Verse to the Subject of the Chapter

That it proves that protection from harm is only from Allah (swt), and so entrusting oneself to any other protector - such as rings, threads etc. is an act of *Shirk*.

..ooOOoo..

It is reported on the authority of Umran Ibn Husain (ra), that Allah's Messenger *(saas)* saw a man with a brass ring in his hand, and he asked him: "What is this?" He replied: "It is for protection from *al-waahinah*."[1] The Prophet *(saas)* answered:

> *"Remove it at once, for verily, it will not increase you except in weakness, and were you to die whilst wearing it, you would never be successful."* (Narrated by Ahmad, with an acceptable *Sanad*)

Umran Ibn Husain (ra) informs us in this Hadith that the Prophet *(saas)* saw a man with a brass ring in his hand, and he asked him for what purpose he was wearing it. The man answered that he was wearing it to protect him from illness, at which the Prophet *(saas)* ordered him to remove it and informed him that it would only cause him to become weak and not protect him from illness at all, and that should he die while wearing it and believing in its power to protect him, he would not succeed in the Hereafter, nor would he know eternal bliss.

Benefits Derived From This Hadith

1. The permissibility of requesting detailed information by the *Mufti.* [2]

2. The importance of intentions.

3. That the method of reproof and rejection may differ according to the individual concerned, so if there is a likelihood that words of wisdom will suffice, force should not be resorted to.

4. Evidence of the ignorance of the polytheists before Islam.

5. Forbiddance of seeking a cure by the use of that which is prohibited.

6. That the prohibited is of no benefit at all: Even though it may help to some degree, the harm it causes is greater.

7. The ignorant man is not excused from the obligation to seek knowledge.

8. That it is by a person's last actions that he will be judged on the Day of Resurrection. [3]

Important Note

a) This Hadith does not contradict the Hadith of `Ali Ibn Al-Husain, which is allegedly from the Prophet *(saas )*, and which states: "Plough (the earth) well, for verily, ploughing is a blessed task. And sow many seeds." This is because the Hadith of `Ali Ibn Al-Husain is *mursal* [4] - one of the *mursal* narration of Abu Dawood, and Abu Dawood has not vouched for the authenticity of his *mursal* narration. But even were it authentic, the reference is to seeds (جماجم), according to a large number of scholars, i.e. taking the required precautions to ensure the success of one's endeavours such as planting many seeds to ensure a good crop or using permitted medicines to alleviate illness, not to some supposed treatment for fever, which involved the laying of hands on the skull [5] of the patient. Taking such precautions is not to be compared to resorting to the forbidden in order to achieve one's goals.

b) The enquiry made by the Prophet *(saas)* might be construed as a rhetorical one, indicating disapproval, and it could also be understood to be a genuine request for more information.

c) Some of the scholars have said that wearing a ring or such like in order to protect oneself against harm is an act of minor *Shirk*, but what is understood from the Hadith of Umran is that it constitutes major *Shirk* because as it is mentioned in the Hadith that to die while doing so would result in failure to achieve everlasting bliss in the Hereafter. It could be that the definition depends upon the beliefs and intentions of the perpetrator if he believed that it could cure him of itself, without Allah's Help, then it would be major *Shirk*; while if he believed it be a cause of the cure, while Allah (swt) is the One Who grants health, then it would be considered to be minor *Shirk* - and Allah (swt) knows best.

Relevance of This Hadith to the Subject of the Chapter

That it proves the obligation to reject the wearing of rings, bangles, chains etc. as a means of protection against harm, because bringing good and avoiding harm are the prerogative of Allah (swt), Alone, and seeking such help from other than Allah (swt) means associating partners with Him.

..ooOOoo..

It is also reported by Ahmad on the authority of `Uqbah Ibn A`mir (ra) in a *marfoo'* [6] form: "Whoever wore a *tamemah*, [7] Allah (swt) will never see his wishes fulfilled, and whoever wears a *wada'ah* [8] Allah will never grant him peace and tranquility." - and in another narration of Ahmad: "Whoever wears a *tamemah* has committed an act of *Shirk*."

`Uqbah Ibn A`mir (ra) informs us in this Hadith that the Messenger of Allah *(saas)* supplicated against every person who wears a talisman or a seashell, believing that it will benefit him without Allah (swt), that Allah (swt) will not allow him to achieve any of his goals nor fulfill his wishes or dreams; rather, He will prevent him from ever finding security and tranquility; and he also informed us that any such action is false; indeed, in another narration, he (swt) informed us that the *tamemah* is a form of *Shirk* because its perpetrator believes that it will benefit him without Allah (swt).

Benefits Derived From This Hadith

1. Denial of any benefit to the one who believes in the use of *tamemah* or *wada'ah*.

2. The permissibility of making supplication against the disobedient ones in general.

3. That some of the Companions were ignorant to this extent, so what of those who came after them?

4. That the *tamemah* is a kind of *Shirk*.

Relevance of This Hadith to the Subject of the Chapter

That it proves that wearing an amulet or talisman, believing that it can benefit one is an act of *Shirk* because benefits come only from Allah (swt), the Almighty, the All-powerful.

..ooOOoo..

It is reported by Ibn Abi Hatim, on the authority of Huzaifah (ra) that he saw a man with a thread in his hand to protect him from fever; he broke it and recited the Words of Allah (ra), Most High:

" *And most of them do not believe in Allah, except that they associate partners with Him"* (Qur'an 12:106)

Huzaifah (ra) visited a sick man and found him wearing a thread on his wrist; and when he asked the man what was the purpose of it, he told him that it was a protection from fever, at which Huzaifah (ra) broke it declaring it to be *Shirk*; and as proof of this, he recited the Words of Allah (swt), Most High: " *And most of them do not believe in Allah, except that they associate partners with Him"* - and the meaning of this verse is that many people believe in Allah (swt), but adulterate their belief with *Shirk*.

Benefits Derived From This Narration

1. Forbidding the detestable by one's own hand, even though the perpetrator may object.

2. That the use of threads and the like to protect from harm is an act of *Shirk*.

3. The obligation to reject the detestable.

4. The deep understanding of the Companions, and the breadth of their knowledge.

5. That *Shirk* is present amongst the people of this *Ummah*.

6. That the heart of a person may contain faith and *Shirk* at the same time.

Relevance of This Narration to the Subject of the Chapter

That it proves that the use of threads as protection from harm is an act of *Shirk*, because protection from harm comes only from Allah (swt), the Almighty, the All-powerful.

Footnotes

1. Al-waahinah: rheumatism.

2. Mufti: An Islamic scholar, who is qualified to deliver formal legal verdicts, based on the Qur'an and Sunnah.

3. See footnote no. 33.

4. Mursal: An incomplete chain of narrators, not reaching to the Prophet (saas).

5. The Arabic word for skulls is also (?????) - jamaajim.

6. Marfoo': With a sanad reaching to the Prophet (saas).

7. Tamemah: Talisman or amulet.

8. Wada'ah: A sea-shell resembling an oyster shell.

Top | Prev | Next

Kitaab At-Tawheed, Chapter: 6

What Has Been Said About the Use of Ar-Ruqi [1] and At-Tamaa`im [2]

It is authentically reported on the authority of Abu Basheer Al- Ansari (ra) that he was with the Messenger of Allah (saas) on one of his journeys when he sent a messenger to tell the people: "Let not any necklace of bowstring, or any other kind of necklace remain on the necks of your camels, except that it is cut off."[3]

Abu Basheer Al-Ansari (ra) informs us that he accompanied the Messenger of Allah (saas) on a journey and he sent a messenger - Zaid Ibn Harithah (ra) - to order the people to cut the bowstrings from around the necks of their camels; this was because the people in the days of ignorance used to believe that it was a protection against *al-'ain.*

Benefits Derived From This Hadith

  1. The obligation to reject the detestable.

  2. The acceptability of information from one reliable person.

  3. The falseness of the belief in the benefit supposedly derived from necklaces, whatever their kind.

  4. That the representative of the leader may act on his behalf in matters entrusted to him.

Relevance of This Hadith to the Subject of the Chapter

That it proves the forbiddance of wearing necklaces in order to protect against harm.

Relevance of This Hadith to the Subject of *Tawheed*

That it proves that such actions are a form of *Shirk* because protection from harm comes only from Allah (swt).

..ooOOoo..

It is reported on the authority of Ibn Mas'ood (ra) that he said: "I heard the Messenger of Allah (saas) say

  That ar-ruqi, at-tamaa`im and at- tiwalah [4] are all forms of Shirk. (Narrated by Ahmad and Abu Dawood)

Important Note

Ar-ruqi is permissible if it meets three conditions:

  i) That it contains the Words of Allah (swt) or mention of His Names and Attributes, or a supplication to Allah (swt), or a request for His Aid.

ii) That it is in Arabic and its meaning is clearly understood.

iii) That it is not believed that the incantation can, of itself bring about any positive result, but that the benefit comes by the Command of Allah (swt) and His Divine Pre-ordination.

Ibn Mas`ood (ra ) informs us that the Prophet (saas ) said that *ar-ruqi* (which means spells and incantations), *at-tamaa`im* (which are made from beads and such like and are hung around the necks of children), and *at-tiwalah* (which is a spell made to cause a husband to love his wife, or a wife to love her husband) are all forms of *Shirk*.

Benefits Derived From This Hadith

1. That *ar-ruqi* are forbidden and are a form of *Shirk*, except what has been permitted by the Law.

2. That *at-tamaa`im* are forbidden and are a form of *Shirk*.

3. The forbiddance of *at-tiwalah*, which is also a form of *Shirk*.

Relevance of This Hadith to the Subject of the Chapter and to the Subject of *Tawheed*

That it proves that *ar-ruqi*, *at-tamaa`im* and *at-tiwalah* are all forms of *Shirk*.

Important Note

Scholars have disagreed concerning *at-tamemah*, if it is from the Qur'an: Some have forbidden it, inferring a general prohibition from this Hadith, while others have permitted it, comparing it to *ar-ruqiyah*, which may be from the Qur'an and is permissible; but the first saying is more correct, and Allah (swt) knows best.

..ooOOoo..

It is reported on the authority of `Abdullah Ibn `Ukaim (ra) in a *marfoo'* form: "Whoever wore something [5] (around his neck) will be put in its charge." (Narrated by Ahmad and At-Tirmizi)

`Abdullah Ibn `Ukaim (ra) tells us that the Prophet (saas) informed him that whoever needed something, he should entrust his affair to Allah (swt), and that whoever depended upon Allah (swt), Alone to fulfill his needs, Allah (swt) will relieve his distress and make his affairs easy, but whoever depended upon something other than Allah (swt), and entrusted his affairs to it, will be left in its charge, i.e. he will have no help from Allah (swt), because it is only by the Hand of Allah (swt) that goodness is achieved, and none but He can benefit.

Benefits Derived From This Hadith

1. The obligation to depend upon Allah (swt), Alone; and this does not contradict the obligation to undertake all possible, permissible measures to ensure success.

2. That whoever sought benefit from other than Allah (swt) will be abandoned.

Relevance of This Hadith to the Subject of the Chapter

That it proves the forbiddance of seeking benefit from other than Allah (swt).

Relevance of This Hadith to the Subject of *Tawheed*

That the Hadith proves that whoever depended upon other than Allah (swt) to bring benefit or protection from harm to him will be abandoned, because granting benefit and protecting from harm are the prerogative of Allah (swt), and seeking such things from others is an act of *Shirk*.

..ooOOoo..

It is reported by Ahmad, on the authority of Ruwaifa' (ra) that he said: "Allah's Messenger (saas) said to me: "Oh, Ruwaifa'! It is probable that your life will be a long one, so inform the people that whoever tied his beard, or wore a bowstring, or cleaned his privates using animal dung or a bone (should know that) Muhammad is innocent of him."

Ruwaifa' (ra) tells us in this Hadith that the Prophet (saas) informed him that he would live a long life, and therefore it was incumbent upon him to tell the people in future that he, Muhammad (saas) was free from blame in the case of anyone who tied his beard, or hung a bowstring around his neck or around the neck of his riding beast in order to be protected from *al-'ain*, or cleaned his private parts after relieving himself with animal dung or a bone.

Benefits Derived From This Hadith

1. The miracle of the Prophet (saas), in knowing that Ruwaifa' (ra) would live a long life.

2. The acceptance of information from a single, reliable source.

3. The forbiddance of tying the beard - though, according to some scholars, this means during prayer, and Allah (swt) knows best.

4. The forbiddance of tying a bowstring around one's neck, or the neck of a riding beast.

5. The forbiddance of cleaning one's privates using animal dung or a bone, because the first is a food for other creatures and the second is a food for the jinn.

Relevance of This Hadith to the Subject of the Chapter

That it proves that it is forbidden to wear a bowstring in order to protect oneself.

Relevance of This Hadith to the Subject of *Tawheed*

That the Prophet (saas) declared himself blameless in the case of anyone who wore a bowstring as a means of protection, because bestowing benefit and granting protection from harm come from Allah (swt), Alone, and so whoever asked them from other than Allah (swt) has committed an act of *Shirk*.

..ooOOoo..

It is reported on the authority of Sa'eed Ibn Jubair (ra) that he said: "Whoever cut (and removed) a *tamemah* from a person, it will be for him as if he had freed a slave." (Narrated by Wakee')

Also from Wakee', on the authority of Ibraheem An-Nakha'i, is that he said: "They (the Companions) used to hate *at-tamaa`im* and they used to remove them (wherever they found them) - whether they were from the Qur'an or from other sources."

In the first narration, Sa'eed Ibn Jubair (ra) informs us that whoever removed an amulet or talisman from a person will have a reward equivalent to the one who freed a slave, because he would by doing so, free that person from the Fire, and from following vain desires and *Shirk*.

As for the second narration, the reporter informs us that the Companions of the Prophet (saas) used to hate, i.e. forbid the wearing of talismans and amulets and ordered their removal, whether they were from the Qur'an or not.

Benefits Derived From the Two Narration

1. The virtue of rejecting the forbidden.

2. The forbiddance of talismans and amulets.

3. The virtue of freeing a slave.

4. The Companions' prohibition of *at-tamaa'im* - whether they contained verses from the Qur'an or anything else.

Relevance of the Narration to the Subject of the Chapter

That both of them prove the prohibition of wearing amulets or talismans, whether they contain Qur'anic verses or not.

Relevance of the Narrations to the Subject of *Tawheed*

That they prove the forbiddance of wearing amulets and talismans as a protection against harm, because protection from harm comes from Allah (swt), Alone, and seeking it from other than Him is an act of *Shirk*.

Footnotes

1. Ar-Ruqi: (sing = ruqiyah) Incantations, magic spells.

2. At-Tamaa`im: (sing. = tameemah) Placing an amulet around the neck to protect the wearer from the effects of al-'ain.

3. Narrated by Bukhari and Muslim.

4. At-Tiwalah: Bewitchment, in order to make a person fall in love with another.

5. i.e. a talisman or an amulet.

Top | Prev | Next

Kitaab At-Tawheed, Chapter: 7

Whoever Seeks Blessing From a Tree, Stone, or Any Such Thing

Allah (swt), says:

> " *Have you seen Al-Laat and Al-`Uzzaa? and another, the third, Manaat? What! Is the male sex for you and the female for Him? That would indeed be a most unfair division!"* (Qur'an 53:19-22)

Allah (swt), Most High, reviles all idol-worshipping polytheists in general and in particular, those who worship the three idols: *Al-Laat,*[1] the idol of the people of Taa'if,[2] *Al-'Uzza,*[3] worshipped by the people of Waadi Nakhlah, and *Manaat,*[4] the idol of the people of Al-Mushallal, near Al-Qadeed,[5] and He challenges them concerning these idols: Can they benefit them in any way, by bringing good or protecting from harm? Or are they simply names which they have given themselves, not sanctioned by Allah (swt)? Allah (swt) also reviles their unfair division: That they appoint those whom they despise, especially the weak females, as children for Allah (swt), the Almighty, the All-powerful, while they prefer for themselves sons, embodying the characteristics of manliness, strength and power.

That being the case, if this is injustice to women, then how about Allah (swt)? Allah (swt) is far above that which they attribute to Him from sons and daughters.

Benefits Derived From These Verses

1. The obligation to reject the forbidden.

2. The falseness of idol-worship.

3. The obligation to reject the attribution of sons and daughters to Allah.

4. The corruption of the *fitrah*[6] in the polytheists, who attributed daughters to Allah, even though they despise them for themselves; and they claimed that their idol-worship was only to bring them closer to Allah.

Relevance of These Verses to the Subject of the Chapter

That they prove that the worship of these idols by the polytheists was a means of seeking protection from harm; and anyone who seeks blessing from a tree, a grave or worships any other created thing seeking benefit or protection from harm is imitating them and commits an act of *Shirk* like them.

Important Note

It has been said concerning *Al-Laat* that he was a pious man who used to prepare *saweeq*[7] for the pilgrims to Makkah, and that when he died, they began to worship at the site of his grave.

It was also said that it was a name given to a carved stone; and in reconciling these two statements, we may say that the carved stone was near to the grave (which is often marked with a stone), and the edifice erected covered both of them, thus making them into one object of worship.

..ooOOoo..

It is reported on the authority of Abu Waqid Al-Laithi (ra) that he said: "We were travelling with the Prophet (saas) to Hunain, when we had only recently abandoned disbelief and the polytheists had a lotus-tree at which they used to worship and upon which they used to hang their weapons. They called it: *Zaatu Anwaat.* So we said to Allah's Messenger (saas):

> *"Make for us a Zaatu Anwaat like theirs," at which the Messenger of Allah (saas) said: "Allaahu Akbar! Verily, that which you have said - by Him in Whose Hand is my soul - is the same as was said by the Children of Israel to Moosa: "Make for us a god such as the gods which they (the polytheist Egyptians) have." Then he (saas) said: "Verily, you are an ignorant people who will follow the way of those who were before you."* (Narrated by At-Tirmizi, who declared it authentic)

Abu Waaqid Al-Laithi (ra) informs us in this Hadith that he accompanied the Prophet (saas) on a journey to the Battle of Hunain, and that they (the Companions) knew that the polytheists had a lotus-tree from which they used to seek blessings and at which they would remain to worship; and because of the fact that they were new to Islam, and because they did not fully realize its goals (i.e. to call people to worship Allah swt , Alone), they asked the Prophet (saas) to designate a tree like it for them that they might also seek blessings from it and worship in its vicinity like the pagans. At this, the Prophet (saas) exclaimed, in vexation: "*Allaahu Akbar*!", [8] then he explained to them that such ignorance was the same as that displayed by the people of Moosa (as) who asked him to make for them an idol like those of the pagan Egyptians which they might worship and this was after Allah (swt) had saved them from Fir'aoun[9] and his people. Then he informed them that this *Ummah* will do as the Jews and Christians do in everything, including *Shirk.*

Benefits Derived From This Hadith

1. The virtue of making clear that which would refute the charge of back-biting, by saying: "...when we had recently abandoned disbelief..."

2. The difficulty man experiences in removing ingrained habits.

3. That devotion (*i'tikaaf*) to a particular place is an act of worship.

4. That the ignorant person is excused by virtue of his ignorance so long as he ceases his mistake once knowledge comes to him.

5. The prohibition of imitating the ignorant people such as the polytheists and others.

6. The permissibility of saying: "*Allaahu Akbar*!" when one is surprised.

7. The obligation to close off all possible routes leading to *Shirk.*

8. That *Shirk* will occur in this *Ummah.*

9. The permissibility of invoking Allah's Name, when delivering a legal verdict.

10. The permissibility of swearing without the intention of making an oath for good reason.

11. That this *Ummah* will do all that the Jews and Christians do.

12. That all the evil deeds done by the Jews and Christians should serve as a warning to us.

Relevance of This Hadith to the Subject of the Chapter

That it proves that taking trees as a source of blessing, and carrying out devotions in their vicinity is *Shirk* and it includes every tree, stone or other object of worship from which blessings are invoked.

Important Note

It has become very common nowadays for people to invoke blessings by the sweat of the righteous, or by touching them or their clothes or by their *tahneek* [10] of children, which they base upon the action of the Prophet (saas); but this is unacceptable because this was something purely and solely for him (saas), not a *sunnah* for all the Muslims. His Companions - who were the best of people in following him and implementing his *Sunnah* did not do so, either in his lifetime or after his death.

Footnotes

1. Al-Laat: Derived from the word: Al-Ilaah, which means: the Deity.

2. Ta`if: A city in the mountains east of Makkah, in present-day Saudi Arabia.

3. Al-'Uzzaa: Derived from the name: Al-'Azeez, which means the Almighty and said to be the name given to a tree in Waadi Nakhlah, which is on the road between Makkah and Ta`if. The pagans had erected a building over it, and covered it with curtains and a gate and it was worshipped by Quraish and the tribe of Banoo Kinaanah.

4. Manaat: Derived from Al-Manaan, which means the Benefactor, it was a structure in Al-Mushallal, near to the town of Al-Qadeed; it was worshipped by the tribes of Khazaa'ah, Al-Aws and Al-Khazraj, and they used to use it as a starting point when making pilgrimage to Makkah.

5. Al-Qadeed: A town lying between Makkah and Madinah in present-day Saudi Arabia.

6. Fitrah: The natural state in which we are born, i.e. believing in the Oneness of Allah (swt).

7. Saweeq: A kind of porridge made from wheat or barley.

8. Allaahu Akbar: Allah (swt) is Greater.

9. Fir'aoun: Pharoah.

10. Tahneek: Putting juice and saliva into the mouth of an infant: It is reported on the authority of 'Aa`ishah (may Allah be pleased with her) that: "The first child born in the Islamic State (Madinah) amongst the Muhaajiroon (Emigrants) was 'Abdullah Ibn Az-Zubair. They brought him to the Prophet (saas). The Prophet (saas) took a date and after chewing it, put its juice in to his mouth. So the first thing that went into the child's stomach was the saliva of the Prophet (saas)." (Narrated by Bukhari)

Top | Prev | Next

Kitaab At-Tawheed, Chapter: 8

What is Said Concerning Slaughter Dedicated to Other Than Allah

Allah (swt), says:

> " *Say: "Verily, my prayer, my slaughter, my life and my death are [all] for Allah, the Lord of the worlds. He has no partner: This am I commanded, and I am the first of those who submit"* (Qur'an 6:162-163)

Allah (swt), Most High, commands His Prophet, Muhammad (saas) to inform the polytheists who worship gods beside Allah (swt) that his prayers - both obligatory and supererogatory - his slaughter of animals, everything which he does in his life, and the correct beliefs [in Islamic Monotheism] and righteous deeds upon which he will die are all purely for Allah (swt), Alone, without partners, and that he was the first of this *Ummah* to submit himself to the Will of Allah (swt), the Almighty, the All-powerful.

Benefits Derived From These Verses

1. That prayer and slaughter are acts of worship.

2. That all of the slave's righteous deeds in this life - if he did them seeking nearness to Allah will become acts of worship.

3. That what counts in deeds is one's final actions.[1]

4. That sincerity in dedicating one's deeds to Allah, Alone is a condition of their acceptance.

Relevance of These Verses to the Subject of the Chapter

That they prove that the slaughtering of animals is not acceptable unless it is done in Allah's Name so that it becomes an act of worship, and dedicating acts of worship to other than Allah (swt) is *Shirk*.

..ooOOoo..

Allah (swt), says:

> " *Therefore pray to your Lord and slaughter [animals in His Name only]"* (Qur'an 8:102)

Allah (swt) orders His Prophet, Muhammad (saas) to approach these two acts of worship with humility and urgency towards Allah (swt), and trusting in Him and desiring to draw near to Him; and the first (prayer) is physical and the second (*halaal* slaughter)[2] is financial.

Benefits Derived From This Verse

1. The obligation to draw near to Allah.

2. The obligation to draw near to Him by *halaal* slaughter - purely and solely for Him.

Relevance of This Verse to the Subject of the Chapter

That it proves that drawing near to Allah (swt) by slaughtering animals will not be achieved unless it is done purely and solely for Allah (swt) - and to slaughter an animal in the name of other than Allah (swt) is an act of *Shirk*.

Important Note

The narration quoted by some, in which `Ali (ra) was said to have explained the Word of Allah (swt) in this verse (*Wanher*) as meaning raising the hands in prayer is rejected by scholars of Hadith and none should follow it or depend upon it.

..ooOOoo..

It is reported on the authority of `Ali (ra) that he said: "Allah's Messenger (saas) told me four things:

> *"Allah (swt) has cursed the one who slaughters in the name of other than Allah (swt);*
> *Allah (swt) has cursed the one who curses his parents; Allah (swt) has cursed the one who*
> *protects and shelters the muhdith;[3] Allah (swt) has cursed the one who alters the land-*
> *marks.* (Narrated by Muslim)

`Ali (ra) informs us that the Prophet (saas) told him that Allah's curse is upon every person who attempts to get nearer to Allah (swt) by slaughtering an animal in the name of other than Him, Most High, and also upon every person who curses his parents, either directly or by inciting others to do so, and upon every person who gives shelter to a criminal or malefactor, and upon every person who alters the landmarks or borders in order to unlawfully seize the land of his neighbour which does not belong to him.

Benefits Derived From This Hadith

1. The prohibition of slaughtering an animal in other than Allah's Name.

2. The forbiddance of cursing one's parents, either directly, or by inciting others to do so.

3. The prohibition of aiding and abetting criminals.

4. The forbiddance of changing borders in order to unlawfully acquire land or territory.

5. The general permissibility of cursing the profligate.

Relevance of This Hadith to the Subject of the Chapter

That the Hadith proves the prohibition of slaughtering an animal in other than Allah's Name, because directing an act of worship to others beside Allah (swt) is an act of *Shirk*.

..ooOOoo..

It is reported from Tariq Ibn Shihab (ra) that the Prophet (saas) said:

*"A man entered Paradise because of a fly, while another entered the Fire because of a fly."
They asked: "How was that possible, oh, Messenger of Allah (saas)?" He replied: "Two
men passed by a people who had an idol, which it was not permissible for anyone to pass
without making a sacrifice to it. They (the people) said to the first man: "Sacrifice
(something)." He said: "I have nothing with which to do so." They said: "Sacrifice something, even if it were only a fly," and so he did so, and they allowed him to continue on his
way and so he entered the Hell-fire. Then they said to the second man: "Sacrifice
(something)." But he said: "I will not sacrifice anything unless it be to Allah (swt), the
Almighty, the All-powerful," so they struck his neck (and he died) and entered
Paradise."* (Narrated by Ahmad)

The Messenger of Allah (saas) informs us in this Hadith that two men - possibly they were from the
Children of Israel passed by a people who had an idol. They requested the two men to sacrifice
something to it, even if it were only something small. The first of them sacrificed a fly, and because of
this, he was thrown in the Hell-fire. The second, due to his strong faith and complete *Tawheed*, refused
to do so and so they killed him and he entered Paradise.

Benefits Derived From This Hadith

1. The enormity of *Shirk*, even though it may be only slight.

2. The existence of Paradise and Hell.

3. That even among the idol-worshipers, the action of the heart is directed to a certain goal.

4. The closeness of man to Paradise and Hell.

5. The warning against sin, even though it may be considered a small sin.

6. Evidence of the breadth of Allah's forgiveness and the severity of His punishment.

7. That the most important deeds are the last ones we do in life. [4]

Relevance of This Hadith to the Subject of the Chapter

That it proves that it is forbidden to slaughter something as a sacrifice to other than Allah (swt), for
such an act of worship is *Shirk*.

Important Note

This Hadith does not contradict the Words of Him, Most High:

*" except he who is forced to do so, while his heart remains steadfast in
faith"* (Qur'an16:106)

Because the Messenger of Allah (saas) said (*fa garrab*): i.e. he attempted to draw closer to Allah (swt)
by sacrificing the fly, and this indicates his acceptance of the deed and it is this which caused him to
enter the Hell-fire because his heart was inclined towards it and did not remain steadfast in faith.

Footnotes

1. See footnonte no. 33.

2. Halaal slaughter: Slaughter in accordance with Islamic rites.

3. Muhdith: A criminal or wrongdoer.

4. See footnote no. 33.

Top | Prev | Next

Kitaab At-Tawheed, Chapter: 9

Do Not Slaughter in the Name of Allah (swt) in a Place Where Animals Are Slaughtered in the Name of Others Beside Him

Allah (swt), says:

> " *Do not ever stand [in prayer] therein. There is a mosque whose foundation was laid on piety from the first day. It is more worthy of your standing [for prayer] therein. In it are men who love to be purified; and Allah loves those who purify [themselves after answering the call of nature]"* (Qur'an 9:108)

Allah (swt), Most High, forbids His Prophet (saas) in this verse, from praying in the Mosque of Harm and Disbelief,[1] which was the first mosque to be built on a foundation of wicked intentions; and He commands them (the Muslims) to pray in the mosque which was built from the first upon a foundation of obedience to Allah (swt) and His Messenger (saas);[2] then Allah (swt) praises the people of that mosque and He tells us that they are meticulous in their cleanliness and ablutions; then He informs us that he loves those who purify themselves from all unclean things, especially when coming from the toilet, or after sexual intercourse, etc. And those who purify themselves from the spiritual `filth' of *Shirk*.

Benefits Derived From This Verse

1. The prohibition of encouraging that which is false.

2. The obligation to deny those deeds which are rejected and whose perpetrators are abandoned.

3. The evidence of the danger of the hypocrites to this *Ummah*, and the obligation to warn against them.

4. The superiority of The Prophet's Mosque and/or Qubaa` Mosque.

5. Confirmation of Allah's Divine Attribute of Love.

6. That Islam encourages cleanliness and purity, both physical and spiritual.

7. The forbiddance of praying in the Mosque of Harm and Disbelief or in the place where it stood, up to the Day of Resurrection.

Relevance of This Verse to the Subject of the Chapter

That it proves that it is forbidden to carry out an act of obedience to Allah (swt) and His Prophet (saas) in a place used to carry out acts of disobedience to Allah (swt) and His Messenger (saas), and that includes slaughtering animals in a place where animals are slaughtered for others besides Allah (swt).

Relevance of This Verse to the Subject of *Tawheed*

That it proves the prohibition of all things which might lead in the end to *Shirk*.

..ooOOoo..

It is reported on the authority of Thabit Ibn Adh-Dhahhak (saas) that he said: "A man vowed to sacrifice a camel at a place called Buwanah, and he asked the Prophet (saas) about it. He (saas) said to him: "Does the place contain any of the idols from the time of the *Jahiliyyah*?"[3] They said: "No." He (saas) then asked: "Did the disbelievers hold any of their (religious) festivals there?" They replied: "No." So the Messenger of Allah (saas) said:

> *"Then fulfill your vow, for verily, vows, which entail disobedience to Allah (swt) or that which is beyond the capacity of the son of Adam should not be fulfilled."* (Narrated by Abu Dawood, with a *Sanad* that meets the conditions of acceptance laid down by Bukhari and Muslim)

Thabit Ibn Adh-Dhahak (ra) informs us that a man made a vow to slaughter a female camel in a place called Buwanah, and so the Prophet (saas) enquired as to whether it had been used as a place of worship for the idols of the *Jahiliyyah* or whether any of their pagan festivals had been celebrated there. When it was made clear to him that this was not the case, he ordered the man to fulfill his vow. In addition to this, he then gave a general ruling binding upon his *Ummah* until the Day of Ressurrection, prohibiting the fulfillment of vows made in disobedience to Allah (swt) or which require of man what is beyond his capacity.

Benefits Derived From This Hadith

1. The obligation to fulfill one's vows so long as it does not entail disobedience to Allah (swt) or some impossible act.

2. The lawfulness of making inquiries on the part of the *Mufti* before delivering judgement.

3. The prohibition of carrying out an act of obedience in a place where acts of disobedience are performed.

4. The forbiddance of fulfilling vows which entail disobedience; instead, an act of recompense is required.[4]

5. That a vow should not be taken to do something which is beyond man's ability.

6. The permissibility of specifying a place or a time for the fulfillment of a vow.

Relevance of This Hadith to the Subject of the Chapter

That it proves the prohibition of carrying out an act of obedience to Allah (swt) in a place where acts of disobedience to Him are performed, and this includes slaughtering animals in a place where animals are dedicated to others than Allah (swt).

Relevance of This Hadith to the Subject of *Tawheed*

That it proves the forbiddance of performing an act which may lead in the end to *Shirk*.

Footnotes

1. This mosque known as Masjid Dhiraar, or, the Mosque of Harm and Disbelief, was built by the hypocrites of Madinah in an attempt to prove their allegiance to Allah (swt) and His Messenger (saas).

2. It is commonly believed that the mosque referred to in this verse is Qubaa` Mosque, on the outskirts of Madinah, as this is the first mosque built by the Muslims after the Hijrah (Migration) of the Muslims from Makkah to Madinah. Ibn Katheer states that some, or a few (???) of the Salaf held this view, while he says that a number ((????? held that it was the Prophet's Mosque in Madinah that was referred to in the verse. While there are some proofs for both views, those who held the latter view drew support from the Hadith reported by Muslim, Ahmad, Ibn Abi Shaibah and others, on the authority of Humaid Al-Kharraat, who said: " I heard Abu Salamah Ibn 'Abdul-Rahman say: "'Abdul-Rahman Ibn Abi Sa'eed Al-Khudri visited me, and I said to him: "What did you hear from your father, concerning the mosque which was built upon a foundation of piety?" He replied: "My father said: "I visited the Messenger of Allah (saas) in the house of one of his wives, and I said to him: "Oh, Messenger of Allah (saas)! Which of the two mosques is it that was built upon a foundation of piety?" The Prophet took a handful of stones and beat the earth with them, then he said: "It is this, your mosque, the Mosque of Madinah." He (Abu Salamah) then said: "I testify that I heard your father say likewise." Ibn Jareer At-Tabari agreed with this, while Ibn Katheer said that there was no contradiction in saying that both mosques were intended - and Allah (swt) knows best.

3. Jahiliyyah: The time of ignorance and polytheism prior to Islam.

4. It is reported on the authority of Ibn 'Abbas (ra) that the Prophet (saas) said: "If anyone takes a vow to do an act of disobedience, its atonement is the same as that for an oath." (Narrated by Abu Dawood) - and concerning the atonement for an oath, Allah (swt), Most High says: [Allah will not call you to account for your unintentional oaths, but He will hold you to account for your deliberate oaths: For expiation, feed ten poor persons, on a scale of what is average for the food of your families; or clothe them; or give a slave his freedom. If that is beyond your means, fast for three days. That is the expiation for the oaths you have sworn] (Qur'an 3:89)

Top | Prev | Next

Kitaab At-Tawheed, Chapter: 10

A Vow to Another Besides Allah (swt) is Shirk

Allah (swt), says:

[They perform their vows, and they fear a Day whose evil is spread far and wide] (Qur'an 76:7)

Allah (swt), Most Glorified, Most High, praises His righteous slaves in this verse because they fulfill the vows which they have made incumbent upon themselves desiring nearness to Allah (swt); and He makes clear to us their certainty of belief on the Day of Resurrection and their fear of Allah's severe chatisement, which will be delivered far and wide on that Day.

Benefits Derived From This Verse

1. The obligation to fulfill one's vows so long as they do not constitute disobedience to Allah.

2. That fear of the Day of Resurrection is one of the attributes of the Believers.

3. Confirmation of the Resurrection of mankind on that Day.

Relevance of This Verse to the Subject of the Chapter

That the verse praises the fulfillment of vows, and Allah (swt) does not praise except that which is obligatory or that which is strongly preferred, or refraining from the prohibited. This is why fulfillment of a vow is considered to be an act of worship, and dedicating an act of worship to other than Allah (swt) is an act of *Shirk*.

..ooOOoo..

Allah (swt), says:

[And whatever you spend in charity or whatever vow you make, be sure Allah knows it all. But the wrongdoers have no helpers] (Qur'an 2:270)

Allah (swt), Most Glorified, Most High, informs us in this verse that whatsoever man gives in the way of charity and whatever vows he makes, seeking nearness to Allah (swt), He knows it, even if the perpetrator were to keep it secret, and He will reward him for it. Then, Allah (swt) warns the people against injustice in charity and in their vows and in all their deeds, and He (swt) informs them that they will find none to help them or protect them should Allah (swt) punish them for their sins.

Benefits Derived From This Verse

1. Evidence of the breadth of Allah's (swt) Knowledge and of the fact that it encompasses every single thing.

2. That taking a vow is an act of worship.

3. The prohibition of all types of injustice.

Relevance of This Verse to the Subject of the Chapter

That the verse proves that Allah (swt), Most Glorified, Most High, has knowledge of each and every vow, and that He rewards the one who makes it, therefore fulfilling a vow is an act of worship and dedicating an act of worship to another besides Allah (swt) is *Shirk*.

..ooOOoo..

It is authentically reported on the authority of `Aa`ishah (may Allah be pleased with her) that the Prophet (r) said: "Whoever vowed to obey Allah (swt), he should do so, and whoever vowed to disobey Him, should not do so.[1]"

Benefits Derived From This Hadith

1. The obligation to fulfill vows so long as they are in obedience to Allah (swt).

2. The prohibition of fulfilling vows if they entail disobedience to Allah (swt). Instead, he must perform the expiation of an oath.

Relevance of the *Hadeeth* to the Subject of the Chapter

That it proves the obligation to fulfill one's vow so long as it does not entail disobedience to Allah (swt). This means that fulfilling a vow is an act of worship, and dedicating an act of worship to other than Allah (swt) is *Shirk*.

Footnotes

1. Narrated by Imam Malik.

Top | Prev | Next

Kitaab At-Tawheed, Chapter: 11

Seeking Refuge in Other Than Allah (swt) is Shirk

Allah (swt), says:

> " *And there were persons among mankind who took shelter with persons among the jinn, but they [only] increased them in rahaq"* (Qur'an 72:6)

Allah (swt), Most Glorified, Most High, informs us in this verse that there were men from among the human race who turned to the men from among the jinn, seeking protection with them, but their supplications only caused to increase the jinn in pride and injustice, and they caused the jinn to increase mankind in fear and misguidance.

Benefits Derived From This Verse

1. The prohibition of seeking protection from other than Allah.

2. That whoever seeks protection from other than Allah, will be disappointed, and he will be guilty of injustice against the one called upon.

3. Confirmation of the existence of the jinn, and of their being composed of men and women.

Relevance of This Verse to the Subject of the Chapter

That it proves the prohibition of seeking shelter or protection with other than Allah (swt), because doing so is an act of worship, and dedicating worship to other than Allah (swt) is *Shirk*.

Important Note

If we understand from Allah's Words:

> " *they [only] increased them in rahaq"*

That `they' refers to mankind, then the meaning would be that the supplication of man only increased the jinn in arrogance and oppression; but if we understand from the verse that `they' refers to the jinn, then the meaning would be that the jinn increased mankind in fear and misguidance.

..ooOOoo..

It is reported on the authority of Khawlah Bint Hakeem (may Allah be pleased with her) that she said: "I heard Allah's Messenger (saas) say:

> *"Whoever visited an abode and said: "I seek refuge in the Most Perfect Words of my Rabb, from the evil of what He has created," no harm shall befall him until he departs from that*

place." (Narrated by Muslim)

Khawlah Bint Hakeem informs us that the Prophet (saas) has approved as a *sunnah* for the Muslims that when they visit a dwelling, they should seek shelter with Allah (swt) rather than with the jinn or others, from the evil of His creatures; and he informed us that whoever seeks refuge and shelter in the Most Complete and Perfect Words of Allah (swt), which are free from every defect and imperfection, Allah will be sufficient protection for him from every evil present in His creatures until he leaves that place.

Benefits Derived From This Hadith

1. Evidence of the blessing of this supplication.

2. That the Qur'an was revealed, not created.[1]

3. That protection is not sought with other than Allah (swt), nor with His Divine Attributes.

4. Evidence that Seeking shelter with Allah (swt) is prescribed by the Religion.

5. Evidence of the completeness and perfection of the Qur'an because, being the Word of Allah (swt), it is necessarily Perfect and Complete.

Relevance of This Hadith to the Subject of the Chapter

That the Hadith proves that seeking protection with other than Allah (swt), or with one of His Attributes is not permissible, because seeking shelter or protection is an act of worship and dedicating an act of worship to other than Allah (swt) is *Shirk*.

Footnotes

1. This is because the Qur'an is the Word of Allah (swt), and as such, it is not created.

Top | Prev | Next

Kitaab At-Tawheed, Chapter: 12

It is Shirk to Seek Aid From Other Than Allah (swt)

Allah (swt), says:

> " *Nor call on any besides Allah, such can neither profit you, nor hurt you. If you do, then you will surely be one of the zalimun"* (Qur'an 10:106)

In this verse, Allah (swt), Most Glorified, Most High, forbids His Prophet, Muhammad (saas) - and the forbiddance applies to the whole *Ummah* - from performing acts of worship, in particular supplication for any other besides Allah (swt), because none beside Him possesses power to benefit or harm. Then Allah (swt) informs His Prophet (saas) that should he do so, he would be one of the *Zalimun*, i.e. the polytheists.

Benefits Derived From This Verse

1. That benefit and protection from harm are only from Allah, the Almighty, the All-powerful.

2. That whoever called upon other than Allah, believing that he possesses the power to benefit or harm him without Allah, has committed an act of *Shirk*.

3. The reference to *Shirk* as *Zulm* (injustice).

..ooOOoo..

Allah (swt), says:

> " *If Allah does not touch you with hurt, there is none can remove it but He: If He designs some benefit for you, there is none can keep back His Favour: He causes it to reach whomsoever of His slaves He wills, and He is the Most Forgiving, Most Merciful"* (Qur'an10:107)

In this verse, Allah (swt), Most Glorified, Most High, informs His Prophet, Muhammad (saas) that both good and evil are determined by Allah (swt), the Almighty, the All-powerful, and that none of His creatures - whoever he may be - has the power to lift harm or prevent benefit coming to anyone; and that all power of disposal is in Allah's Hands. He forbids whom He wills, in His Wisdom, and He gives to whom He wills from His Bounty, and He is Oft-forgiving to whomsoever turns in repentance to Him; even to the one who has committed shirk, He is Full of Mercy.

Benefits Derived From This Verse

1. That all goodness and evil is at Allah's Disposal.

2. Confirmation of Allah's Divine Attribute of *Iradah* (i.e. Wish, Decree).

3. Confirmation of Allah's Divine Attribute of *Mashee`ah* (i.e. Will).

4. Confirmation of the totality of Allah's Dominion and Rulership.

5. Confirmation of two of Allah's Names: *Al-Ghafoor* (the Most Forgiving) and *Ar-Raheem* (the Most Merciful to all in this world and to the Believers in the Hereafter) and both of these names encompass the Attributes of Forgiveness and Mercy.

Relevance of This Verse to the Subject of the Chapter

That it proves that preventing or removing harm and the granting of benefit come only from Allah (swt), the Almighty, the All-powerful, and seeking them from other than Allah (swt) is an act of *Shirk*.

..ooOOoo..

Allah (swt), says:

> " *You do naught but worship idols besides Allah, and you invent falsehood. The things that you worship besides Allah have no power to give you sustenance: Then seek you sustenance from Allah, worship Him and be grateful to Him: To Him will you return"* (Qur'an 29:17)

Allah (swt), Most Glorified, Most High tells us in this verse about Prophet Ibraheem (as), how he made clear to his people the truth concerning the idols which they worshipped, that they possessed no power to harm or to benefit, and that they had invented a lie by attributing such powers to them, for goodness may only be sought from Allah (swt), and from none other; and that He, Alone is the One Who has the right to be worshipped, and to be praised and Who deserves our gratitude because all creatures will return to Him when they die; then they will be resurrected and they will receive the recompense of their deeds.

Benefits Derived From This Verse

1. That the original Religion of all the Prophets is *Tawheed*.

2. The falseness of worshipping idols.

3. That all goodness and evil is within Allah's power.

4. The obligation to worship Allah and to be grateful to Him.

5. Confirmation of the coming of the Day of Resurrection.

Relevance of This Verse to the Subject of the Chapter

That it proves that sustenance must not be sought except from Allah (swt), because supplicating for sustenance from other than Allah (swt) is an act of *Shirk*.

..ooOOoo..

Allah (swt), Most High says:

> " *And who is more astray than one who calls upon other than Allah, such as will not answer him until the Day of Resurrection, and who are [even] unaware of their calls to them. And*

when mankind are gathered [on the Day of Resurrection], they [the false deities] will become enemies to them and will deny their worshipping" (Qur'an 46:5-6)

Allah (swt), Most Glorified, Most High, informs us in this verse that none is further astray nor more ignorant than the one who rejects the worship of the All-hearing, the One Who answers, and instead, worships things which are unable to answer him until the Hour comes, either because they themselves are slaves of Allah (swt), who are bound to worship Him, such as the angels, the Prophets and the righteous, or because they are inanimate objects, such as idols. Then Allah (swt) makes clear to us that mankind will be gathered together on the Day of Resurrection, then the worshipers will be shown the uselessness of their deeds because their objects of worship will declare themselves innocent of them and their actions; indeed they will become their enemies, rejecting them and all that they did.

Benefits Derived From These Verses

1. That the most ignorant and farthest astray of all people are those who call upon other than Allah.

2. Confirmation that their objects of worship are ignorant of them and cannot answer them.

3. That this supplication is a kind of worship.

4. That their calling upon these false gods will be the cause of those deities' enmity towards those who worshipped them on the Day of Resurrection.

5. Evidence that these objects of worship will declare themselves innocent of their worshipers on the Day of Resurrection.

Relevance of These Verses to the Subject of the Chapter

That they prove that there is none more ignorant, none farther astray than the one who calls upon other than Allah (swt), because supplication is an act of worship, and dedicating an act of worship to other than Allah (swt) is *Shirk.*

Important Note

The rejection by those objects of worship, such as the angels, the Prophets and the righteous will be by their mouths, obviously. As for those inanimate objects, such as idols, trees, stones, etc., it has been said that Allah (swt) will create for them the power of speech, and they will speak, denouncing their worshipers and their deeds; and it has also been said that they will reject them by their silence and inanimity.

..ooOOoo..

Allah (swt), says:

" Is not He [better than your gods] Who responds to the distressed one, when he calls Him, and Who removes the evil, and makes you inheritors of the earth [generation after generation], is there any deity with Allah? Little it is that you bear in mind [the warning]" (Qur'an 27:62)

Allah (swt), Most High, defines some of the Attributes which are purely for Him, and nobody else, such as responding to those in dire straits, lifting harm from them and protecting mankind. Then Allah (swt), Most Glorified, Most High, makes clear that those who will not be warned by this, nor fear the consequences, and do not worship Allah (swt), Alone, will not heed any warning.

Benefits Derived From This Verse

1. That making one's *du'aa`* [1] purely for Allah will ensure its acceptance.

2. Confirmation of the blessing of *Du'aa`*.

3. That goodness and evil are within Allah's power.

4. Proof of *Tawheed* of worship through *Tawheed* of *Rabb*ship.

5. That Allah (swt) answers the *Du'aa`* of the distressed and the oppressed.

6. Knowledge of Allah (swt) through the *fitrah*.

Relevance of This Verse to the Subject

That the verse proves that none can answer the oppressed or the distressed except Allah (swt), Most Glorified, Most High, because *Du'aa`* is a form of worship and dedicating an act of worship to other than Allah (swt) is *Shirk*.

..ooOOoo..

At-Tabarani reports that: "In the time of the Prophet (saas) there was a hypocrite[2] who used to harm the Believers, and some of them said: "Come, let us seek aid from the Messenger of Allah (saas) against this hypocrite." But the Prophet (saas) said: "Aid must not be sought from me; aid must only be sought from Allah (swt)."

The narrator informs us in this Hadith that a man from amongst the hypocrites used to harm the Companions in any way he could, and so some of them went to the Prophet (saas) to seek his aid in stopping this harm. And even though the Prophet (saas) was able to do so, he forbade them from seeking help from him and instead, he guided them towards that which was better for them - to seek aid from Allah (swt), to ask Him to alleviate their distress and protect them from their enemies in accordance with the dictates of *Tawheed*.

Benefits Derived From This Hadith

1. Evidence that the hypocrites used to do their utmost to harm the Muslims.

2. The prohibition of seeking help from other than Allah (swt) in those things which are beyond their power.

Relevance of This Hadith to the Subject of the Chapter

That it proves the forbiddance of seeking aid from other than Allah (swt), in those things which are beyond the capabilities of all but Allah (swt) because seeking aid is an act of worship, and dedicating acts of worship to other than Allah (swt) is *Shirk*.

Important Note

There is no contradiction between this Hadith and the Words of Allah (swt), Most High:

" And the man from amongst his own people appealed to him for aid" (Qur'an 28:15)

Because this verse tells us that it is permissible to seek aid from one of Allah's creatures in those things which are within their power. Secondly, the Hadith does not prohibit that, but the Messenger of Allah (saas) forbade them, seeking to guide them to that which is better - that is to seek aid from Allah (swt), the Almighty, the All-powerful, for Allah (swt) says:

" And when my slaves ask you [O, Muhammad!] about me, [inform them that] verily, I am near [i.e. in His Knowledge, His Hearing and His Seeing]. I answer the request of every supplicant when he calls upon Me" (Qur'an 2:186)

Footnotes

1. Du'aa`: Supplication.

2. It is likely that the hypocrite referred to here is 'Abdullah Ibn Ubayy.

Top | Prev | Next

Kitaab At-Tawheed, Chapter: 13

Concerning Allah's Words:

> " *Will they associate [with Me] those that do not create, but are [themselves] created - those that can bring them no victory?"* (Qur'an 7:191-192)

Allah (swt) rejects and censures the polytheists from among the Arabs and the non-Arabs in this verse, and those false gods which they worship beside Allah (swt) which can not bring into being anything - for they are themselves created from nothing, and cannot help those who worship them - in fact, they cannot even help themselves, should some misfortune befall them! And this is the ultimate in weakness and powerlessness.

Benefits Derived From These Verses

1. Evidence of the ignorance of the polytheists.

2. Confirmation of the weakness and powerlessness of all that is worshipped beside Allah, and that therefore, logically, they are not fit to be worshipped.

Relevance of These Verses to the Subject of the Chapter

That they prove the negation of all worship except that of Allah (swt), and that to do so is false and rejected, and this includes everything to which people turn besides Allah (swt), such as graves, trees and such like.

Relevance of These Verses to the Subject of *Tawheed*

That they prove that turning towards other than Allah (swt) in order to obtain some benefit or protection from harm is an act of *Shirk*.

Important Note

The warning here is against worshipping those who are blessed with the power of thinking and logic, though many objects of worship are inanimate, and unaware of what is said or believed concerning them.

..ooOOoo..

Allah (swt), says:

> " *He merges the night into the day [i.e. the decrease in the hours of the night is added to the hours of the day] and He merges the day into the night [i.e. the decrease in the hours of the day is added to the hours of the night]. And He has subjected the sun and the moon: Each runs its course for a term appointed. Such is Allah, your Lord; His is the Dominion. And those whom you call upon instead of Him, own not even a qitmeer [the thin membrane covering a date-stone]. If you call upon them, they hear not your call and even were they to hear, they could not grant it [your request] to you. And on the Day of Resurrection, they*

will disown your ascribing them as partners [with Allah]. And none can inform you [oh, Muhammad!] like He [the All-knowing]" (Qur'an 35:13-14)

Allah (swt), Most Glorified, Most High, informs us in these verses that He decreases the hours of the night, and adds them to the hours of daylight, and vice versa, according to the changing seasons, by Allah's Will and in accordance with His Divine Decree. And He has subjected the sun and the moon. These two lights bring innumerable benefits to mankind, by Allah's Will, and He Who is Able to do all things has the exclusive right of Rabbship and to be worshipped alone, without partners - How could it be otherwise, when His is the Dominion over all created things, and everything that is worshipped besides Him possesses nothing, not even the covering of a date-stone, and does not hear the supplication of those who call upon him? And even were they able to hear, they would be incapable of responding to it; indeed, they will reject those who worshipped them and their *Shirk* on the Day of Resurrection, and none besides Allah (swt), the All-knowing, could inform the Messenger (saas) of the truth of these matters and their outcome.

Benefits Derived From These Verses

1. That the sun and moon move in their orbits and are not stationary.

2. That idols do not possess any power to benefit or harm those who worship them, either in this world or in the Hereafter.

3. That *Shirk* will be the cause of enmity between the worshipers and the worshipped.

4. That knowledge should be taken from its original source - in this case, Allah, Who is the source of all knowledge.

Relevance of These Verses to the Subject of the Chapter

That the verses reject and condemn the idea that those deities worshipped besides Allah (swt) have any power to benefit or harm the worshipers.

Relevance of These Verses to the Subject of *Tawheed*

That the verses prove that making *Du'aa`* to other than Allah (swt) is *Shirk*.

..ooOOoo..

It is authentically reported on the authority of Anas (ra) that the Prophet (saas) was struck during the battle of Uhud, and one of his molar teeth was broken, at which he said: "How can a people ever be successful, when they strike their Prophet?" and so it was revealed:

" *The matter is not for your decision: Whether He turns in mercy to them or punishes them; for verily, they are the wrongdoers"* (Qur'an 3:128) [1]

Anas Ibn Malik (ra) informs us in this Hadith that the Prophet (saas) received an injury to his head, which bled and one of his teeth was broken during the Battle of Uhud, and he became despondent of the prospect of their accepting Islam because of this outrage against the personage of Allah's chosen Messenger and the enmity which they showed for him. Then Allah (swt) revealed this verse:

" *The matter is not for your decision...*"

And so it became clear to him the path that he must follow and that forgiveness or punishment for these polytheists rests with Allah (swt), Most Glorified, Most High, Alone and with no other.

Benefits Derived From This Hadith

1. That the Prophets are subject to illness and injury, which is proof of their humanity and a rejection of those who ascribe Divine Attributes to them.[2]

2. That the Prophets are unable to do anything, except what Allah (swt) Wills for them, so how about other lesser creatures?

3. None knows what a person's last actions will be except Allah (swt).

4. That turning to Allah (swt) in sincere repentance wipes out all previous sins.

5. That wrongdoing (i.e. *Shirk*) will be punished.

Relevance of This Hadith to the Subject of the Chapter

That it proves that the Prophets, who are the best of people do not possess any power to benefit or harm, so what about other lesser creatures?

Relevance of This Hadith to the Subject of *Tawheed*

That the Hadith proves that benefit or harm comes only from Allah (swt), and requesting it from other than Him is *Shirk*.

..ooOOoo..

It is reported on the authority of Ibn `Umar (ra) that he heard the Messenger of Allah (saas) saying as he raised his head from bowing, in the second *rak'ah* of *fajr* prayer: "Oh, Allah (swt)! Curse so-and-so and so-and-so," after saying: "*Sami' Allahu Liman Hamidah*," and: "*Rabbanaa wa Lak Al-Hamd*." And so Allah (swt) revealed:

" *The matter is not for your decision...*"." [3]

In another narration, it is reported that he (saas) made *Du'aa`* against Safwaan Ibn Umayyah, Suhail Ibn `Amr and Al-Harith Ibn Hisham, and so this verse was revealed:

" *The matter is not for your decision...*"

`Abdullah Ibn `Umar (ra) informs us in this Hadith that the Prophet (saas), while straightening up from bowing in the second unit of the dawn prayer, said: "Allah hears the one who praises Him," and: "Our *Rabb*! To You is due all praise." Then he invoked Allah's Curse on the heads of a number of the pagans of Quraish, in one narration, naming them; then Allah (swt) revealed to him a verse prohibiting him from doing so because of Allah's Knowledge of what the future held for some of them, who would eventually embrace Islam, and become good Muslims.

Benefits Derived From This Hadith

1. That the Imam recites *"Sami' Allahu Liman Hamidah,"* as well as *"Rabbanaa wa Lak Al-Hamd."*

2. The lawfulness of invoking Allah (swt) upon someone in times of need.

3. Proof that the Qur'an is revealed, not created.

4. Evidence that the Prophets do not possess any power to benefit or harm anyone, nor do they have knowledge of the unseen.

Relevance of This Hadith to the Subject of the Chapter

That it proves that the Prophets, though they are the best of people, do not have power to benefit or harm, so what of lesser creatures?

Relevance of This Hadith to the Subject of *Tawheed*

That it proves that benefit and harm are in Allah's power only, and so seeking them from other than Him is an act of *Shirk*.

Important Note

It has been authenticated that the three persons mentioned in the Hadith, Safwaan Ibn Umayyah, Al-Haarith Ibn Hishaam and Suhail Ibn `Amr all later embraced Islam.

..ooOOoo..

It is reported on the authority of Abu Hurairah (ra) that when this verse was revealed:

" *And warn your nearest kinsmen" (Qur'an 26:214)*

Allah's Messenger (saas) stood up and said: "Oh, you people of Quraish (or something similar)! Save your own souls! I possess nothing with which to protect you from Allah (swt). Oh, `Abbas Ibn `Abdul Muttalib! I possess nothing with which to protect you from Allah (swt). Oh, Safiyyah, aunt of the Messenger of Allah (saas)! I possess nothing with which to protect you from Allah (swt). Oh, Fatimah Bint Muhammad! Ask me of what I have anything you which; I possess nothing with which to protect you from Allah (swt)."

Abu Hurairah (ra) informs us in this Hadith, that when the Words of Allah:

" *And warn your nearest kinsmen"*

Were revealed, the Messenger of Allah (saas) stood amongst them and addressed them, requesting them to save themselves from the punishment of Allah (swt) by obeying Him and His Messenger (saas) and that he could not save them or protect them from Allah's severe chastisement. Then he addressed some of his close family members, one at a time, so that they should not be proud or conceited and depend upon their relationship to him.

Benefits Derived From This Hadith

1. That the Qur'an is revealed, not created.

2. That nothing can benefit a person except his good deeds.

3. The falseness of relying on one's ancestry or family ties to save him from Allah's punishment, rather than good deeds.

4. Those closest to Allah's Messenger (saas) are those who obey him, not those who claim close family ties.

5. The permissibility of asking the Messenger of Allah (saas) for that which was in his power while he was alive.

Relevance of This Hadith to the Subject of the Chapter

That the Hadith proves that the Prophets do not possess any benefit for any person, nor any harm, so how could any lesser person?

Relevance of This Hadith to the Subject of *Tawheed*

That it proves that bringing benefit or harm is the special prerogative of Allah (swt), Alone and therefore seeking them from other than Him is an act of *Shirk*.

Important Note

There is no contradiction between this Hadith and the Ahadith which confirm the Prophet's intercession, because the latter inform us that he will intercede for the Believers after Allah (swt) Allows him to do so, while the former Hadith rejects the idea that he can save us of his own self.

Footnotes

1. Narrated by Muslim.

2. Such as the Jews who claimed that 'Uzair (as) was their god, and the Christians, who claimed that Eesa (u) was the son of God, and the deviant Braillawis, who ascribe divine Attributes to the Prophet Muhammad (saas).

3. Reported by An-Neesaaboori in "Asbaab An-Nuzool", who said: "It was narrated by Bukhari. and by Muslim.

Top | Prev | Next

Kitaab At-Tawheed, Chapter: 14

The Words of Allah (swt), Most High:

" *No intercession can avail with Him, except for those whom He allows so [much so] that, when terror is removed from their hearts, they will say: "What is it that your Lord has said?" They will say: "The Truth; and He is the Most High, the Most Great."*" (Qur'an 34:23)

Allah (swt), Most Glorified, Most High, informs us in this verse that none can intercede on behalf of another on the Day of Judgement - whosoever he might be - unless Allah (swt), the Almighty, the All-powerful Permits him to do so, and that all, including the angels, will be prostrate due to their fear of Him. Then when the fear is removed from the angels' hearts, they will begin to ask one another concerning what Allah (swt) has said and what He has revealed; and some of them will answer that He has said naught but the Truth, and He (swt) is the Most High, the Most Great.

Benefits Derived From This Verse

1. That none may intercede except if Allah Wills it.

2. Confirmation of Allah's Greatness and His Fearfulness.

3. Confirmation of Allah's Divine Attribute of Speech.

4. That the Words of Allah are free from all falseness.

5. Confirmation of His Divine Attribute of being Above all of His creation - in His Self and in His Attributes.

6. Confirmation of two of His Names, which are: The Most High and the Most Great.

Relevance of This Verse to the Subject of the Chapter

That the verse proves that even the angels fear Allah (swt) and are humbled before Him.

Relevance of This Verse to the Subject of *Tawheed*

That it proves that the angels themselves fear their Lord, so how can anyone call upon them instead of Allah (swt)? And if such acts of worship are rejected, whether they are worshipped directly or as intercessors with Allah (swt), then what must be said about worshipping others such as the inhabitants of graves? - they have even less right to be worshipped.

..ooOOoo..

It is authentically reported from Abu Hurairah (ra) that the Prophet (saas) said: "When Allah (swt) orders a matter in the heaven, the angels beat their wings in humility and submission to His Words, and the sound is like the sound of a chain on smooth rocks; they continue to do so until it enters their hearts. Then, when fear has been removed from their hearts, they (i.e. some of the angels) say: "What has your

Lord said?" They (the others) reply: "The Truth, and He (swt) is the Most High, the Most Great," and the listening thief and (another listening thief) hears it, so, one above another," Sufyaan (one of the narrators) described it by spreading out his fingers, "...and he (the thief) hears the Words (of Allah swt) and transmits them to the one below him and he transmits it to the one below and so on, until it reaches the tongue of the magician or the fortune-teller, and sometimes the meteorite strikes him (the thief) before he can convey the news, and sometime he conveys it before he is struck, and then he adds a hundred lies to what he hears, and it is said: "Did not he (the fortune-teller) tell us such-and-such on such-and-such a day?" Then he is believed because of these Words which were overheard from the heaven." [1]

Allah's Messenger (saas) informs us in this Hadith that when Allah (swt), Almighty, All-Powerful, decrees a matter in the heaven, the angels fall prostrate in fear of Him and in glorification of Him; then, when the fear is removed from their hearts, they begin to ask one another about what the Lord, Almighty, All-powerful has said. One of them (probably Jibreel as)[2] replies that Allah (swt) has spoken the uncompromising Truth, of which there is no doubt; and it could be that the listening thief, who is a devil, overhears what is said and transmits it to the awaiting magician or the fortune-teller, although a meteorite might strike the devil and incinerate him before he has the chance to pass on what he has heard, or it might be passed on before he is destroyed - all in accordance with Allah's Will. And the devil, the magician or the fortune-teller adds a hundred lies to what he has heard and the people hear and believe ninety-nine lies because of this one scrap of Truth which was heard from the heaven.

Benefits Derived From This Hadith

1. Confirmation of Allah's being above His creation.

2. Evidence of Allah's Greatness.

3. Confirmation of Allah's Divine Attribute of Speech.

4. Confirmation that the devils overhear what the angels are saying in the heaven, and that Allah (swt) has allowed them to do so as a test and a trial for them.

5. The permissibility of the use of practical examples in order to explain abstract matters.

6. That the devils are the source of knowledge for both the magician and the fortune-teller.

7. The attachment of some souls to that which is vain and futile.

8. Evidence that the sorcerors and fortune-tellers are liars and cheats.

Relevance of This Hadith to the Subject of the Chapter

That it shows the position of the angels, that they fear and revere their Lord.

Relevance of This Hadith to the Subject of *Tawheed*

That the Hadith proves that the angels themselves worship Allah (swt) and fear Him, and so, if it is not permissible to worship them, whether by calling upon them as intercessors, or as gods, then it is eminently clear that calling upon them is even more obviously futile.

..ooOOoo..

An-Nawwaas Ibn Sam'aan (ra) reported that Allah's Messenger (saas) said: "When Allah (swt), Most High, wishes to reveal something, He speaks out the Revelation and the heavens begin to shake (or he said: thunder heavily) due to fear of Allah (swt), the Almighty, the All-powerful, and when the inhabitants of the heavens hear it, they fall down in prostration to Allah (swt), and Jibreel (as) is the first to raise his head; then Allah (swt) speaks to him and Allah (swt) gives him the Revelation according to His Will. Then Jibreel (as) passes by the angels, and every time he passes through a different heaven, its angels ask him: "What Has our Lord revealed, oh, Jibreel as ?" Jibreel (as) then answers: "He has spoken the Truth, and He (swt) is the Most High, the Most Great." Then they all repeat the same after him, and then Jibreel (as) proceeds to the destination commanded by Allah (swt), the Almighty, the All-powerful."

Allah's Messenger (saas) informs us in this Hadith that when Allah (swt) speaks the Revelation which He wishes, it causes the heavens to shake with thunder and convulsions and the angels to fall down prostrate, in fear of His Majesty; then the first of them to recover and raise his head is the angel Jibreel (as), and Allah (swt) then speaks to him as He (swt) Wills, after which Jibreel (swt) departs with the Revelation to wheresoever Allah Commands him; and every time he passes through one of the heavens, its inhabitants from among the angels enquire of him as to what the *Rabb*, Almighty, All-powerful has commanded. And each time he gives the same reply: That Allah (swt) has spoken the evident Truth, and He (swt) is the Most High, above all His creation, the Most Great, without equal in greatness.

Benefits Derived From This Hadith

1. Confirmation of Allah's Divine Attribute of *Iradah*. [3]

2. Confirmation of Allah's Divine Attribute of *Kalaam* (speaking) and that His (saas) Speech is heard.

3. Evidence of Allah's unparalleled Might.

4. Evidence that all of the heavens are inhabited.

5. Proof of Jibreel's superiority over the rest of the angels.

6. Confirmation of Allah's Divine Attribute of *Qawl*. [4]

7. Confirmation of two of Allah's Names: The Most High and the Most Great.

Relevance of This Hadith to the Subject of the Chapter

That the Hadith clearly shows the position of the angels that they fear Allah (swt).

Relevance of This Hadith to the Subject of *Tawheed*

That the Hadith proves that the angels, who are amongst Allah's finest creations, fear Allah (swt), and so worship of them by others is false and an act of *Shirk*.

Footnotes

1. Narrated by Bukhari

2. Since he is the leader of the angels and the greatest of them.

3. Iradah: Want, wish, will, decree.

4. It is not easy to adequately translate the words Qawl and Kalaam into English, but we may say that Qawl is when we say: "Such-and-such a person said: "...", whereas Kalaam refers to the spoken words of Allah (swt), which are spoken to whom He wills from amongst the angels or Prophets (alayhum-as-salaam).

Top | Prev | Next

Kitaab At-Tawheed, Chapter: 15

Intercession

Allah (swt) says:

> " *And warn by it, those who fear to be gathered to their Lord: Besides Him they will have no protector nor intercessor: That they may become pious, God-fearing"* (Qur'an 6:51)

Allah (swt), Most High commands His Prophet, Muhammad, (saas) in this verse to inform and strike fear into those who are convinced of the truth of the Day of Resurrection: That they will stand before their Lord on that Day, and that they will find no helper, nor intercessor to intercede between them and Allah's punishment, that hopefully, they will fulfill the commands of Allah (swt) and abstain from that which He has forbidden.

Benefits Derived From This Verse

1. That warnings profit not except those who believe.

2. Confirmation of the Resurrection.

3. That there will be no intercession except and until its conditions have been fulfilled.

Relevance of This Verse to the Subject of the Chapter

That the verse proves that no intercession will be excepted unless and until its conditions have been met.

Relevance of This Verse to the Subject of *Tawheed*

That the verse proves that none can intercede on his own initiative; therefore, to seek such intercession from one of Allah's creatures is an act of major S*hirk*. Likewise, seeking intercession from idols which their worshippers claim can intercede with Allah (swt) on their behalf is a *Shirk*.

..ooOOoo..

Allah (swt), says:

> " *Say to Allah belongs all intercession. To Him belongs the dominion of the heavens and the earth and to Him you shall all return"* (Qur'an 39:44)

Allah (swt), Most Glorified, Most High, commands His Prophet, Muhammad (saas) in this verse to inform the people, whatever their philosophy or creed, that the right to grant every manner of intercession is purely and solely for Allah (swt), the Almighty, the All-powerful, and none may contend with Him in it, nor can any intercede except by His permission; then He affirms that He is the One and Only Disposer of affairs in the heavens and the earth and all that they contain and that there is no escaping from the Day when all mankind will be returned to Allah (swt); then those who took others as intercessors will know the futility of their deeds.

Benefits Derived From This Verse

1. The plurality of intercession.

2. That intercession is the dominion of Allah and none may intercede unless He Wills it and is pleased by the one for whom intercession is made.

3. Confirmation of the truth of the Resurrection.

Relevance of This Verse to the Subject of the Chapter

That the verse proves that every kind of intercession is the dominion of Allah (swt) and it will not be granted to anyone unless Allah (swt) permits it and Is pleased by the one for whom intercession is sought.

Relevance of This Verse to the Subject of *Tawheed*

That the verse confirms that intercession is the dominion of Allah (swt), to which none other than He is entitled. Therefore, seeking it from other than Allah (swt) is an act of major *Shirk*, including those idols which people worship, claiming that they are doing so in order to obtain intercession.

Important Note

Allah's Words: " *to Allah belongs all intercession"* Prove that intercession is of many different kinds and the scholars have mentioned eight of them:

1. Major Intercession: It is that which will fall upon the shoulders of the Prophet Muhammad (saas) after all the other Prophets and Messengers have refused to accept it on the Day of Resurrection: The people will ask all of the previous Prophets and Messengers to intercede with Allah (swt) on their behalf but they will refuse, saying: "Myself! Myself!" Then they will come to the Messenger of Allah (saas), and he will accept, and go to his *Rabb* and prostrate before Him for as long as He wills, then he will be given permission to raise his head and intercede on behalf of the believing people, and none other than he (swt) shall be given this right and privilege.

2. Intercession for the People of Paradise: This has been confirmed by the long Hadith of Abu Hurairah (ra) which has been narrated by Bukhari and Muslim and which mentions that the Prophet (saas) will intercede with Allah (swt) on behalf of the People of Paradise that they may be allowed to enter therein.

3. Intercession for the Disobedient Muslims: He (saas) will intercede with his Lord on behalf of those Muslims who may have committed sins of disobedience to their *Rabb*, Almighty, that they may not be placed in the Fire.

4. Intercession for the Disobedient People of *Tawheed*: He (saas) will intercede with Allah (swt) on behalf of those Muslims who have entered the Hell-fire because of their sins, that they may be removed from it. The authentic narration concerning this has been widely reported and all of the Companions and *Ahl As-Sunnah* are agreed upon it.

5. Intercession for Increasing the Reward of the People of Paradise: The Messenger of Allah (saas) will intercede on behalf of a people from amongst the People of Paradise, that they may have their reward increased and their status elevated; and there is none who disputes this.

6. Intercession of the Prophet (saas) for his Uncle: He (saas) will intercede on behalf of his uncle Abu Talib, that his punishment in the Hell-fire may be lightened.

7. Intercession of the Children: Those children who died while still below the age of reason will intercede on behalf of their believing parents.

8. Intercession of Some of the Believers for Others: It is authentically confirmed that some of the Believers will intercede on behalf of their believing brothers.

..ooOOoo..

Allah (swt), says:

> " *Allah! There is none has the right to be worshipped but He, the Living, the Ever-lasting. Neither slumber or sleep overtakes him. His are all things in the heavens and the earth. Who is it that can intercede in His presence, except as He permits? He knows what is before them and what is behind them. Nor shall they compass aught of His Knowledge, except as He Wills. His Kursi extends over the heavens and the earth and He feels no fatigue in guarding and preserving them, for He is the Most High, Most Great"* (Qur'an 2:255)

Allah (swt), Most Glorified, Most High informs us in this verse that there is none who has the right to be worshipped besides Him, because He is the Living, Whose Life is complete and without beginning or end, Who gives life to His creatures, but is in no need of anything and is afflicted by nothing which affects His slaves, such as tiredness, sleep, hunger etc. His Lordship is complete and all-encompassing: His is the Dominion of the heavens and the earth and all that is in them and none can gainsay Him in anything concerning them, including the matter of intercession, and none possesses power to intercede except as He Wills and permits, and whose intercession pleases Him. And He informs us that none encompasses anything of His Knowledge except Him whom He blesses and grants knowledge, whether Revelation or other wisdom. And He tells us that His *Kursi*[1] extends over all of the heavens and the earth and that guarding and protecting them causes Him no fatigue or discomfort, for He (swt) is the Most High, above all of His creation, and He is the Most Great, Greater than all others who claim greatness.

Benefits Derived From This Verse

1. Affirmation of five of Allah's Names: (i) Allah (swt); (ii) *Al-Hayy* (the Living); (iii) *Al-Qayyoom* (the Ever-lasting); (iv) *Al-'Ali* (the Most High); (v) *Al-'Azeem* (The Most Great).

2. That Allah (swt) does not succumb to slumber or sleep, for He is in no need of them; they are attributes of His creatures which indicate imperfection and He is far above any imperfection.

3. That none may intercede with Him on his own initiative but only as He permits.

4. Evidence of Allah's Will.

5. Confirmation of intercession after Allah (swt) permits it.

6. Proof of the existence of Allah's *Kursi*.

7. Evidence of Allah's Complete Power and Knowledge.

8. Affirmation of Allah's Divine Attribute of being Above, both literally and metaphorically.

9. Evidence of Allah's Greatness.

Relevance of This Verse to the Subject of the Chapter

That the verse negates any intercession by Allah's creatures on their own initiative without His permission.

Relevance of This Verse to the Subject of *Tawheed*

That it negates any intercession by Allah's creatures of their own volition, and therefore seeking such intercession from other than Allah (swt), is an act of major *Shirk* including idols which their worshipers claim can intercede with Allah (swt) on their behalf.

Important Note

This blessed verse has been described in authentic Hadith as the greatest verse in the Qur'an, and it is reported that whoever recites it in the evening, will be protected from Satan until he wakes in the morning, and also that whoever recites it in the morning will be protected from Satan until the evening, in accordance with His Will.

..ooOOoo..

Allah (swt), says:

> " *And no matter how many be angels in the heavens, their intercession will avail nothing except after Allah has given leave for whom He Wills and pleases"* (Qur'an 53:26)

Allah (swt), Most Glorified, Most High, informs us in this verse that in the heavens there are hosts of angels, but in spite of their large numbers, and their elevated status in the sight of Allah (swt), they cannot benefit anyone unless Allah (swt) grants them leave to intercede and is Pleased with their intercession.

Benefits Derived From This Verse

1. Proof that all of the heavens are inhabited by angels.

2. Evidence that intercession will only be granted on two conditions: (i) That Allah has permitted the intercession, and (ii) that He is pleased with the one for whom intercession is sought. And Allah is not Pleased with any save the People of *Tawheed* as is confirmed by the Hadith: "On behalf of whom will your intercession be most pleasing (to Allah), oh, Messenger of Allah?" He replied: Him who says: *Laa ilaaha illal-laah*, sincerely, from his heart." [2]

3. Confirmation of Allah's Divine Attribute of Will.

4. Confirmation of Allah's Divine Attribute of Pleasure.

Relevance of This Verse to the Subject of the Chapter

That it proves the negation of intercession by every created thing unless two conditions are fulfilled: (i) That Allah's permission is granted to the intercessor, and (ii) that Allah (swt) is pleased with the one for whom intercession is sought.

Relevance of This Verse to the Subject of *Tawheed*

That the verse proves that intercession is not granted except after Allah (swt) permits it and is pleased with the person for whom intercession is sought, which proves that intercession belongs to Allah (swt) and therefore, seeking it from other than Him is an act of major *Shirk*, especially including the worship of idols in the belief that they can intercede with Allah (swt).

..ooOOoo..

Allah (swt), says:

> " *Say: "Call upon those whom you claim [as gods] besides Allah: They have no power, not the weight of an atom - in the heavens or on the earth. No share have they therein, nor is any of them a helper to Allah. No intercession can avail with Him, except for those for whom He has granted permission. So much so that, when terror is removed from their hearts, they will say: "That which is true and just; and He is the Most High, Most Great.""* (Qur'an 34:22-23)

In these verses, Allah (swt), Most Glorified, Most High, challenges the polytheists to ask their objects of worship which they have set up as partners with Allah (swt), for they will not be able to grant any benefit or protect anyone from harm because they possess not an atom's weight of goodness or evil in the heavens or the earth, nor do they have any share in the heavens or the earth, nor are they helpers for Allah (swt), nor intercessors. Not even the angels or any other of Allah's creations possess the power to intercede on behalf of anyone except by His permission. Then Allah (swt) makes plain that the angels, who are the most powerful of Allah's creatures, fall down in fear and submission to Allah (swt) and His aweful Majesty. Then, when the fear is removed from their hearts, they ask one another concerning what their *Rabb*, the Almighty, the All-powerful has Said; and some of them answer that it is the firm truth, and He (swt) is the Most High, the Most Great.

Benefits Derived From These Verses

1. Negation of all the polytheists' claims regarding the idols they worship - that they possess any power or dominion in the heavens or the earth, or that they have any share in that, or in Allah's Help, or that they have the power of intercession with Allah (swt).

2. Confirmation of intercession after Allah (swt) permits it and negation of it without His permission.

3. Evidence of the awesomeness of Allah (swt) and His Greatness.

4. Affirmation of Allah's Divine Attribute of Speech.

5. Confirmation of two of Allah's Names: (i) *Al-'Ali*, and (ii) *Al-Kabeer*.

Relevance of These Verses to the Subject of the Chapter

That they prove the negation of intercession without Allah's leave.

Relevance of These Verses to the Subject of *Tawheed*

That the verses prove the negation of intercession for all of Allah's creatures on their own initiative, and that granting intercession is the exclusive right of Allah (swt), and therefore, to seek it from other than Allah (swt) is an act of *Shirk*. This includes the worship of idols which their worshipers claim have the power of intercession.

Important Note

Abul `Abbas said: "Allah (swt) has negated all that the polytheists do in worship: Such as the belief that any besides Allah (swt) possesses sovereignty or has any share in sovereignty, or aid, so that naught remains except intercession; and He has made plain that intercession is not possible except by His permission for the intercessor and the Hadith of Major Intercession also supports this, for in it is (reported the Words of Allah (swt) on the Day of Resurrection: "Raise your head and ask and it shall be given; intercede and it will be accepted." (Narrated by Bukhari)

And it will not be accepted unless Allah (swt) is Pleased with the one for whom intercession is sought, as is proved by the Words of Him (swt), Most High:

" *And they offer no intercession except for those with whom He is well-pleased*" - and Allah (swt) is not well-Pleased except with the people of *Tawheed* as evidenced by the Hadith: On behalf of whom will your intercession be most Pleasing (to Allah swt), Oh, Messenger of Allah (saas)? He replied: "Him who says: *Laa illaha illallah*, sincerely, from his heart."

Footnotes

1. Kursi: It has been authentically reported that the Kursi is the resting place of the Feet of the Beneficent, and it is the largest of all created things after the 'Arsh (Throne).

2. Narrated by Bukhari, on the authority of Abu Hurairah (ra)_.

Top | Prev | Next

Kitaab At-Tawheed, Chapter: 16

The Words of Allah (swt), Most High:

" Verily, you will not guide everyone whom you love, but Allah guides whom He wills and He knows best those who Will guided" (Qur'an 28:56)

Allah (swt) informs the Prophet (saas) that his assiduous pursuit of his uncle, Abu Talib in order to call him to Islam will be of no avail, that he will not be guided; for Allah (swt) knows all things - past, present and future, and none other than Allah (swt) has knowledge of the unseen. And He informs His Messenger (saas) that successful guidance comes only by His will, and He makes successful the guidance for whosoever of His slaves He Wills and that is because He knows best who deserves to be guided to success.

Benefits Derived From This Verse

1. That successful guidance comes only through Allah.

2. That the natural love of a person for his disbelieving kin - so long as they do not fight against Islam - does not conflict with true faith and belief.

3. Confirmation of Allah's Divine Attribute of Will.

The Relevance of This Verse to the Subject of the Chapter

That the verse proves that there can be no successful guidance through the Prophet (saas) alone in spite of the fact that he is the noblest of all mankind; and if he cannot guide anyone of his own Will, then obviously, no lesser human being can do so.

The Relevance of This Verse to the Subject of *Tawheed*

That the verse proves that successful guidance comes only from Allah (swt) and therefore seeking it from other than Allah (swt) is of *Shirk*.

Important Note

There is no contradiction between this verse and the Words of Allah (swt), Most High:

" And verily, you do guide [men] to the Straight Path" (Qur'an 42:52)

For in the former verse, Allah (swt) is negating the ability of the Prophet (saas) to make people accept his guidance, while in the latter He says that His Messenger (saas) Calls people to the Straight Path.

..ooOOoo..

It is authentically reported on the authority of Ibn Al-Musyyib from his father, that he said: "When death approached Abu Talib, Allah's Messenger (saas) came to him, and with him were `Abdullah Ibn Abi Umayyah and Abu Jahl. The Prophet (saas) said to his uncle: "Oh uncle! Say: *Laa ilaaha illallaah,* a word by which I will plead for you with Allah (swt )." But they said: "Will you reject the faith of `Abdul Muttalib?" And the Messenger of Allah (saas) repeated his words, and again they repeated their question, and so the last testament of Abu Talib was that he reamined upon the religion of `Abdul Muttalib and he refused to say: *Laa ilaaha illallaah.* So the Messenger of Allah (saas) said: "Verily, I will continue to ask forgiveness for you until I am forbidden to do so." Then Allah (swt) revealed:

> " *It is not for the Prophet or those who believe with him to ask forgiveness for the polytheists, even though they be their close relative after it has been made plain to them that they are of the people of the Hell-fire"* (Qur'an 9:113)

And concerning Abu Talib, He revealed: " *Verily, you will not guide everyone whom you love, but Allah guides whom He wills and He knows best those who will be guided"* [1]

Sa'eed Ibn Al-Musayyib (ra) informs us in this Hadith, that when death approached Abu Talib, the Prophet (saas) requested him to pronounce the words of *Tawheed* (i.e. *Laa ilaaha Iilallaah*) so that he might be a witness for him to Allah (swt); but Abu Talib's two wicked visitors aroused in him the passion of the *Jahiliyyah*, reminding him that it was the religion of his ancestors, and so Abu Talib refused to embrace Islam an died upon the religion of his people, after which the Prophet said that he would continue to ask forgiveness for him until Allah (swt) forbade him to do so. This he did, until Allah (swt) revealed the above-mentioned verse.

Benefits Derived From This Hadith

1.   The permissibility of visiting the sick, even though he may be a polytheist if the purpose in so doing is the desire to call him to Islam.

2.   That whoever said: *Laa ilaaha illallaah* at the time of death, will be judged by appearances to be a Muslim, even though he may never have done any good deeds or acts of worship in Islam.

3.   That the most important deeds are one's final in life.

4.   The obligation to strive in the cause of propagating Islam, to be patient and persevering in that cause, and to order the good and forbid the evil.

5.   Refutation of the claim of those who assert that `Abdul Muttalib and his forebears were Muslims.

6.   The harm inflicted by the evil people upon the good.

7.   The forbiddance of seeking forgiveness from Allah (swt) for the disbelievers and polytheists, even though they be close family members and even though they might perform services for Islam and the Muslims.

Relevance of This Hadith to the Subject of the Chapter

That the Hadith proves the negation of successful guidance through the Prophet (saas) and since he is the noblest of mankind, it stands to reason that no lesser mortal may be assured of successful guidance.

Relevance of This Hadith to the Subject of *Tawheed*

That it proves that successful guidance is from Allah (swt), Alone and therefore seeking it from other than Him is an act of *Shirk.*

Footnotes

1. Narrated by Bukhari.

Top | Prev | Next

Kitaab At-Tawheed, Chapter: 17

**What Has Been Said Concerning the Reason for
Mankind's Disbelief and Rejection of Their
Religion-it is Exaggerated Praise of the Righteous**

Allah (swt), says:

> " *Oh, you People of the Book! Commit not excesses in your religion, nor say of Allah anything but the truth. The Messiah, `Eisa, the son of Maryam is no more than a Messenger of Allah, and His Word, which He bestowed upon Maryam, and a Spirit proceeding from Him: So believe in Allah and His Messengers. Say not "Three"-desist: It will be better for you: For Allah is one God, glory be to Him [Far exalted is He] above having a son. To him belong all things in the heavens and on earth. And enough is Allah as a Disposer of affairs*" (Qur'an 4:171)

In this verse, Allah (swt), Most High, forbids the Jews and Christians from exaggeration and excess in their religion, such as the deification by the Christians of `Eisa (as), the son of Maryam, while the Jews went to the opposite extreme, rejecting him, but Allah (swt) refutes the claims of both, by describing Eisa (as) as His Messenger and a Spirit from amongst the spirits created by Allah (swt), and therefore they are obliged to believe truly in Allah (swt), Alone, without attributing fathers, sons, wives or companions to Him, and to believe in all of the Messengers and not to belie them and not to elevate them above their true status, and to reject the belief in the trinity, and to affirm their belief in Allah (swt) as the only God Who has the right to be worshipped, as the only *Rabb*, Owner and Creator of the whole universe, and the sole Guardian of all creatures.

Benefits Derived From This Verse

1. The forbiddance of excess in religion.

2. The prohibition of speaking according to one's own opinion in matters of religion without evidence.

3. Affirmation of the Prophethood and Messengership of Eisa.

4. A refutation of the claims of the Jews and Christians regarding the status of Eisa.

5. Affirmation of Allah's Divine Attribute of Speech.

6. Evidence of the falseness of the belief in the trinity.

7. That every aspect of *Tawheed* represents goodness.

Relevance of This Verse to the Subject of the Chapter

That the verse proves that the cause of the People of the Book leaving their religion was, in the case of the Christians, their excessive praise and glorification of Eisa (as), and in the case of the Jews, their vilification of him.

Relevance of This Verse to the Subject of *Tawheed*

That the Christians exceeded in their praise of Eisa (as) until they deified him and worshipped him as a partner with Allah (swt).

..ooOOoo..

Allah (swt), says:

> " *And they said: "Do not abandon your gods: Do not abandon Wadd, nor Yaghooth, or Ya'ooq, or Nasr," and they have led many astray. And [oh, Allah!] Grant increase to the wrong-doers save error"* (Qur'an 71:23-24)

Allah (swt), Most Glorified, Most High, informs us in this verse about polytheists: That they are devoted to the worship of their idols as evidenced by their advising each other to worship them and not to abandon them, in particular, those mentioned in the verse. Then He, Most Glorified, Most High, makes plain that they have caused many to go astray by their false advice, and they are described as wrong-doers who deserve their punishment and who are far astray from the Straight Path of Allah (swt).

Benefits Derived From This Verse

1. That *Shirk* was present among the former communities.

2. That these five names mentioned in the verse are the names of the idols of the people of Nooh.

3. Evidence of the mutual cooperation of the people who practice falsehood in the perpetuation of that falsehood.

4. That permissibility of supplicating Allah against the unbelievers in general.

Relevance of This Verse to the Subject of the Chapter

The relevance of this verse to the subject of the chapter may be realized from the *tafseer*[1] of some of the *mufassiroon*[2]: It is stated that these names were the names of righteous men and that their people became excessive in their love of them so that when they died, Satan whispered to them that they should make pictures of them in order to remember them; then later, when those people died, the original purpose of the pictures was forgotten and the succeeding generations began to worship them.[3]

Relevance of Verse to the Subject to *Tawheed*

That the verse proves that exaggeration and excessive veneration of the righteous is an act of *Shirk* because doing so means that one attributes to a created being what should only be attributed to Allah (swt), thus making them partners with Allah (swt).

..ooOOoo..

It is reported on the authority of `Umar (ra) that the Messenger of Allah (saas) said:

"Do not extoll me as the Christians extolled the son of Maryam (as); I am no more than a slave (of Allah) and so (instead), say: Allah's Slave and His Messenger."[4]

In this Hadith, the Prophet (saas) forbids his *Ummah* to praise him excessively so that they may never raise him above the status in which Allah (swt) has placed him. Then he makes plain that the correct way in which to speak of him is as a dependent, worshiping slave of Allah (swt), Most Blessed, Most High, and His (saas) Messenger; and this entails believing him in all that he says, and obeying him in what he commands abstaining from what he forbids and knowing that Allah (swt) may not be worshipped except in accordance with the Law which He has ordained.

Benefits Derived From This Hadith

1. The forbiddance of exceeding in praise of the Prophets and the righteous.

2. The care taken by the Prophet to prevent any means that might lead to sin.

3. Evidence of the Christians' exaggeration in their praise of Eisa (as).

4. Refutation of those who claim that Muhammad (saas) was more than a Messenger.

Relevance of This Hadith to the Subject of the Chapter

That is proves that excessive praise and glorification of the Prophet (saas), who is the best of mankind, will lead the Muslim out of the fold of Islam, just as the Christians left their religion because of excessively extolling Eisa (as).

Relevance of This Hadeeth to the Subject of *Tawheed*

That it proves that excessive praise and glorification of Allah's creatures may lead to worship of them.

..ooOOoo..

The Messenger of Allah (saas) said:

"Beware of exaggerated praise, for it was only this which led those before you to destruction."[5]

In this Hadith, the Prophet (saas) forbids us from excess in religion and exaggerating the praises of Allah's creatures so that we may not be destroyed like the communities that came before us when they practised excess in their religion and exceeded all bounds in worship.

Benefits Derived From This Hadith

1. The forbiddance of excess in religious matters.

2. That excess in religious matters is a cause of destruction.

Relevance of This Hadith to the subject of the Chapter

That the Hadith proves that the reason for the destruction of former people was their excess in matter of religion.

Relevance of This Hadith to the subject *Tawheed*

That it proves that excess in matters of religion, or excessive praise and reverence of Allah's creatures removes a person from the legal bounds set by Allah (swt) because the one who does so is following his own vain desires, which means that he is elevating those desires to the level of partners with Allah (swt), and this is *Shirk*, and is in contradiction with the pure Islamic concept of *Tawheed.*

..ooOOoo..

It is reported by Muslim on the authority of Ibn Mas'ood (ra) that the Messenger of Allah (saas) said:

"Destroyed are those who are extreme"

And he repeated it three times.

Because the Prophet (saas) was sent to us with Law, he warned his community against extremism and severity in all things, particularly in matters of religion which have been prescribed by Allah (swt), Most Glorified, Most High; and he made clear for us the limits of that Religion and he repeated his words three times in order to emphasise their importance to the listening Companions that they should understand and be warned of transgressing those limits.

Benefits Derived From This Hadith

1. The prohibition of extremism in all matters.

2. The virtue of stressing important matters.

3. The ease and flexibility of Islam.

Relevance of This Hadith to the Subject of the Chapter

That the Hadith proves that extremism in all matters, including reverence and praise of the righteous, is a cause of destruction.

Relevance of This Hadith to the Subject of *Tawheed*

That it proves that extremism in religious matters, or in excessive praising of the righteous puts a person beyond the limits imposed by Allah (swt), because he spends his life in pursuit of his own vain desires and this is an act of *Shirk*.

Footnotes

1. Tafseer: Explanation of the meanings of the Qur'an.

2. Mufassiroon: Scholars of tafseer

3. Ref.: Tafseer Ibn Katheer.

4. Narrated by Bukhari.

5. Narrated by Ahmad, An-Nassa'I and Ibn Majah.

Top | Prev | Next

Kitaab At-Tawheed, Chapter: 19

What Has Been Said About Exaggeration
in Raising up the Graves of the Righteous
and How They Tend to Become Idols Worshiped Besides Allah (swt)

Imam Malik has reported in his book, *Al-Muwatta`*, that the Messenger of Allah (saas) said:

> *"Oh, Allah! Do not let my grave become an idol that is worshiped: Allah's Wrath is*
> *immense against those peoples who turned the graves of their Prophets into mosques."*

The narrator informs us in this Hadith, that the Prophet (saas) adjured his *Rabb* that He protect his grave from being taken as an object of worship besides Allah (swt); then he made clear that Allah's Wrath is upon all of His slaves who take the graves of the Prophets as places of worship - then what may be said of those who take the graves' inhabitants as objects of worship?

Benefits Derived From This Hadith

1. Glorifying graves worship is an act of *Shirk* however close to Allah (swt) was the grave's inhabitant.

2. Confirmation of Allah's Divine Attribute of Anger.

3. Prohibition of building places of worship over graves.

4. The forbiddance of praying near graves even if there is no building erected over the grave.

Relevance of This Hadith to the Subject of the Chapter

That the Hadith proves that the graves will be taken as idols by some of this *Ummah*; this is why the Prophet (saas) asked Allah (swt) to protect his grave from being taken as an object of worship.

Relevance of This Hadith to the Subject of *Tawheed*

That the Hadith proves that taking the graves as places of worship will lead to worship of their inhabitants, and this is an act of *Shirk*.

..ooOOoo..

In addition, Ibn Jareer reports, on the authority of Sufyaan, from Mansoor, from Mujahid (that he said):
"" *Have you seen Al-Laat and Al-'uzzaa and another, Manaat, the third [deity]?"* [1] - He (*Al-Laat*) used to prepare *saweeq* for the pilgrims, and when he died, the people began to sit at his grave."

Relevance of This Narration to the Subject of the Chapter and the Subject of *Tawheed*

That it shows that *Al-Laat* was originally the name of a righteous man who used to prepare *saweeq* for the pilgrims; then, after he died, the people began to exaggerate their praises of him, sitting at his grave and taking it as an object of worship besides Allah (swt). For this reason, every grave whose inhabitant is praised in an exaggerated manner by the people is likely to become an object of worship, even though they may not refer to it as such.

It is reported on the authority of Ibn `Abbas (ra) that he said: "Allah's Messenger (saas) said:

> *"Cursed those women who visit the graves and those who take them as places of worship and hang lights around them."* (Narrated by Abu Dawood, At-Tirmizi and Ibn Maajah)

The Prophet (saas) cursed in this Hadith three groups: (i) Women who visit graves, because of the inherent weakness in them which may lead them to mourn excessively the departed; (ii) those who take the graves as places of worship, because this leads to the glorification of the graves' inhabitants and worship of them; (iii) those who adorn the graves with lights, because this is a waste of wealth without purpose and it leads to the glorification of the graves' inhabitants, very similar to the glorification of idols by those who make them. And the Hadith is a warning and an admonition to every person who would build places of worship over the graves of the righteous and the leaders and praise them excessively, and experience a state of humility which they do not feel when they go to the mosque - and this is among the greatest of sins; indeed it is one of the major sins, which should be eradicated, as the Prophet (saas) has made clear in this Hadith, for he did not curse except those who committed major sins.

Benefits Derived From This Hadith

1. The general permissibilty of cursing the corrupt.

2. The prohibition of women visiting graves.

3. The forbiddance of taking graves as places of worship and adorning them with lights.

4. The wisdom of Islamic Law lies in its forbidding everything which may lead to *Shirk*.

5. The prohibition of using up wealth without purpose.

Relevance of This Hadith to the Subject of the Chapter and to the Subject of *Tawheed*

That the Hadith prohibits excessive praise and glorification of the graves and their inhabitants, by building mosques or other places of worship over them and decorating them with lights because this leads to them being taken as idols and worshiped.

Important Note

(a) The purpose of prohibiting both the building of places of worship over graves and of adorning them with lights is in that these practices may lead to worship of the graves' inhabitants, not because graves are unclean.

(b) There is no conflict between this Hadith and the saying of the Prophet (saas):

> *"I had forbidden you to visit the graves, but (now I say:) visit them."*[2]

Because the former is an exception for women from the general license granted by the latter.

Footnotes

1. Qur'an An-Najm 53:19-20.

2. Narrated by Malik, Muslim and Abu Dawood.

Top | Prev | Next

Kitaab At-Tawheed, Chapter: 18

What Has been Said Concerning the Condemnation of One Who Worships Allah (swt) at the Grave of a Righteous Man - and Therefore of One Who Worships its Inhabitant

It is authentically reported on the authority of `Aa`ishah that Um Salamah (May Allah be pleased with them both) told the Messenger of Allah (saas) about a church she had seen in Abyssinia in which there were pictures. The Prophet (saas) said: "Those people, when a righteous member of their group or a pious slave (of Allah swt) dies, they build a mosque over his grave and make images therein; by so doing, they combine two evils: (i) The evil of the graves and (ii) the evil of images." [/]

`Aa`ishah tells us that Um Salamah informed her that she had told the Prophet (saas) about a church in Abyssinia which she saw when she migrated there with her husband in which there were images. The Prophet (saas) then explained to her the significance of what she had seen: That the Christians, when a pious man from among them died, would build an edifice over his grave and place his image in it in order to remember him and be inspired by his piety; and he added that these people were the worst of people in the sight of Allah (swt) because they had combined two sins: (i) The sin of building over graves which may lead eventually to the worship of their occupants; and (ii) the sin of making images of living creatures which may also lead to worship of those images when the original purpose of their making has been forgotten.

Benefits Derived From This Hadith

1. The acceptability of the evidence of a truthful woman.

2. That placing images in places of worship is among the deeds of the Christians.

3. The forbiddance of building mosques over graves.

4. The prohibition of placing images over graves.

Relevance of This Hadith to the Subject of the Chapter

That the Hadith proves that building a place of worship over the grave of a righteous man is strongly condemned - and therefore what may be said of one who actually worships its occupant?

Relevance of This Hadith to the Subject of *Tawheed*

That the Hadith proves the forbiddance of building mosques over graves because it entails glorification of their inhabitants and glorification is a form of worship, and dedicating worship to other than Allah (swt) is an act of *Shirk*.

..ooOOoo..

Al-Bukhari and Muslim report that `Aa`ishah said: "When the Messenger of Allah (saas) was close to death, he covered his face with a cloth, and then when it became difficult for him to breathe, he uncovered his face and said:

"May Allah (swt) curse the Jews and Christians who took the graves of their Prophets as places of worship - do not imitate them."

And, (added `Aa`ishah,) "if it had not been for this, his grave might have been raised above ground, but it was feared that it would be taken as a place of worship."

`Aa`ishah informs us in this narration that when the Prophet (saas) was near to death and in a state of delirium, he invoked Allah's curse on the Jews and Christians because they built places of worship over the graves of their Prophets. Then `Aa`ishah explains that the Prophet (saas) intended by this to warn his *Ummah* against doing what the Jews and Christians had done; and she made clear that the reason for his forbidding the Companions from burying him outside his house was to prevent them from taking his grave as a place of worship.

Benefits Derived From This Hadith

1. Evidence that the Prophet (saas) was afflicted by the agonies of death.

2. That the Prophet (saas) cared deeply for his *Ummah*.

3. The general permissibility of invoking Allah's curse on the disbelievers.

4. The general prohibition of building over graves.

5. That the Hadith is a reply to those who claim that building over graves - in particular those of Muslim scholars - is permissible.

6. That building over graves is a custom of the Jews and Christians.

7. Evidence of `Aa`ishah's knowledge and understanding in matters of *fiqh*.

8. Evidence of the reason for burying the Prophet (saas) in his house.

Relevance of This Hadith to the Subject of the Chapter

That it proves that it is prohibited to build places of worship over graves or to worship Allah (swt) beside them. Therefore, what may be said of one who worships the occupant of the grave?

Relevance of This Hadith to the Subject of *Tawheed*

That the Hadith proves that it is forbidden to build places of worship over graves because this entails glorification of their inhabitants and glorification is an act of worship and directing such an act to other than Allah (swt) is *Shirk*.

..ooOOoo..

Muslim narrates on the authority of Jundub Ibn `Abdillah (ra) that he said: "I heard the Prophet (saas) say five days before his death:

"Verily, I bear witness before Allah (swt) that I have taken none of you as my Khaleel,[2] for

truly, Allah (swt) has taken me as His Khaleel, just as He took Ibraheem (as) as a Khaleel. If I were to take any man from my Ummah as a khaleel, it would be Abu Bakr. Your predecessors used to take their Prophets' graves as places of worship, so do not make graves into places of worship for I have forbidden you to do this."

Jundub Ibn `Abdillaah (ra) informs us that the Prophet (saas), shortly before his death, rejected that he had taken any man as his *Khaleel*, and this was because his heart was completely filled with love for Allah (swt) as was the heart of his ancestor, Ibraheem (as). Then he said that were he to take any man as his *Khaleel*, the one with most right to be considered would be Abu Bakr As-Siddeeq (ra) because of his many virtues, his unceasing efforts in the cause of Islam and his help and support of the Prophet (saas); and when he knew that the Companions loved him and were influenced by him in everything they did, he began to fear that they might build an edifice over his grave for the purpose of worship as the Jews and Christians had done with their Prophets, and so he expressly forbade the building of places of worship over graves especially his own.

Benefits Derived From This Verse

    1. Confirmation that the Prophet is Allah's *Khaleel*.

    2. Affirmation of Allah's Divine Attribute of Love.

    3. Confirmation that Ibraheem is Allah's *Khaleel*.

    4. Evidence of the virtue of Abu Bakr and therefore of his right to be the first *Khaleefah* (Caliph) of Islam, because the most loved of mankind in the eyes of the Prophet naturally has more right than any other to be his successor.

    5. That building places of worship over graves was the practice of the former nations.

    6. The prohibition of taking graves as places of worship.

    7. The obligation to take precautions against that which is undesirable.

Relevance of This Hadith to the Subject of the Chapter

That the Hadith proves the forbiddance of building places of worship over graves, and so what may be said of those who worship their inhabitants?

Relevance of This Hadith to the Subject of *Tawheed*

That the Hadith clearly prohibits the building of places of worship over graves because this entails glorification of their inhabitants, and glorification is a kind of worship, and directing acts of worship to other than Allah (swt) is *Shirk*.

..ooOOoo..

It is narrated by Ahmad, with a good *sanad*,[3] on the authority of Ibn Mas'ood (ra), in a narration traced back to the Prophet (saas) himself, the following:

"Verily, the most wicked of people are those who, when the Hour overtakes them, are still

alive, and those who take graves as places of worship." (Also Narrated by Abu Hatim in his *Saheeh*)

The Messenger of Allah (saas) informs us in this Hadith about the two categories of people upon whom the Hour (i.e. the Day of Judgement) will fall: (i) Those who build places of worship over graves and (ii) those who pray at those places of worship, since this is implicit in the phrase: "taking the graves as places of worship," for they glorify the occupants of the graves and deify them and seek blessings from their graves, which actions are totally unacceptable to the person who has an uncorrupted soul and is still upon the *fitrah*, and which no person with an ounce of faith in his heart can accept it because conflicts with all authentic sources, whether in the Qur'an or the *Sunnah*.

Benefits Derived From This Hadith

1. The miracle of the Messenger's prophecy being fulfilled as he had predicted that some members of his *Ummah* would build places of worship over graves.

2. That the Hour will not fall upon the Believers.

3. Confirmation that the Hour will come.

4. Prohibition of building places of worship over graves and praying close to them, even without building anything over them because a place of worship does not have to be a building but may be any place used for worship, even if it is outdoors.

Relevance of This Hadith to the Subject of the Chapter

That it proves that building places of worship over graves is prohibited, and therefore, what may be said of those who actually worship their inhabitants?

Relevance of This Hadith to the Subject of *Tawheed*

That the Hadith describes those who build places of worship over graves as the wickedest of people because that entails glorification of their inhabitants, and glorification is a form of worship, and dedicating acts of worship to other than Allah (swt) is *Shirk*.

Important Note

The rules of the grave are four:

1. For men to visit them without undertaking a journey to do so, is a favourable act because it reminds them of the Hereafter.

2. Building over graves and burning lights over them is totally forbidden because it leads inevitably to *Shirk*.

3. Taking the occupants of graves as intercessors, or supplicating them directly is an act of major *Shirk* because supplication is a form of worship and directing it to other than Allah (swt) is an act of *Shirk*.

4. For women to visit graves is prohibited as the Prophet (saas) said: "Allah (swt) has

cursed those women who visit the graves."[4]

What *Shaikh Al-Islam* Ibn Taymiyah Said Concerning This Matter

He (saas) forbade it (building over graves) towards the end of his life and cursed whoever did so, likewise praying near them, even if no building is erected over them, and this is the intended meaning here, since none of the Companions would have built a mosque over the grave of the Messenger of Allah (saas), for every place where the intention for prayer is made is a place of worship; indeed, every place which is used as a place of prayer may be classified as a mosque, as He (saas) said: "The whole earth has been made for me a pure and clean mosque." [5]

Footnotes

1. Narrated by Bukhari.

2. Khaleel: A special, most beloved friend.

3. Sanad: Chain of narrators.

4. Narrated by Abu Dawood.

5. Narrated by Abu Dawood.

Top | Prev | Next

Kitaab At-Tawheed, Chapter: 20

What Has Been Said Concerning the Prophet's Protectiveness of Tawheed and His Blocking of Every Path Leading to Shirk

Allah (swt), says:

> " *Verily, there has come to you a Messenger from amongst your-selves: It grieves him that you should perish: He is ardently anxious over you. To the Believers He is Most Kind and Merciful"* (Qur'an 9:128)

In this verse, Allah (swt) has bestowed a great blessing upon mankind, in particular, the Arabs, because He sent to them a Messenger from amongst themselves who spoke their language, whose lineage, nobility and trustworthiness were well-known to them; and Allah (swt) has described him as possessing certain Divinely-given qualities which make it incumbent upon all of us to follow him and believe in him, for he is troubled and grieved by whatever troubles and grieves his *Ummah*, and he ardently seeks that which is beneficial to them and earnestly desires that they be guided aright and he is full of compassion for them.

Benefits Derived From This Verse

1. Evidence of the great blessing which Allah has bestowed upon mankind, in particular, the Arabs by His sending a Prophet to them from their own community, through whom Allah saved them from the abyss of *shirk* and humiliation.

2. Evidence of the Prophet's ardent care for his *Ummah*.

Relevance of This Verse to the Subject of the Chapter and to the Subject of *Tawheed*

That the verse proves the care taken by the Prophet (saas) over his *Ummah*, especially his protection of their *tawheed* and his great efforts to prevent them from falling into whatever might lead to shirk, including his prohibition of glorifying graves, by building structures over them, in particular, his own grave - may Allah's Peace and Blessings be upon him.

..ooOOoo..

It is reported on the authority of Abu Hurairah (ra) that he said: "Allah's Messenger (saas) said:

> *"Do not make your homes into graves, nor make my grave into a place of celebration. Send your prayers and blessings upon me, for they will be conveyed to me wherever you may be."* (Narrated by Abu Dawood with a good *sanad,* and all of its narrators are trustworthy)

Abu Hurairah (ra) tells us in this Hadith, that the Prophet (saas) forbade us from abandoning our homes and making them into graves where acts of worship are not performed and Allah's Name is not mentioned. And he forbade us from taking his grave as a place of celebration where people come to visit on a specific date, for a specific occasion. Then the Messenger of Allah (saas) ordered us to send prayers and blessings upon him and informed us that the prayers and blessings of any Muslim, whoever he may be and wherever he may be, will be conveyed to him.

Benefits Derived From This Hadith

1. The forbiddance of abandoning worship in the home.

2. The prohibition of praying towards graves.

3. The prohibition of visiting the grave of the Prophet (saas) on a special occasion or for that matter, of visiting any grave in this manner.

4. The obligation to send prayers and blessings upon the Prophet (saas).

5. That prayers and blessings upon the Prophet (saas) reach him wherever the supplicator may be.

6. That the dead can benefit from the prayers and blessings of the living Believers.

Relevance of This Hadith to the Subject of the Chapter and to the Subject of *Tawheed*

That the Hadith proves that it is prohibited in Islam to take graves as places of celebration, and that this demonstrates the Prophet's protectiveness towards his *Ummah* from the danger of every path that might lead to shirk.

Important Note

Some people have claimed that the Prophet's forbiddance of making his grave into a place of celebration necessitates that we should zealously cling to and visit his grave: As if he (saas) had said: "Don't make my grave an annual place of celebration, but visit it all the time." However, this explanation is totally false and without substance, for the following reasons: (i) That this explanation is unclear and is therefore in contradiction with the established *Sharee'ah*,[1] which is always clear. (ii) Had the Prophet (saas) intended what they claim, his family and Companions would have implemented it and ordered others to do likewise. (iii) It has not been reported that the Companions ordered anyone to do this or that they did so themselves - and they were the most knowledgeable about the meaning of the Prophet's sayings.

..ooOOoo..

It is reported on the authority of `Ali Ibn Al-Husain that he saw a man approaching a small niche before the grave of the Prophet (saas) and he went into the niche and began to supplicate. So he (`Ali) prevented the man from doing so, saying: "Shall I not tell you a Hadith (of the Prophet (saas) which I heard from my father, who in turn, heard it from my grandfather [i.e. `Ali Ibn Abi Talib (ra)], who reported from Allah's Messenger (saas) that he said:

> *"Do not take my grave as a place of celebration, nor your homes as graves; send prayers and blessings upon me, for your salutations will reach me, wherever you may be."* (Narrated by Al-Maqdasi, in *Al-Mukhtarah*)

`Ali Ibn Al-Husain informs us in this narration, that he saw a man supplicating Allah (swt) at the grave of the Prophet (saas) and that he prevented him from doing so, using as evidence, a Hadith which contains a forbiddance of taking his grave as a place of celebratory visits and of abandoning worship of Allah (swt) in the home and then he ordered us to send prayers and blessings upon him, saying that they would be conveyed to him wherever the Muslim who sent them may be.

Benefits Derived From This Hadith

1. The obligation to reject wickedness.

2. The prohibition of intentionally making supplication at the Prophet's grave or any other grave.

3. The prohibition of abandoning worship and remembrance of Allah (swt) in the home.

4. The forbiddance of praying at the graves.

5. Evidence that the prayers and salutations which a Muslim sends upon the Prophet (saas) will be conveyed to him whether the Muslim is near or far from his grave.

6. That the dead Believer can benefit from the supplications of the living Believer.

Relevance of This Hadith to the Subject of the Chapter and to the Subject of *Tawheed*

That it proves that it is forbidden to take the grave of the Prophet (saas) as a place of celebration in order to worship there and this shows the Prophet's protection of the purity of *tawheed* and his desire to close off every avenue that might lead to *shirk*.

Important Note

Setting out on a journey with the express intent of visiting the grave of the Prophet (saas) is prohibited, because of his words:

"Do not saddle up your riding beasts, except to three mosques: "The Sacred Mosque (in Makkah), this my mosque and Al-Aqsa Mosque (in Jerusalem)."[2] *In light of this, it is clear that whoever undertook a journey in order to pray in the Prophet's Mosque, is not guilty of any sin, while whoever did so in order to worship at the grave has disobeyed the Prophet."*

Footnotes

1. Sharee'ah: Islamic Law.

2. Narrated by Bukhari, Muslim and others.

Top | Prev | Next

Kitaab At-Tawheed, Chapter: 21

What Has Been Said Concerning Those of This Ummah, Who Worship Idols

Allah (swt) says:

> " *Do you not see those who were given a portion of the Book? They believe in Al-Jibt* [1] *and At-Taaghoot and say to the unbelievers that they are better guided than the Believers!*" (Qur'an 4:51)

In this verse, Allah (swt), Most Glorified, Most High, directs the attention of His Messenger, Muhammad (saas) and that of all the Muslims, to the evil deeds of some of the Jews, who believed in the worship of idols and preferred that to the Believers' worship of their *Rabb*, even though the Jews knew from their Revealed Books that the Religion of Islam was better than the worship of idols and that the Messenger of Allah (saas) spoke the truth from his *Rabb*. But their hatred and jealousy blinded them and prevented them from speaking the truth and instead, caused them to praise and flatter the unbelievers; but Allah (swt) will complete His Light and Guidance, even though the disbelievers may detest that.

Benefits Derived From This Verse

1. Confirmation that the Jews had distorted the teachings of their Scriptures.

2. That false flattery in matters of religion and concealing the truth are amongst the characteristics of the Jews.

3. The existence of *Shirk* amongst the People of the Book.

Relevance of This Verse to the Subject of the Chapter and to the Subject of *Tawheed*

That the verse proves the existence of shirk amongst the People of the Book and it has been authentically reported from the Prophet (saas) that the Muslims will imitate the People of the Book, and this includes in committing *Shirk*.

Important Note

The reason for the revelation of this verse has been narrated by Imam Ahmad, on the authority of Ibn `Abbas (ra), who said: "When K'ab Ibn Al-Ashraf approached Makkah, Quraish said: "Do you not see this orphan, who is cut off from his family? He claims that he is better than us, while we are the patrons of the pilgrims and the Custodians (of the Sacred Mosque)," at which K'ab replied: "You are better (than he)." Then this verse was revealed:

> " *Verily, he who despises you will be cut off [from hope of mercy and forgiveness in the Hereafter]*" (Qur'an 108:1)

..ooOOoo..

Allah (swt) says:

" Say: "Shall I inform you of something much worse than this [as judged] by the treatment it received from Allah? Those who incurred the curse of Allah and His wrath, those of whom some He transformed into apes and some into swine, those who worshipped At-Taaghoot - they are worse in rank and far astray from the even Path" (Qur'an 5:60)

Allah (swt) says, addressing the Prophet (saas): Say, oh, Muhammad, to these disbelievers from amongst the People of the Book: "Shall I tell you about those who will receive the worst punishment on the Day of Resurrection? They are those of you whom Allah (swt) has banished from His Mercy and His wrath is upon them and He (swt) has turned them into apes and swine, and they worship idols." Because of these evil attributes, Allah (swt) has informed us that they are the worst of people and the farthest astray.

Benefits Derived From This Verse

1. The permissibilty of cursing the disbelievers in general.

2. Confirmation of Allah's Divine Attribute of Anger.

3. Confirmation of Allah's having transformed some of the People of the Book into pigs and apes.

4. The presence of *Shirk* amongst the People of the Book.

5. That disobedience to Allah's Will can result in chastisement in this world as it does in the Hereafter.

Relevance of This Verse to the Subject of the Chapter and to the Subject of *Tawheed*

That it proves the existence of *Shirk* among the People of the Book by their worship of *At-Taghoot*; and it has been authentically reported that this *Ummah* will imitate the Jews and Christians and this includes committing *Shirk*.

Important Note

Allah (swt) transformed some of the Jews into apes because the ape outwardly resembles the human being, although they are separate and distinct from them. Likewise, the Jews used to commit transgressions which, in some ways, outwardly appeared to be good deeds, while in fact they were false.

..ooOOoo..

Allah (swt) says:

" And thus did We make their case known to the people that they might know that the Promise of Allah is true, and that there can be no doubt about the Hour [of Judgement]. When they disputed among themselves about their affair, [some] said: "Construct a building over them." Their Rabb knows best about them: Those who prevailed over their affair said: "Verily, we will build a place of worship over them."" (Qur'an 18:21)

Allah (swt), Most High, informs us in this verse that He (swt) drew the attention of the people to the situation of the People of the Cave; and the wisdom behind that was to prove to them that man can be resurrected after death. Then He (swt), Most High, informs us about the dialogue which took place between their people: That some of them believed that they should build structures over the People of the Cave although that which was incumbent upon them was for Allah (swt) to decide while others preferred that they should build a place of worship over them.

Benefits Derived From This Verse

1. Confirmation of the story of the People of the Cave.

2. Confirmation of the truth of resurrection after death.

3. That making places of worship over graves was the practice of former peoples.

Relevance of This Verse to the Subject of the Chapter and to the Subject of *Tawheed*

That the verse proves that the People of the Book used to build structures over graves, and the Prophet (saas) cursed them because of this as their actions led to the worship of the graves' inhabitants; and it has been authentically reported that some of the people of this *Ummah* will imitate them, building mosques over graves and worshipping their inhabitants.

..ooOOoo..

It is reported on the authority of Abu Sa'eed Al-Khudri (ra) that the Messenger of Allah (saas) said:

> *"Surely, you will follow the ways of those before you, just as the flight of one arrow resembles another, so much so, that even if they entered the hole of a lizard, you would enter it." They said: "(Do you mean) the Jews and Christians?" He (saas) replied: "(If not them,) then whom?"* (Narrated by Bukhari and Muslim)

Abu Sa'eed Al-Khudri (ra) tells us in this Hadith that the Messenger of Allah (saas) informed the Companions that this *Ummah* will imitate the previous nations in their customs, their politics and even their religion; indeed in all matters, as the flight of one arrow resembles another. Then he further impressed upon us this fact, saying that even were those previous nations to enter the hole of a lizard, the people of this *Ummah* would try to follow them. Then when the Companions asked him as to the identity of those people, were they the Jews and Christians? he (saas) replied in the affirmative.

Benefits Derived From This Hadith

1. Evidence of a Prophetic miracle, since the Messenger of Allah (saas) predicted correctly that the Muslims would one day imitate the Jews and Christians.

2. That making things clear by using powerful similes is an Islamic method of teaching.

3. The forbiddance of imitating the People of the Book.

4. The permissibility of asking questions of the people of knowledge.

Relevance of This Hadith to the Subject of the Chapter and to the Subject of *Tawheed*

That it proves that this *Ummah* will do as the People of the Book do; and amongst their actions is the worship of idols.

..ooOOoo..

It is narrated by Muslim, on the authority of Thawban (ra) that the Messenger of Allah (saas) said:

"Verily, Allah (swt) folded the earth for me, so much so that I saw its East and its West: The kingdom of my Ummah will reach as far as the earth was folded for me. The two treasures, both the red and the white were given to me. I prayed to my Rabb that He may not destroy my Ummah by a widespread drought and not give sovereignty over them to an enemy who annihilates them in large numbers except from among themselves. And then verily, my Rabb said: "Oh, Muhammad (saas)! When I issue a decree, it is not withdrawn: I have promised your Ummah that I will not destroy it by a widespread drought and I shall not give sovereignty of them to an enemy who exterminates them in large numbers, even if they are stormed from all sides of the earth except from among themselves. Only a portion of them will destroy another portion and a portion will take another portion prisoner." This was also narrated by Al-Barqaani, who added: "I fear for my Ummah those leaders who will send them astray: When the sword is used among my people, it will not be withdrawn from them until the Day of Resurrection and the Hour will not come until a tribe from among my Ummah attach themselves to the polytheists and numbers of my people worship idols; and there will be among my Ummah thirty liars, all of them claiming that he is a prophet, though I am the Seal of the Prophets - none will come after me. But some of my Ummah will continue to hold to the truth and they will be victorious and they will not be harmed by those who oppose them until Allah's Command comes."

The Prophet (saas) tells us in this Hadith that Allah (swt) gathered together for him all of the earth, and he saw all that lay between the east and west. And he saw that the kingdom of his people would stretch across all of the earth then he asked his *Rabb*, Almighty, All-powerful not to destroy his *Ummah* through drought or famine nor allow any enemy from without to rule over them and who would slaughter them in large numbers. And his *Rabb* granted his request, but that they would quarrel amongst themselves, fight each other, kill each other and take each other prisoner. Then he (saas) made clear that the most dangerous thing that he fears for his *Ummah* is those leaders who will misguide the people, for they will follow them and will be ruled by them, though they have no knowledge; thus they will be astray themselves and will send others astray; and should the killing begin, it will not end until the Day of Resurrection; and a number of his *Ummah* will worship idols, and that there will appear among them thirty liars who will claim prophethood, but the Messenger of Allah (saas) has informed us that he is the Seal of the Prophets and that none will come after him. And finally, in order that we despair not he (saas) informs us that a number of his *Ummah* will hold fast to the true Religion, that they will be aided by Allah (swt) and they will not be harmed by those who abandon them or those who plot against them until the Command of Allah (swt) comes.[2]

Benefits Derived From This Hadith

1. Evidence of a miracle of the Prophet (saas) in predicting the future - some of which has come to pass and some of which has yet to happen.

2. The permissibility of taking war booty for the Muslims.

3. The Prophet's care for the fate of his *Ummah*.

4. Confirmation of Allah's Divine Attribute of Speech.

5. That the cause of destruction of this *Ummah* will be quarrelling and warring amongst themselves.

6. Evidence that the danger to this community will come from misguided leaders who will send their people astray.

7. The presence of *Shirk* in this *Ummah*.

8. The rejection of all those who claim to be Prophets after Allah's Messenger, Muhammad (saas).

9. That Muhammad (saas) is the Seal of the Prophets.

10. The continuation of the Truth among some of this *Ummah* until comes the Command of Allah (swt).

Relevance of This Hadith to the Subject of the Chapter and to the Subject of *Tawheed*

That the Hadith proves that some of this *Ummah* will worship idols.

Footnotes

1. Al-Jibt: A false idol.

2. This would appear to be a reference to the wind which Allah (swt) will send and which will take away the souls of all the believers so that when the Trump is sounded, there will be none alive except the unbelievers - and Allah (swt) knows best.

Top | Prev | Next

Kitaab At-Tawheed, Chapter: 22

What Has Been Said Concerning Sorcery

Allah (swt), says:

> " *They followed what the devils gave out against the power of Sulaiman: Sulaiman did not blaspheme, but the devils did blaspheme, teaching the people sorcery and such things as came down at Babylon to Haroot and Maroot. But neither of these taught anyone [such things] without saying: "We are but a trial; so do not blaspheme." They learnt from them the means to sow discord between man and wife. But they could not thus harm anyone except by Allah's permission. And they learned what harmed them, not what profited them and they knew that the buyers [of magic] would have no share in the Hereafter. And miserable was the price for which they sold their souls, if only they knew!"* (Qur'an 2:102)

Allah (swt), Most High, informs us in this verse that the Jews and Christians turned away from the Book of Allah (swt) and instead devoted themselves to the study of sorcery which the devils claimed was from the time of Sulaiman (as) and they further falsely claimed that they had learnt it from Sulaiman (as) himself; but Allah (swt) makes it clear that Prophet Sulaiman (as) did not commit an act of disbelief as they claimed, but it was the devils who blasphemed by their teaching the people sorcery. Then He says that one of the objects of those who taught magic was to cause discord between men and their wives, but that there can be no result from the machinations of the magician unless Allah (swt) permits it and that whoever abandons his Religion in favour of magic will have no reward on the Day of Resurrection and wretched will be the lot which he has purchased for himself by his actions, if only he knew it.

Benefits Derived From This Verse

1. That sorcery is one of the works of the devils.

2. That Sulaiman was innocent of practising magic.

3. That learning magic and teaching it are acts of disbelief.

4. Proof that magic has no effect unless Allah Wills it.

5. That there is no benefit in magic.

6. The vileness and wretchedness of the sorceror.

Relevance of This Verse to the Subject of the Chapter

That the verse proves that practising magic is an act of disbelief.

Relevance of This Verse to the Subject of *Tawheed*

That the verse warns against practising magic which cannot be performed without committing *shirk*, and *shirk* is a negation of *Tawheed*.

Important Note

(a) The Arabic word *sihr* (سحر) linguistically means: That which its cause is hidden. In Islamic terms, it means: The practice of writing spells on paper, or tying knots which effect the heart and the body until the person becomes ill and dies, or it means to cause a rift between a man and his wife.

(b) According to Imam Ahmad, Malik and Abu Haneefah, magic is an act of disbelief.

..ooOOoo..

Allah (swt) says:

" *Do you not see those who were given a portion of the Book? They believe in Al-Jibt and At-Taghoot and they say to the unbelievers that they are better guided than the believers!*" (Qur'an 4:51)

Allah (swt) directs the attention of the Muslims, in particular, the Messenger of Allah (saas) to the practices of some of the People of the Book which deviate from the Truth such as their preferring magic and obedience to Satan to the Book of Allah (swt) and the knowledge and guidance it contains, and their lying assertion that the polytheists are better than the Muslims and closer to the Straight Path.

Benefits Derived From This Verse

1. Evidence that some of the People of the Book were astray.

2. The presence of magic among the People of the Book.

3. That flattery, lies and hypocrisy are among the characteristics of the Jews.

Relevance of This Verse to the Subject of the Chapter

That the verse proves the forbiddance of practising magic and censures those who do so.

Relevance of This Verse to the Subject of *Tawheed*

That it proves that engaging in magic is an act of disbelief, because its origin is in *shirk*.[1]

Note

Muhammad Ibn `Abdul Wahhab said: "`Umar (ra) said: "*Al-Jibt* (here) means magic and *At-Taaghoot* means the devil." Jabir said: "*At-Tawagheet*[2] are fortune-tellers to whom the devils used to descend, one to every neighbourhood."

..ooOOoo..

It is reported on the authority of Abu Hurairah (ra) that the Messenger of Allah (saas) said:

"*Avoid the seven destroyers.*" They (the Companions) asked: "Oh, Messenger of Allah *(saas)! What are they?" He (saas) replied: "Shirk (associating partners) with Allah (swt), sorcery, taking the life which has been prohibited by Allah (swt), except in truth (i.e. in accordance with Islamic Law), devouring usury, consuming the property of the orphans, running away on the day of battle and making false charges against the chaste, unmindful[3] women."* (Narrated by Bukhari and Muslim)

Because sins are the cause of loss and destruction, the Messenger of Allah (saas) has commanded his *Ummah* to avoid the following major sins which cause the destruction of their perpetrators in this life and in the Hereafter:

1. *Shirk* (Associating partners with Allah swt): This is because it ensnares a person in that which debases him - the worship of other created beings.

2. Magic: This is because it leads to many sicknesses in society such as swindling of gullible people, superstition and ignorance, fraud and cheating people out of their money by lying and deception.

3. Taking the life which Allah (swt) has forbidden: This is because willful murder leads to a state of chaos and disorder and breakdown of law and order, causing the people to exist in a state of fear and insecurity.

4. Devouring Usury (*Ribaa*): This is because the presence of usury, or interest[4] in society causes loss of the peoples wealth and property, as greedy and unscupulous money-lenders rook people of their honestly earned money, growing fat at the expense of hard-working people, with no benefit to the society but only to themselves.

5. Usurping the property of the orphan: This is because such behavour constitutes injustice against one who is a minor, without any who can help him or support him except Allah (swt).

6. Running away from the enemy without cause or reason: This is because such an act of betrayal to ones Muslim brothers, weakening their forces and breaking their morale.

7. Unjustly accusing chaste women of adultery: This is because it destroys their reputations and results in loss of trust in them and sows doubts concerning the paternity of their children.

Benefits Derived From This Verse

1. That sins cause destruction and loss to the perpetrator.

2. The prohibiton of associating partners with Allah, for it is the greatest sin against Allah.

3. The forbiddance of learning and teaching magic.

4. The prohibition of taking a life which has not been sanctioned by Allah.

5. The forbiddance of devouring usury.

6. The prohibition of appropriating the property of the orphan.

7. The forbiddance of running away from the field of battle unless there is a valid reason such as to deceive the enemy, or lend aid on another front etc.

8. The prohibition of slandering chaste women, whether be maidens or married women.

Relevance of This Hadith to the Subject of the Chapter

That the Hadith proves the prohibition of learning and teaching magic.

Relevance of This Hadith to the Subject of *Tawheed*

That magic is forbidden because it is based upon *shirk*.

..ooOOoo..

It is reported from Jundub (ra) in a *marfoo'* [5] form: "The punishment for the magician is that he be struck (i.e. beheaded) by the sword."[6]

Because magic is such a serious problem for society, indeed a sickness from which results all manner of corruption and evil, such as killing, stealing, cheating, fraud, discord between spouses etc., Allah (swt) has provided a drastic cure for it which is the execution by beheading of the magician so that society may be freed from the evil which results from his actions.

Benefits Derived From This Hadith

1. The prohibition of learning sorcery and of teaching it.

2. That the punishment for practising magic is death by beheading.

Relevance of This Hadith to the Subject of the Chapter

That the Hadith proves that the punishment for sorcery is beheading, which shows that it is forbidden.

Relevance of This Hadith to the Subject of *Tawheed*

That the Hadith proves that learning and teaching magic is forbidden, because it is built upon a foundation of *shirk*.

..ooOOoo..

It is narrated by Bukhari, on the authority of Bajalah Ibn 'Ubadah, that he said: "'Umar Ibn Al-Khattab (ra) wrote: "Execute every sorceror and sorceress." "So, continued Bajalah," we executed three sorcerors."

And it is reported authentically from Hafsah (may Allah be pleased with her) that she ordered the execution of her slave for practising magic upon her, and she was executed. Such an event has also been reported from Jundub (ra). According to Imam Ahmad, execution of sorcerors is authentically reported from three Companions (i.e. `Umar, Hafsah and Jundub ra).

Relevance of These Narration to the Subject of the Chapter

The writer (Muhammad Ibn `Abdul Wahhab) has mentioned these narrations in this chapter in order to make it clear that the opinion of the above-mentioned Companions was that the magician be killed.

Footnotes

1. This is because the magician places his faith not in Allah (swt), but in the devils among the jinn whom he supplicates.

2. At-Tawagheet: Plural of At-Taghoot.

3. Unmindful: Innocent or naive.

4. There is no difference between these two terms; the idea propagated by some Muslim "modernists" that ribaa means excessive interest rates, and that moderate interest is therefore permissible, is totally without foundation and is in contradiction with the Qur'an, the Sunnah and the confirmed practices of the Companions who were the best people after the Prophet (saas) in understanding the Sunnah and who used to avoid even those permissible transactions that in any way resembled ribaa.

5. Marfoo': A report from one of the Companions which suggests, without explicitly saying so, that he heard it from the Prophet (saas), such as the above report of Jundub (ra), in the which he states the punishment for a certain crime, for it is not possible that he would have used his own judgement in such a matter.

6. Narrated by At-Tirmizi, who said: "The correct saying is that it is mawqoof (i.e. a saying of Jundub)." - and Allah (swt) knows best.

Top | Prev | Next

Kitaab At-Tawheed, Chapter: 23

Clarification of a Number of Types of Sorcery

Imam Ahmad narrates, on the authority of Muhammad Ibn J'afar, on the authority of `Awf Ibn Hayyaan Ibn Al-'Alaa`, who said: "Qutun Ibn Qabeesah informed us from his father that he heard the Prophet (saas) say: "Verily, *al-'iyaafah*,[1] *at-tarq*[2] and *at-tiyarah*[3] are all acts of sorcery.

Because the Muslims at the beginning of Islam had recently come from the *Jahiliyyah* (Days of Ignorance), they still carried with them many of the customs and superstitions of that time; Islam ordained for them freedom from such ignorant superstition which Revelation and common sense reject and for which no practical evidence can be produced. Such beliefs and practices include: *Al-'iyaafah*, which is the belief that one's fortune is affected by the flights of birds, their species or their cries; *at-tarq*, which is to draw lines in the soil or sand and throwing stones in order to supposedly reveal secrets of the unseen; and *at-tiyarah*, which is to believe in omens and portents. The Messenger of Allah (saas) has made plain that these three are acts of sorcery and it is confirmed that practising magic, learning it and teaching it are all prohibited and it is incumbent upon every Muslim to avoid it and to declare his innocence of any such beliefs and practices and their adherents.

Benefits Derived From This Hadith

    1. Evidence that *al-'iyaafah, at-tarq* and *at-tiyaarah*.

    2. The prohibition of magic.

Relevance of This Hadith to the Subject of the Chapter

That it proves that the three above-mentioned practices are acts of sorcery.

Relevance of This Hadith to the Subject of *Tawheed*

That it proves that these three practices are acts of magic, and magic is built upon a foundation of *Shirk*.

..ooOOoo..

It is reported on the authority of Ibn `Abbas (ra) that he said: "Allah's Messenger (saas) said:

> *"Whoever learns a part of astrology, has learnt a part of magic. Those who learn more accumulate more (sin)."*

Because knowledge of the unseen is for Allah (swt) Alone, the Prophet (saas) negated all attempts to uncover it, including astrology, according to which belief, one may know the future by understanding the supposed influence produced by the movement of the stars and the planets on peoples' lives. And He (saas) has made clear that learning such things is an act of sorcery, and that the more a person learns, the more he is guilty of sin.

Benefits Derived From This Hadith

1. Evidence that the study of astrology is a kind of magic.

2. That magic is of more than one kind.

Relevance of This Hadith to the Subject of the Chapter

That it proves that the study of astrology is a kind of magic.

Relevance of This Hadith to the Subject of *Tawheed*

That the Hadith proves that the study of astrology is a type of sorcery and sorcery is founded upon *Shirk*.

Important Note

Attempting to uncover the secrets of the physical unknown using practical methods such as the working of the Universe, biology, physics etc. are not considered acts of magic; rather, they are a fulfillment of the Command of Allah (swt) and His Prophet (saas) to seek knowledge.

..ooOOoo..

An-Nasaa`i reports on the authority of Abu Hurairah (ra) that he said:

> *"Whoever tied a knot and blew on it has committed an act of sorcery, and whoever commits an act of sorcery has committed an act of Shirk, and whoever wore an amulet will be left to its control."*

The Prophet (saas) tells us in this Hadith that anyone who makes knots in ropes and then blows upon them is guilty of practising magic; and He (saas) makes it clear that he who practises magic has committed *Shirk*; likewise, anyone who wears an amulet or talisman, believing that it will protect him from harm, he will be abandoned to its protection, which is, of course, non-existent; whereas he who gives his heart to Allah (swt) and is filled with confidence in Him, Most High, and depends upon Him Alone, this will suffice him. And whoever depended upon Allah's creatures - sorcerors and others - he will attain only evil - in this life and in the Hereafter because he has placed his faith in other than Allah (swt), while Allah (swt) is Sufficient for His slaves.

Benefits Derived From This Hadith

1. The forbiddance of practising magic.

2. That blowing on knots is a form of magic.

3. Evidence that the sorceror is a *mushrik*.

4. The prohibition of wearing anything as a means of protection, or a provider, or a granter of wishes, etc.

5. That whoever depends upon other than Allah (swt) is abandoned.

6. That whoever depends upon Allah (swt), this will suffice him.

Relevance of This Hadith to the Subject of the Chapter

That the Hadith proves that the wearing of amulets or the like and blowing upon knots are acts of sorcery.

Relevance of This Hadith to the Subject of *Tawheed*

That the Hadith proves that magic is *Shirk*.

..ooOOoo..

It is reported on the authority of Ibn Mas'ood (ra) that the Messenger of Allah (saas) said:

"Shall I not tell you what al-'adhdhah[4] is? It is an-nameemah." [5] (Narrated by Muslim)

In order to focus the attention of his Companions on what he was saying, because of the great love and affection that he had for them, he used the form of a question, which he then proceeded to answer himself: He (saas) asked them about *al-'adhdhah*; then he explained to them that it is *an-nameemah*, which means to carry tales about someone behind his back by quoting something he said about a person to that person, the result of which is to sow discord between those two people and to fill their hearts with enmity.

Benefits Derived From This Hadith

1. That asking questions is a part of the Islamic way of teaching.

2. The prohibition of *an-nameemah*, and that it is a major sin.

Relevance of This Hadith to the Subject of the Chapter

That the Hadith proves that *an-nameemah* is a kind of sorcery, because it produces the same effect as magic, or worse causing division among the people.

Relevance of This Hadith to the Subject of *Tawheed*

That the Hadith proves that *an-nameemah* is a kind of sorcery, and, as we have seen, sorcery is a form of *Shirk*.

Important Note

The person who is guilty of *an-nameemah* is not considered a disbeliever, nor is it ordered that he be killed, but the sorceror is guilty of *kufr* because he is depending upon other than Allah (swt) to supply his wants and needs, while the tale-bearer is not, but because of its similarity in some respects to sorcery, it is incumbent upon every Muslim to avoid it.

..ooOOoo..

It is reported by Bukhari and Muslim, on the authority of Ibn `Umar (ra) that the Messenger of Allah (saas) said:

"Verily, some eloquence (can be so beautiful); it constitutes sorcery.

In this Hadith, the Prophet (saas) has compared excessive eloquence and expressiveness with words to magic, for the eloquent man may on occasions succeed in making the false appear true or vice versa. He (saas) distorts the truth by throwing dust in peoples' eyes, robbing some of their rights by deception and falsehood. The truth of this may be seen by anyone who visits a court of law and watches a lawyer at work.

Benefits Derived From This Hadith

1. The forbiddance of some eloquence, i.e. that which attempts to make truth appear as falsehood and vice versa.

2. The derogatory comparison of some eloquence with magic.

Relevance of This Hadith to the Subject of the Chapter

That it defines some eloquence as comparable to sorcery because it deflects the heart as does sorcery.

Relevance of This Hadith to the Subject of *Tawheed*

That it compares excessive eloquence to sorcery, and as we have seen, sorcery is an act of *Shirk*.

Important Note

It is not to be understood from this Hadith that the capacity of expressiveness with words constitutes *kufr*, but that since some forms of eloquence result in corruption and usurpation of rights, they are in some ways comparable to sorcery, and therefore it is incumbent upon us to abstain from them.

Footnotes

1. Al-'Iyaafah: Foretelling events by the flight of birds.

2. At-Tarq: Drawing lines in the earth to predict events.

3. At-Tiyarah: Omens and portents.

4. Al-'Adhdhah: Literally, biting.

5. An-Nameemah: Tale-bearing, such as one's saying: "Such-and-such a person says you are untruthful." - even though what that person says may be true, it is still considered to be carrying tales.

Kitaab At-Tawheed, Chapter: 24

What Has Been Said About Fortune-tellers and Their Like

Muslim has narrated, on the authority of one of the wives of the Prophet (saas) (Hafsah - may Allah be pleased with her), that Allah's Prophet (saas) said:

"Whoever went to a fortune-teller and asked him about some matter (i.e. of the unseen) and believed him, will have his prayer rejected for forty days."

The Prophet (saas) informs us in this Hadith that if anyone visited a fortune-teller and asked him about a matter of the unseen - about which, in reality, none possesses knowledge except Allah (swt) - and believed in what fortune teller said, Allah (swt) will not accept his prayers, nor reward them for forty days - and this is a punishment for the major sin which he has committed.

Benefits Derived From This Hadith

1. The prohibition of fortune-telling.

2. The forbiddance of believing the prophesies of soothsayers and fortune-tellers.

3. That a person may lose the reward of his prayers as a punishment for his sins.

Relevance of This Hadith to the Subject of the Chapter

That the Hadith proves the forbiddance of fortune-telling and the belief in it.

Relevance of This Hadith to the Subject of *Tawheed*

That the Prophet (saas) has condemned whoever visits a fortune-teller for he has made him a partner with Allah (swt) in possessing knowledge of the unseen.

Important Note

It has been mentioned by the scholars - may Allah (swt) have mercy on them - that whoever believed in what the fortune-teller says does not have to repeat his prayers for this period of forty days, but that he receives no reward for them.

..ooOOoo..

It is reported on the authority of Abu Hurairah (ra) that the Prophet (saas) said:

"Whoever went to a fortune-teller and believed in what he said, has disbelieved in what was revealed to Muhammad."

The Prophet (saas) informs us in this Hadith, that whoever visited a fortune-teller and asked him about the unseen and believed in his words, has committed an act of disbelief in the Qur'an and *Sunnah*, this is because both of these Revelations have belied fortune-telling, for Allah (swt) is Alone in His

Knowledge of the unseen.

Benefits Derived From This Hadith

1. The forbiddance of fortune-telling.

2. The accusation of lying against the fortune-teller.

3. That believing the words of fortune-tellers is considered disbelief.[1]

4. That the Qur'an is revealed, not created.

Relevance of This Hadith to the Subject of the Chapter

That the Hadith proves clearly that the fortune-teller is a disbeliever.

Relevance of This Hadith to the Subject of *Tawheed*

That the Hadith is clear evidence that fortune-telling is *kufr*; this is because the fortune-teller depends upon methods of *shirk*.

The same thing was narrated on the authority of Abu Hurairah by "the four"[2] and by Al-Haakim, who said that it is authentic according to the strict conditions of acceptance laid down by Bukhari and Muslim.

It has also been reported, with a good *sanad*, on the authority of Abu Y'alaa (ra) that he said the same thing, but in a *mawqoof* form.[3]

..ooOOoo..

On the authority of `Imran Ibn Husain (ra), in a *marfoo'* form, it is reported: "Whoever practises *at-tiyarah*, or tells fortunes or seeks advice from a fortune-teller, or practises magic or asks another to do so, is not one of us; and whoever goes to a soothsayer and believes what he tells him has disbelieved in that which was revealed to Muhammad." (Narrated by Al-Bazzaar, with a good *Sanad* and by At-Tabarani, in his book, *Al-Awsat*, with a good *sanad*, but without the words: "...and whoever goes to a soothsayer etc...")

In this Hadith, the Prophet (saas) declares himself free and innocent of three kinds of people: (i) The one who seeks omens or their interpretation, (ii) the one who tells fortunes or seeks advice from fortune-tellers and (iii) the one who practises magic, or seeks the services of a magician. Then He (saas) adds, as an extra warning to the fortune-teller and his clients, that whoever believes in the words of the fortune-teller has disbelieved in the Revelation (the Qur'an and the *Sunnah*) given to him (saas); this is because Allah and His Messenger (saas) have informed us that knowledge of the unseen is only with Allah (swt), therefore belief in the fortune-teller is a rejection of Allah's Words and those of His Prophet (saas).

Benefits Derived From This Hadith

1. The prohibition of interpreting omens, of sorcery and fortune-telling.

2. The forbiddance of seeking these three things.

3. That believing the prophesies of the fortune-teller is *kufr*.

4. That the Qur'an is Revelation, not created.

Relevance of This Hadith to the Subject of the Chapter

That the Hadith proves without doubt, that the fortune-teller is a disbeliever.

Relevance of This Hadith to the Subject of *Tawheed*

That the Hadith proves without question, that the fortune-teller is a disbeliever, because he depends upon *shirk* in order to predict the future.

Muhammad Ibn `Abdil Wahhab says: "Al-Baghawi said: "The seer (*al-'arraaf*) who claims to know the unseen depends upon knowledge stolen (by the jinn, who overheard it from the lowest heaven) and falsehood and the like; It has been said that he is the same as the fortune-teller (*al-kaahin*), but the latter is, in fact, one who claims knowledge of the unseen events of the future. It has also been said that he is one who knows the secrets of the mind." Abul `Abbas Ibn Taimiyah said: "The seer is a name for the fortune-teller, the astrologer, the thrower of sand, and all those who claim knowledge of these matters by such means." Ibn `Abbas (ra) said, concerning a people who wrote *Abaajaad* [4] and practised astrology: "I do not consider that those who do this will have any share (of blessings or reward) with Allah (swt)."

Footnotes

1. It has been said by some scholars, based upon this Hadith, that one who believes the prophecies of a fortune-teller is a disbeliever. However, other scholars maintain that what is intended here is that he who believes the words of a fortune-teller has committed an act of disbelief. This is because, in the previous Hadith, the Prophet (saas) informed us that one who visits a fortune-teller and believes in what he says will have his prayers rejected for forty days, while if it were true that he were a disbeliever, his prayer would not be accepted at all.

2. The Four: That is, Bukhari, Muslim, At-Tirmizi and An-Nasaa`i.

3. Mawqoof: That is, the statement of a Companion, which he does not attribute to the Prophet (saas).

4. Abaajaad: An ancient system of prediction based on use of the letters of the alphabet.

Top | Prev | Next

Kitaab At-Tawheed, Chapter: 25

What has Been Said About An-Nushrah [1]

It is reported on the authority of Jabir (ra) that Allah's Messenger (saas) was asked about *an-nushrah* and he said:

> *"It is one of the works of Satan."* (Narrated by Ahmad with a good *Sanad* and by Abu Dawood

Who said: "Ahmad was asked about these matters and he answered that Ibn Mas'ood detested all such things.")

Because *an-nushrah* was one of the actions of the *Jahiliyyah*, and the Companions had no desire or liking for the *Jahiliyyah* or its deeds, they asked the Prophet (saas) about *an-nushrah*. He (saas) replied that it is one of the works of Satan, and it is well-known that Satan orders not except that which is corrupt and detestable to the Believer. As for that which is permissible and not from the works of Satan, there is *ar-ruqyah*, seeking refuge (with Allah swt) and the use of all permissible medicines (i.e. those which do not contain forbidden substances such as alcohol, pig fat etc.) and the Hadith is not a forbiddance of these things.

Benefits Derived From This Hadith

1. The prohibition of *an-nushrah*, i.e. of using methods which involve sorcery or *shirk* in order to counteract the effects of magic.

2. That the works of Satan are all forbidden.

Relevance of This Hadith to the Subject of the Chapter

That the Hadith proves the prohibition of *an-nushrah*.

Relevance of This Hadith to the Subject of *Tawheed*

That it proves that *an-nushrah*, which is from the *Jahiliyyah*, and cannot be performed without committing *shirk*, is forbidden, and that the one who does so is a magician.

..ooOOoo..

It is reported by Bukhari, on the authority of Qatadah that he said: "I said to Ibn Al-Musayyib: "A man is under the influence of a magic spell, or is unable to have sex with his wife - should we treat him with *an-nushrah* or use some other means to cure the spell?" Ibn Al-Musayyib replied: "It is permissible (to use *an-nushrah*), since they intend by it restoration or mending. That which is beneficial is not prohibited."[2]

It is reported that Al-Hasan Al-Basri said: "Magic is not counteracted by its like except by a magician."

Relevance of This Narration to the Subject of the Chapter

That it shows that Al-Hasan Al-Basri considered that counteracting magic with magic is forbidden and that the one who does so is a sorceror.

Muhammad Ibn `Abdul Wahhaab said: "Ibn Al-Qayyim said: "*An-Nushrah* is counteracting the effects of magic and it consists of two kinds:

> 1. Counteracting magic with its like and this is the work of the devil.

> 2. *An-Nushrah* by means of *ar-ruqyah*, seeking refuge with Allah (swt), permissible medicines and making supplications to Allah (swt) - these are all permitted forms of *an-nushrah*.

Important Note

It might be said, with some justification, that these words of Ibn Al-Qayyim sum up the message of this chapter.

Footnotes

1. Counteracting magic with magic.

2. This is not a permission to use magic against magic; what is permitted here is the use of ar-ruqyah, seeking refuge with Allah (swt), using permitted medicines etc. For how could Ibn Al-Musayyib make permissible that which the Prophet (saas) had forbidden?

Top | Prev | Next

Kitaab At-Tawheed, Chapter: 27

What Has Been Said About *At-Tanjeem* [1]

Bukhari narrates in his *Saheeh*, that Qatadah said:

> *"Allah created these stars for three reasons: (i) To adorn the heaven, (ii) as missiles against the devils and (ii) as signs by which (the traveller) may be guided; and so whoever claims more than this for them has is emoneous and has lost his reward (on the Day of Resurrection) and taken upon himself that of which he has no knowledge."*

In this narration, Qatadah informs us that Allah (swt), Most High, Created the stars for only three things: The first, to beautify the night sky; the second, as projectiles against the devils who approach the lowest heaven in order to overhear the angels speaking of the Commandments of Allah (swt) which they then attempt to convey to the fortune-tellers and soothsayers; [2] and the third, as guidance for the wayfarer at night, whether on land or at sea. He (saas) added that anyone who claims more than this for the stars such as the claims of astrologers, that the positions of the stars and planets exert an influence on our daily lives, is acting out of ignorance, and will receive no reward from Allah (swt) on the Day of Judgement and has gone astray from the Straight Path.

Benefits Derived From This Narration

1. The wisdom of creating the stars.

2. The falseness of the claims of those who say otherwise.

3. The forbiddance of belief in astrology.

4. The punishment prescribed for those who practice or believe in astrology.

Relevance of This Narration to the Subject of the Chapter

That it informs us of the view of Qatadah concerning astrology, that it is false and forbidden.

Relevance of This Narration to the Subject of *Tawheed*

That Qatadah rejected that which the astrologers claim concerning the stars and knowledge of the unseen because it is an act of *Shirk* to claim knowledge of the unseen; as such knowledge is only with Allah (swt).

Harb informs us that while Qatadah disliked the studying of the lunar phases, Ibn `Uyainah forbade it, and Ahmad and Ishaq permitted it.

Important Note

(a) Study of the stars is of three kinds: (i) That which is *kufr*, and that is the belief that the heavenly bodies themselves decide the events of our daily lives. (ii) The belief that events may be predicted by studying the courses and relative positions of the stars and planets which they claim is by Allah's Ordainment and His Will and there is no doubt of the forbiddance of this nor of its being a form of *Shirk*. (iii) The study of the stars and the planets in order to have knowledge of their cycles for the purpose of aiding travellers in order to know the direction of the *Qiblah* [3] and to know the time and season and this is permissible.

(b) The suggestion that Allah's Words:

" *And marks and signs; and by the stars they are guided"* (Qur'an 16:16)

Are an indication that astrology is permissible is totally false and baseless, because its forbiddance has been reported in many authentic Ahadith and therefore, it is clear that the meaning of this verse is not as the ignorant and misguided have claimed, but that Allah (swt) has placed in the earth many natural sign-posts such as mountains, valleys, rivers, trees, rocks, etc.; and in the heaven stars to help the traveller find his way and that we may know the time and the season.

..ooOOoo..

It is reported on the authority of Abu Moosa (ra), that he said: "Allah's Messenger (saas) said:

"There are three who will not enter Paradise: (i) The habitual wine drinker, (ii) the one who cuts family ties and (iii) the one who believes in sorcery."

The Messenger of Allah (saas) informs us in this Hadith that there are three categories of people who will not enter Paradise because of the major sins which they committed, all of which are harmful to themselves and to the whole community: The first of them is the alcoholic because when he is under the influence of alcohol, his rationality and his inhibitions depart and he is likely to commit any number of sins. The second is the one who breaks family ties, because in so doing he causes strife, division and enmity between members of his family - the result of this may be the breakdown of the family unit which is the basis of a healthy society. The third is the one who believes in sorcery which includes fortune-telling, astrology, palm-reading etc., because this leads to cheating, fraud and deception for the purpose of stealing the money of the innocent and the gullible.

Benefits Derived From This Hadith

1. The prohibition of alcoholic drinks.

2. The obligation to maintain family ties.

3. The forbiddance of belief in sorcery.

Relevance of This Hadith to the Subject of the Chapter

That it proves that it is forbidden to believe in all kinds of sorcery, including astrology.

Relevance of This Hadith to the Subject of *Tawheed*

That the Hadith forbids belief in sorcery, including astrology, because belief in astrology necessitates the belief that someone other than Allah (swt) possesses knowledge of the unseen and such a belief is *Shirk*.

Footnotes

1. At-Tanjeem: Astrology.

2. This refers to meteorites, not stars, which are referred to in Arabic also as stars, as indeed they are in English (shooting stars, falling stars).

3. Qiblah: The direction towards which we face when we pray i.e. the K'abah in Makkah.

Top | Prev | Next

Kitaab At-Tawheed, Chapter: 28

What Has Been Said Concerning *Al-Anwaa`*

Allah (swt), says:

> " *And instead [of thanking Allah] for the provision He gives you, on the contrary, you deny [Him] by disbelief"* (Qur'an 56:82)

Allah (swt), Most Glorified, Most High, rebukes those who reject His Blessings upon them, such as the rain which gives life to the land, causing the crops and fruits of the earth to grow; instead, they attribute it to the movements of the stars which can neither harm nor benefit, saying: "We have been given rain by virtue of the movement of the moon and the stars."

Benefits Derived From This Verse

1. That good and evil are ordained by Allah.

2. That the rain is a blessing from Allah.

3. Attributing blessings to other than Allah is an act of disbelief in Him.

Relevance of This Verse to the Subject of the Chapter

That it proves that whoever attributes blessings such as the rain to the movements of the moon and stars is a disbeliever.

Relevance of This Verse to the Subject of *Tawheed*

That it rejects the claims of those who attribute blessings to other than Allah (swt), such as the sending of the rain, because such a belief is *shirk*.

..ooOOoo..

It is reported on the authority of Ibn Malik Al-Ash'ari (ra) that the Messenger of Allah (saas) said:

> *"There are four traits remaining from the Jaahiliyyah to be found in my Ummah, which they will not abandon: (i) Pride in the nobility of one's ancestors, (ii) defaming the ancestors of others, (iii) seeking rainfall from the stars and excessive mourning and wailing for the dead." And he (saas) added: "The wailing woman, if she does not repent before she dies, will be raised on the Day of Resurrection with a dress of liquid tar and a cloak of mange or scabies."* (Narrated by Muslim)

It being the intention of Islam to cut off every connection with the iniquitous customs of the *Jahiliyyah*, the Messenger of Allah (saas) informs us in this Hadith, in a spirit of censure and rebuke, that four customs of the Days of Ignorance will remain in this *Ummah*: The first is pride in the nobility of one's lineage for this leads to slackness and idleness, as one rests on the laurels of one's forebears; the second is the disparagement of the ancestry of others which leads to a situation in which people spend their time in seeking out weaknesses and defects in each others' backgrounds which causes the reputation of Islam and the Muslims to suffer and results in division and enmity amongst them; the third is seeking rainfall from the stars because it causes the hearts to become attached to other than Allah (swt) and humility before His creations which possess no power to benefit or harm; and the fourth is excessive mourning and bewailing of the dead and eulogising them in loud voices for this suggests non-acceptance of Allah's Ordainments, and adversely affects the deceased's family and spreads depression and despair; because of this, the Prophet (saas) stressed the punishment of such wailing women, should they not repent to Allah (swt) before they die.

Benefits Derived From This Hadith

1. The refutation of the evil customs practised during the *Jahiliyyah*.

2. The prohibition of pride in one's ancestry, of defaming the lineage of others, and of excessive mourning and bewailing of the dead.

3. That those who seek rain from the stars in the belief that they can, of their own accord send rain, are disbelievers, while those who believe that the stars are the cause of rain, but that Allah (swt) made them so, are guilty of an act of disbelief, without being considered disbelievers.

4. The acceptance of repentance as long as it is before the death of the penitent.

5. Confirmation of the miracle of the Prophet (saas), since his prophesy has proved true in every respect.

6. Confirmation of the reality of the Resurrection and the Requital.

Relevance of This Hadith to the Subject of the Chapter

That the Hadith proves the forbiddance of seeking rain from the movements of the stars.

Relevance of This Hadith to the Subject of *Tawheed*

That the Hadith rejects seeking rain from the stars as this necessitates requesting blessings from other than Allah (swt), which is *shirk*.

Important Note

It is permissible to mention a person by a nickname such as "the son of the tall one" or "the son of the thin man" or "the son of the lame one" etc., even though the person so named may dislike it, if it is the only way in which he can be identified.

..ooOOoo..

It is narrated by Bukhari and Muslim, on the authority of Zaid Ibn Khalid Al-Juhani (ra) that he said: "Allah's Messenger (saas) prayed the morning prayer with us in Al-Hudaibiyyah after it had rained during the night, and when he had finished, he addressed the people, saying: "Do you know what your *Rabb* said?" They said: "Allah (swt) and His Messenger (saas) know best!" He (saas) said: (Allah swt said:) "Some of My slaves this morning are true Believers in Me and others are disbelievers: As for those who say: "We have received rain from the Bounty of Allah (swt) and His Mercy," they are Believers in Me and disbelievers in the stars, while those who say: "We have received rain from the movements of such-and-such a star," are disbelievers in Me and believers in the stars."

Zaid Ibn Khalid (ra) tells us in this Hadith that the Prophet (saas) led the people in *fajr* prayer in the area known as Al-Hudaibiyyah, after a night of rain. After the prayer, facing the people, He (saas) addressed them, wishing to encourage them to do good and to increase their knowledge; He (saas) told them that Allah (swt) had revealed to him that regarding the rain, the people are divided into two categories: (i) Those who thank Him and (ii) those who are ungrateful to Him. As for those who are grateful and believe in Him, they are the ones who attribute the blessing of rain to Allah (swt); and as for those who are ungrateful and disbelieve in Him, they are the ones who attribute the rainfall to the positions of the planets and stars.

Benefits Derived From This Hadith

1. The virtue of the Imam addressing the congregation after finishing the prayer.

2. The virtue of infusing knowledge by asking: "Do you know.?"

3. Confirmation of Allah's Divine Attribute of Speech.

4. The correct manner of responding to a question in religious matters when one does not know the answer.

5. The forbiddance of rejecting Allah's Blessings.

6. Confirmation of Allah's Divine Attribute of Mercy.

7. That attributing Allah's Blessings to other than Allah is *kufr*.

8. The forbiddance of saying: "We have received rain due to the position of such-and-such a star."

Relevance of This Hadith to the Subject of the Chapter

That the Hadith proves that attributing rainfall to the movements or positions of stars is forbidden.

Relevance of This Hadith to the Subject of *Tawheed*

That the Hadith shows that whoever attributes rainfall to the stars' movements is a disbeliever because he has attributed blessings to other than Allah (swt), Who is the Source of all blessings.

..ooOOoo..

It is reported by Bukhari and Muslim, on the authority of Ibn `Abbas (ra) a Hadith carrying the same meaning as the previous Hadith: "Some (of the people) said: "The promise of rain of such-and-such a star has come true." Then Allah (swt) revealed the following verses:

" *Furthermore, I call to witness the setting of the stars - and that is indeed a mighty oath, did you but know it - that this is indeed a Qur'an most honourable, in a Book well-guarded, which none has touched except the pure ones [i.e. the angels]: A Revelation from the Lord of the worlds. Is it such a Message as you would deny? and instead [of thanking Allah] for the provision He gives you, on the contrary, you deny [Him] by disbelief"* (Qur'an 56:75-82)

In these verses, Allah (swt), Most High, swears by the setting of the stars concerning the greatness of the Qur'an and its blessings, that it is preserved in a Book, which is in the hands of the angels, touched by none but the angels, and that it was revealed from the Owner of creation and the Director of its affairs, and that it is not, as the disbeliever's claimed, poetry, or magic. Then Allah (swt) rebukes those who support the disbeliever's in the Qur'an and abet them by attributing to the stars that which is for Allah (swt), Alone, i.e. the rain, for this is a denial of the Qur'an which clearly states that it is Allah (swt) Who sends the rain.

Benefits Derived From This Verse

1. That it is for Allah (swt) to swear by anything He Wills, but it is not permissible for His slaves to swear except by Allah (swt), or one of His Divine Attributes.

2. Confirmation of the greatness of Qur'an and that Allah (swt) has preserved it from all corruption and change.

3. That the Qur'an was revealed, not created.

4. Confirmation of Allah's Divine Attribute of being Above His creation.

5. The forbiddance of friendly relations at the expense of religion.

6. The prohibition of attributing the rain to the movements of the heavenly bodies.

Relevance of This Verse to the Subject of the Chapter

That it proves that whoever attributed blessings to other than Allah (swt) is a disbeliever.

Relevance of This Verse to the Subject of *Tawheed*

That the verse rejects the claim that blessings come from other than Allah (swt); this includes attributing the rain to the movements of the stars and planets, because this is *shirk*.

Top | Prev | Next

Kitaab At-Tawheed, Chapter: 29

Allah's Words: (swt) And Among the People Are Those Who Take [for Worship] Partners Besides Allah (swt)

Allah (swt), says:

> " *And among the people are those who take [for worship] partners besides Allah; they love them as they should love Allah, but those of faith are greater in their love for Allah. If only the evil-doers could see. Behold! They would see the punishment: That to Allah belongs all power, and Allah will strongly enforce the punishment"* (Qur'an 2:165)

Allah (swt), Most Glorified, Most High, informs us in this verse that some of the people set up partners with Allah (swt), whom they love and glorify as they do Allah (swt). Then Allah (swt) makes it clear that the Believers love Allah (swt) more, for their love is a pure unadulterated love, which is only for Allah (swt), while the love of the polytheists is corrupted and spoiled by their equal love of the other deities whom they have taken as partners with Allah (swt). Then Allah (swt) warns that those polytheists, when they see the punishment that is theirs on the Day of Resurrection, will know that all power belongs to Allah (swt) and that His punishment is condign.

Benefits Derived From This Verse

1. That love of Allah is a form of worship.

2. The love of the polytheists for Allah does not benefit them at all because of their *shirk*.

3. That *shirk* invalidates one's deeds.

4. That pure love for Allah is sign of true faith.

5. Confirmation of Allah's Divine Attribute of Power.

Relevance of This Verse to the Subject of the Chapter and to the Subject of *Tawheed*

That it proves that whoever loves someone or something as much as Allah (swt), has set up a partner with Allah (swt) and this is an act of *shirk*.

Important Note

In order that there should be no confusion in this matter, it is important to point out that love falls into two categories: (i) That which is pure, and that is worshipful love which necessitates humility, submissiveness, exaltation and complete obedience; none has the right to such love except Allah (swt); (ii) The second kind of love is shared love: This includes natural love, such as the love of certain foods, certain aromas, etc., the love of family, such as that of a child for his parents and vice versa, and the love that a person may have for a friend. Such love may come and go, strengthen and weaken, unlike the first category, for it is incumbent upon us to love Allah (swt) to the utmost of our ability.

..ooOOoo..

Allah (swt), says:

> " *Say:* "*If it be that your fathers, your sons, your brothers, your wives, your kindred, the wealth that you have gained, the commerce in which you fear a decline and the dwellings in which you delight are dearer to you than Allah and His Messenger, and striving hard, and fighting in His Cause, then wait until Allah brings about His Decision - and Allah guides not the rebellious*" (Qur'an 9:24)

In this verse, Allah (swt), Most Glorified, Most High, commands His Prophet, Muhammad (saas) to make plain to the people that whoever places his love of worldly things above his love of Allah (swt), and His Prophet (saas) and defence of his religion, verily, he will see what awaits him of chastisement from Allah (swt), because Allah (swt) does not grant success to those who do not submit themselves to Him Alone.

Benefits Derived From This Verse

1. The forbiddance of placing one's love of worldly things above one's love of Allah (swt).

2. The permissibility of love for such things as long as it does not interfere with one's love for Allah (swt).

3. That love of Allah (swt) and His Messenger (saas) are both obligatory, and love of one without the other is not acceptable.

4. That the guidance of success comes only from Allah (swt) and no other.

Relevance of This Verse to the Subject of the Chapter

That it proves the prohibition of placing one's love of worldly things above that of Allah (swt).

Relevance of This Verse to the Subject of *Tawheed*

That it proves the obligation to love Allah (swt) and His Messenger (saas); therefore, this kind of love is an act of worship, and directing worship to other than Allah (swt) is *shirk*.

..ooOOoo..

On the authority of Anas (swt), it is reported that Allah's Messenger (saas) said:

> *"None of you truly believes until I am more beloved by him than his sons, his father and all of mankind. "* (Narrated by Bukhari and Muslim)

Allah's Messenger (saas) informs us in this Hadith that none has complete faith, nor can he achieve the necessary level of faith by which he may enter Paradise without punishment, unless and until he places his love of the Prophet (saas) before his love of parents, children and all mankind. This is because love of the Messenger of Allah (saas) means love of Allah (swt), for the Messenger (saas) is the one who brings to us Allah's Revelation and Guidance to His Religion and love of Allah (swt) and His Messenger (saas) is not true unless it leads to the implementation of all of Allah's Laws and abstinence from all that He has forbidden - and love of Allah's Messenger (saas) is not demonstrated merely by singing his praises or by celebrating his birthday, which is a despicable innovation unknown to the

Prophet (saas) and his Companions.

Benefits Derived From This Hadith

1. That the negation of complete faith in this Hadith does not necessitate exclusion from the fold of Islam.

2. That deeds are a part of faith, for love is an action of the heart.

3. The obligation to place one's love of the Messenger (saas) before love of parents, children and all of mankind.

Relevance of This Hadith to the Subject of the Chapter

That it proves the obligation of placing one's love of Allah (swt) and His Messenger (saas) before love of all others.

Relevance of This Hadith to the Subject of *Tawheed*

That it proves the obligation of placing one's love of Allah (swt) and His Messenger (saas) before that of all others; this proves that love is an act of worship and directing an act of worship to other than Allah (swt) is an act of worship.

..ooOOoo..

Also reported by Al-Bukhari and Muslim, on the authority of Anas (ra) is that he said: "Allah's Messenger (saas) said:

"Whoever possesses the following three qualities will have the sweetness of faith: (i) The one to whom Allah (swt) and His Messenger (saas) are more loved than anything else; (ii) the one who loves a person purely and solely for Allah's sake; and (iii) the one who hates to return to kufr after Allah (swt) has saved him, as he would hate to be thrown into the Fire." *and in another narration: "None of you will find the sweetness of faith until..."*

Allah's Messenger (saas) informs us in this Hadith that faith has a sweetness, and that this sweetness will not be experienced by any except him who places his love of Allah (swt) and His Messenger (saas) before that of all others and who does not love anyone except for Allah's sake and none other, and who hates disbelief and the idea of returning to it as much as he hates the Hell-fire and as much as he would hate to be thrown into it.

Benefits Derived From This Hadith

1. Confirmation of the sweetness of faith and that it is not achieved by every Believer.

2. The obligation of placing love of Allah (swt) and His Messenger (saas) above love of all others.

3. The permissibility of referring to Allah (swt) and His Messenger (saas) together.

4. That loving a person for Allah's sake is a part of faith.

5. The obligation to hate *kufr* and its adherents.

Relevance of This Hadith to the Subject of the Chapter

That the Hadith proves the obligation to love Allah (swt) and His Messenger (saas) more than all others.

Relevance of This Hadith to the Subject of the Chapter

That the Hadith proves that placing one's love of Allah (swt) and His Messenger (saas) before love of all others is an obligation which shows that love is a form of worship and directing an act of worship to other than Allah (swt) is *shirk*.

..ooOOoo..

It is reported on the authority of Ibn `Abbas (ra) that he said: "Whoever loved for Allah's sake and hated for Allah's sake and befriended for Allah's sake and showed enmity for Allah's sake, will achieve by this Allah's friendship and the slave will not attain the real taste of *eemaan* (faith), even though he may pray much and fast much, until he does all these things. Today, most of the people maintain relationships and love only for some worldly reason, but this will not profit them anything (on the Day of Judgement)." (Narrated by Ibn Jareer At-Tabari)

Relevance of This Narration to the Subject of the Chapter and to the Subject of *Tawheed*

That it shows that Ibn `Abbas (swt) considered that love is a form of worship and directing an act of worship to other than Allah (swt) is *shirk*.

Ibn `Abbas (ra) said, concerning Allah's Words:

> *" And all relations between them would be cut off" (Qur'an 2:166)*

that it refers to relations of love.

Relevance of This Narration to the Subject of the Chapter and to the Subject of *Tawheed*

That it shows that Ibn `Abbas (ra) explained this verse as follows: That if love is not for Allah's sake, it will be wasted and a source of loss to the one who loved on the Day of Judgement for it is tantamount to *shirk*.

Top | Prev | Next

Kitaab At-Tawheed, Chapter: 26

What Has Been Said About At-Tatayyur [1]

Allah (swt) says:

> " *And when good came to them, they said: "This is due to us." But when evil befell them, they ascribed it to omens connected with Moosa and those with him! Verily, in truth the omens of evil are theirs in Allah's sight, but most of them understand not!"* (Qur'an 7:131)

In this verse, Allah (swt), Most High, describes the ways of Fir'aoun and his people in their dealings with Moosa (as) and his companions: That when any good came to them, they would claim the credit for it themselves, not attributing it to Allah (swt); but when any calamity befell them, they would blame it on the presence of Moosaa (as) and his people. Then Allah (swt) makes plain the falseness of their claims, Confirms that whatever evil comes to them is from Allah (swt) and it is what they have earned by their disbelief and rejection of the Signs of Allah (swt). Then He (swt), Most High, explains the reason for their behaving in this manner, which is their ignorance and lack of knowledge that Allah (swt) is the Ordainer of all good and evil.

Benefits Derived From This Verse

1. That good and evil are ordained by Allah.

2. The prohibition of denying Allah's Blessings.

3. The forbiddance of belief in omens.

4. That ignorance is the cause of all evil.

Relevance of This Verse to the Subject of the Chapter

That the verse proves the prohibition of *at-tatayyur*.

Relevance of This Verse to the Subject of *Tawheed*

That it proves that *at-tatayyur* is *Shirk* because it is an attachment of the heart to other than Allah (swt) and a belief that the cause of events is other than He.

..ooOOoo..

Allah (swt), Most High, says:

> " *They said: "Your evil omens are with yourselves." If you are admonished [do you deem it an evil omen?] No! But you are a people transgressing all bounds"* (Qur'an 36:19)

In this verse, Allah (swt), Most Glorified, Most High, explains that the Messengers who came to their people with warnings and reminders were considered evil omens by them, but that those Messengers rejected this, saying to them that whatever afflicts the unbelievers is because of their disbelief and rejection of Allah's Signs for they were peoples who transgressed all decent limits and were estranged from the Truth, preferring disbelief over faith - and this is the end result for the disbeliever.

Benefits Derived From This Verse

1. The prohibition of belief in evil omens and of pessimism based upon those omens.

2. The forbiddance of exceeding the limits of Allah.

3. That exceeding Allah's prescribed limits is the cause of destruction and humiliation.

Relevance of This Verse to the Subject of the Chapter

That it proves the forbiddance of *at-tataayyur*.

Relevance of This Verse to the Subject of *Tawheed*

That the verse rejects *at-tiyarah* because it causes the heart to become attached to other than Allah (swt) and this is *Shirk*.

..ooOOoo..

It is reported on the authority of Abu Hurairah (ra) that the Messenger of Allah (saas) said:

> *"There is no `adwaa,² no tiyarah and no haamah ³ and no Safar. ⁴"* (Narrated by Bukhari and Muslim)

Muslim, in his *Saheeh*, adds: "...and no *naw`* and no *ghool*." ⁵

Benefits Derived From This Hadith

1. That illness cannot spread except by Allah's Will.

2. The falseness of believing in omens and their effect.

3. The falseness of the beliefs of the *Jahiliyyah* regarding the flight of nocturnal birds.

4. The falseness of pessimism due to the approach of the month of *Safar*.

5. The falseness of the beliefs of the *Jahiliyyah* regarding ghosts and ghouls.

Relevance of This Hadith to the Subject of the Chapter

That the Hadith proves the falseness of belief in omens.

Relevance of This Hadith to the Subject of *Tawheed*

That the Hadith proves the invalidity of belief in omens because such beliefs cause an attachment of the heart to other than Allah (swt) and this is *Shirk*.

Important Note

There is no conflict between this Hadith which states: "There is no `adwaa...*" and that in which the Prophet (saas) said:

"Flee from the leper as you would flee from a lion,"

Because in the former Hadith, what is intended is that no disease may affect us except by Allah's leave, while the latter Hadith instructs us to undertake the necessary measures to ensure as best we can that we do not become ill, and this is the true meaning of *at-tawakkul* (dependence on Allah swt), to do that which is in your power in order to attain your objective and *then* to depend upon Allah (swt).

..ooOOoo..

Bukhari and Muslim report on the authority of Anas (ra) that he said: "Allah's Messenger (saas) said:

> *"There is no `adwaa and no tiyarah, but al-f al [6] pleases me." They asked: "What is al-f al?" He (saas) replied: "It is the good word."*

Because good and evil are ordained by Allah (swt), the Prophet (saas) negated the idea that infectious disease of itself may affect a person or that omens may affect us, either adversely or positively. And then He (saas) endorsed and approved optimism because optimism means to think well of Allah (swt) and to be filled with positive zeal to achieve one's objectives - as opposed to pessimism which produces lethargy and depression.

Benefits Derived From This Hadith

1. The negation of the belief that disease may affect us of itself, without Allah's leave.

2. The absolute falseness of belief in omens.

3. The desirabilty of optimism, rather than pessimism.

Relevance of This Hadith to the Subject of the Chapter

That the Hadith proves that belief in omens is false.

Relevance of This Hadith to the Subject of *Tawheed*

That the Hadith rejects the belief in omens because such belief is a denial of Allah's *Qadr* [7] and because it causes the heart to become attached to other than Allah (swt), and this is *Shirk*.

..ooOOoo..

It is authentically reported by Abu Dawood, on the authority of `Uqbah Ibn `Amir (ra), that he said: "*At-tiyarah* was mentioned before the Messenger of Allah (saas) and he said: "The best form of it is *al-f al*, for it does not prevent a Muslim (from achieving his objective). Whenever any of you sees something he dislikes, he should say: "Oh, Allah (swt)! None but You Brings good things. None but You can prevent evil things. There is no power and no strength except in You."

Because *at-tiyarah* is a sickness in society, which held sway over peoples' souls in the *Jahiliyyah*, it was mentioned during a gathering in which the Prophet (saas) was present and so he informed the Companions that such beliefs were baseless, and that while *al-f al* is a form of *tiyarah*, it is much superior because it necessitates thinking good of Allah (swt), and encourages positive thinking and optimism for the good. Then He (saas) informed them that *at-tiyarah* will not prevent any Muslim whose beliefs are correct from attaining his goals, nor weaken his resolve. Then He (saas) described an effective treatment for whomsoever is confonted by such supposed omens which is to place; the matter in Allah's Hands, that He may attract the good and repel the evil, by Allah's leave and continue to depend only upon Allah (swt) in order to fulfill all his goals.

Benefits Derived From This Hadith

1. That *al-f al* is a (permissible) form of *tiyarah*.

2. The desirability of optimism because it strengthens one's trust in Allah (swt).

3. The legality of supplicating Allah (swt) should any trace of this belief in omens take hold of one's heart.

4. That good and evil are ordained by Allah (swt).

Relevance of This Hadith to the Subject of the Chapter

That it proves the falseness of *at-tiyarah*.

Relevance of This Hadith to the Subject of *Tawheed*

That it rejects *at-tiyarah* because it negates belief in Allah's *Qadr* and because it causes the heart to become attached to other than Allah (swt) and this is *Shirk*.

..ooOOoo..

On the authority of Ibn Mas'ood (ra), in a *marfoo'* form, it is reported that he said: "*At-tiyarah* is *Shirk*, *at-tiyrah* is *Shirk*. There is none among us who is not afflicted by it, but Allah (swt), by true dependence on Him removes it from the heart." (Narrated by Abu Dawood and At-Tirmizi, who said it is authentic, but considered the last part of it to be Ibn Mas'ood's own statement)

Ibn Mas'ood informs us in this narration that the Prophet (saas) described *at-tiyarah* as *Shirk*, and he emphasised this by repeating it. And he said that there is none who is not afflicted by it to some degree at sometime or other, but that Allah (swt) will remove it from the heart of the one who places his complete trust in Him and depends upon Him Alone.

Benefits Derived From This Hadith

1. That *at-tiyarah* is *Shirk*.

2. The desirability of emphasising important matters.

3. That true dependence on Allah (swt) causes *at-tiyarah* to be removed from the heart.

Relevance of This Hadith to the Subject of the Chapter

That the Hadith proves the falseness of belief in omens.

Relevance of This Hadith to the Subject of *Tawheed*

That the Hadith rejects belief in omens because it necessitates negation of belief in Allah's *Qadr* and because it causes the heart to become attached to other than Allah (swt), which is *Shirk*.

..ooOOoo..

Imam Ahmad reports, on the authority of Ibn `Amr (ra), that the Prophet (saas) said:

> *"Whoever is turned back from his objective by a bad omen has committed Shirk." They asked: "And what is the expiation for that?" He (saas) replied: "It is to say: "Oh, Allah (swt)! There is no good except that which You bestow and there is no evil except that which You bestow and there is none has the right to be worshipped but You."*

The Messenger of Allah (saas) informs us in this Hadith that whoever allowed pessimism due to omens to deflect him from his intentions has committed a form of *Shirk*, and when the Companions asked him what the penance due for this major sin is, He (saas) replied that it is to supplicate Allah (swt), rejecting the belief in good and evil omens and affirming their belief in His *Qadr*, His Oneness and His sole right to be worshipped.

Benefits Derived From This Hadith

1. Confirmation of the *Shirk* of those who allow themselves to be guided by omens.

2. The acceptance of the repentance of the *mushrik*.

3. Guidance as to what the one who succumbs to the temptation of *at-tiyarah* should say as expiation.

4. That all good and all evil occur in accordance with Allah's *Qadr*.

Relevance of This Hadith to the Subject of the Chapter and to the Subject of *Tawheed*

That it proves the *Shirk* of those who allow themselves to be turned away from their goals by omens.

..ooOOoo..

Also narrated by Imam Ahmad, on the authority of Al- Fadhl Ibn Al-'Abbas is: "*At-tiyarah* is that which causes you to carry out some act or turns you away from some deed.

This is an excellent summing up of this chapter for the kind of *tiyarah* which has been forbidden is that which determines our course of action or prompts us to abandon a course of action. Even *al-f'al* may fall under this category of prohibition if the person relies upon optimism alone, without remembering dependence upon and trust in Allah (swt), for he is the same as the one who depends upon omens of good or evil. Likewise, when a person hears or sees something which he dislikes and become pessimistic due to it, or allows it determine his actions, he is also guilty of *at-tiyarah*.

Benefits Derived From This Hadith

1. The forbiddance of *at-tiyarah*, which causes one to take a certain course of action or deflects one from acting.

Relevance of This Hadith to the Subject of the Chapter

That it proves the prohibition of *at-tiyarah* when it causes us to alter our plans or abandon them.

Relevance of This Hadith to the Subject of *Tawheed*

That it rejects *at-tiyarah* as forbidden because it causes the heart to become attached to other than Allah (swt) and it negates belief in Allah's *Qadr*, both of which amount to *Shirk*.

Footnotes

1. At-Tatayyur: Belief in omens.

2. 'Adwaa: Infectious or contagious disease. What is meant here is that disease cannot be contracted unless Allah (swt) wills it.

3. Haamah: Interpreting omens based on the flight of a nocturnal bird.

4. Safar: Some scholars said that it refers to parasites which infest the stomach and intestines of mankind and cattle, while others said that it refers to the pagan belief that the arrival of the month of Safar in the Muslim calendar bodes ill, while the dictionary defines safar as jaundice - and Allah (swt) knows best.

5. That is, there is no foundation to the belief that the positions of the stars affect the climate and there are no such things as ghosts and ghouls.

6. Al-F`al: Optimism.

7. Qadr: Divine Preordination: That all events - both good and bad - were written and ordained by Allah (swt), before their creation.

Top | Prev | Next

Kitaab At-Tawheed, Chapter: 30

Allah's Words:

" *It is only Satan who suggests to you the fear of his awliyaa` [supporters and friends]. Do not fear them, but fear Me, if you are of the Believers"* (Qur'an 3:175)

Because fear of Allah's creatures might cause the Muslims to refrain from supporting and raising the flag of Islam, Allah (swt), Most High, informs us in this verse that any such fear which may enter our hearts is only the deception of Satan and his followers, that delegation often takes the form of spreading falsehood by various methods. Then Allah (swt) commands the Muslims not to pay any heed to the whispers of these devils, but to fear Allah (swt), Alone - if they are truthful in their belief, for fear of Allah must take precedence over any other fears.

Benefits Derived From This Verse

1. The forbiddance of abandoning one's obligations due to fear of Allah's creatures.

2. The obligation to fear Allah, Alone, sincerely.

3. That fear of Allah is a sign of faith.

Relevance of This Verse to the Subject of the Chapter

That it proves the obligation of fearing Allah (swt) Alone, sincerely.

Relevance of This Verse to the Subject of *Tawheed*

That the verse proves the obligation of fearing Allah (swt), Alone, in sincerity; therefore, it is clear that fear is a form of worship and directing an act of worship to other than Allah (swt) is *shirk*.

Important Note

Fear consists of four kinds: (i) The fear that someone other than Allah (swt) will cause one some form of illness, poverty or other misfortune by his power and will - whether he claimed that this was due to the feared one's independent power or because of his supposed position as an intercessor with Allah (swt): This kind of fear is forbidden, for it equates the one who is feared with Allah (swt), which is an act of major *shirk*; (ii) fear of one of Allah's creatures which leads the one in fear to seek a solution from that which has been forbidden, or to abandon his obligations; this is forbidden; (iii) fear of Allah's promised recompense for the disobedient: This type of fear is the highest level of faith; (iv) natural fear, such as the fear of another of Allah's creatures e.g. a lion, a snake, etc. Such fear is permissible.

..ooOOoo..

Allah (swt), says:

" *The mosques of Allah shall be maintained only by those who believe in Allah and the Last Day, offer prayers perfectly, give zakah and fear none but Allah: It is they who are most likely to be on true guidance"* (Qur'an 9:18)

Allah (swt), Most Glorified, Most High, tells us in this verse that, because the mosques are places of worship for the Muslims and centres of knowledge, leadership and guidance, He has placed the responsibility of their building and maintenance in obedience to Allah (swt) and His Messenger (saas) on the shoulders of the Muslims. He (swt), Most High, adds that none should perform this duty except those who believe in the Oneness of Allah (swt) and in the Day of Recompense and Accounting, who perform the obligations commanded by Allah (swt) in the prescribed manner and do so purely for Him, Alone. Then He (swt), Almighty, All-powerful, confirms that such people will be successful, by Allah's Will and His facilitation.

Benefits Derived From This Verse

1. That the building and maintenance of mosques for the purpose of worship is a sign of faith.

2. The obligation to perform the five prayers correctly.

3. The obligation to give *zakah* to those who are entitled to it.

4. The obligation to fear and glorify Allah (swt), Alone.

Relevance of This Verse to the Subject of the Chapter

That the verse proves the obligation to fear and glorify Allah (swt), Alone.

Relevance of This Verse to the Subject of *Tawheed*

That the verse proves the obligation to fear and glorify Allah (swt), Alone, therefore such fear and glorification is a form of worship and to direct such worship to other than Allah (swt) is an act of *shirk*.

Important Note

It has been said that by building and maintaining mosques, what is meant here is being responsible for their planning, financing supervision, regularly organizing teaching and lectures by scholars therein; and it has been said that what is intended is the physical construction, repair and maintenance, cleaning etc. But it is more correct to say that the verse covers both meanings, since they do not contradict each other.

..ooOOoo..

Allah (swt), says:

" *Then there are among men those who say: "We believe in Allah," but when they suffer affliction in Allah's cause, they treat men's oppression as if it were the punishment of Allah! And if help comes to you [oh, Muhammad] from your Lord, they will surely say: "We have [always] been with you!" Does not Allah know best all that is in the hearts of the `aalameen [the worlds of mankind and the jinn]?"* (Qur'an 29:10)

Allah (swt), Most High, informs us in this verse that some of the people (i.e. the hypocrites) affect to believe by their words, but when hurt comes to them from others because of their professed faith, they compare this temporary punishment of man to the lasting punishment of Allah (swt) and abandon their faith. Then when Allah (swt) aids his followers and slaves from among the Believers, and blesses them with victory and spoils, they affect to believe once more in order that they may receive a share of the spoils along with the believers. Then Allah (swt) warns them that He (swt) knows the hypocrisy that is in their hearts and that He (swt) will recompense them for it.

Benefits Derived From This Verse

1. Patience in the face of affliction borne for the sake of one's religion is a part of faith.

2. The forbiddance of hypocrisy in religion.

3. That it is the way of the hypocrite to flee from the enemy in terror when he advances, but to advance in avarice and greed when the enemy is in retreat.

Relevance of This Verse to the Subject of the Chapter

That it proves the forbiddance of likening fear of Allah (swt) with fear of His creation.

Relevance of This Verse to the Subject of *Tawheed*

That it proves the obligation to place one's fear of Allah (swt) above fear of His creation; this shows that fear is a form of worship, and directing worship to other than Allah (swt) is *shirk*.

..ooOOoo..

It is reported on the authority of Abu Sa'eed Al-Khudri (ra), in a *marfoo'* form that he said: "It is from a lack of certainty (of faith) that a person pleases people and by so doing, invokes Allah's Anger, and that he praises them for the livelihood which Allah (swt) has given him and that he blames them for the things not bestowed by Allah (swt). Not even the avarice of the greediest of people can bring Allah's Blessings, nor can the aversion of the one who hates it prevent it."

Abu Sa'eed informs us in this narration, which is attributable to the Prophet (saas), that it is weakness of faith and uncertainty which causes a person to gratify people by his speech and actions at the expense of his religion, increasing their pleasure with him at the same time as they decrease Allah's Pleasure with them and thanking them for the blessings which Allah (swt) has given them and holding them to blame for those blessings which Allah (swt) does not ordain for him, forgetting that the One Who grants or withholds is Allah (swt). Then Abu Sa'eed mentions that all bounty comes from Allah's Hand - He grants to whom He wills and He withholds from whom He wills, and that none can attract such bounty, even though he may be the most avaricious of people, nor can he withhold it from any, even though he may violently oppose it.

Benefits Derived From This Narration

1. That faith may increase and decrease, strengthen and weaken.

2. That righteous deeds are a part of faith.

3. Confirmation of Allah's Divine Attribute of Anger.

4. The forbiddance of thanking people, if it is believed that the blessing came from them independently, without Allah's having ordained it.

5. The forbiddance of blaming people for what Allah (swt) has not ordained for us.

6. That good and evil are ordained by Allah (swt).

Relevance of This Narration to the Subject of the Chapter

That it proves the prohibition of abandoning an obligation due to fear of men.

Relevance of This Narration to the Subject of *Tawheed*

That the narration shows that fear is a form of worship, and directing worship to other than Allah (swt) is *shirk*.

Important Note

(a) This narration has some weakness in its *sanad* but other narrations strengthen and support it.

(b) There is no contradiction between this narration and the Hadith which states: "Whoever does not thank people does not thank Allah (swt)," because here what is intended is thanking people for doing something which was in their power and which they have in fact, done, such as giving financial aid; this is quite unlike thanking a person for making it rain or thanking him for making the sun shine. Also, it is forbidden to thank a person for something believing that he acted independently, without Allah having ordained it.

..ooOOoo..

On the authority of `A`ishah (may Allah be pleased with her) it is reported that Allah's Messenger (saas) said:

"Whoever seeks Allah's Pleasure at the expense of men's displeasure, will win Allah's Pleasure and Allah (swt) will cause men to be pleased with him. And whoever seeks to please men at the expense of Allah's Displeasure, will win the Displeasure of Allah (swt) and Allah (swt) will cause men to be displeased with him." (Narrated by Ibn Hibban in his *Saheeh*)

The Prophet (saas) informs us in this Hadith that whoever sought Allah's Pleasure by obeying His Commands and abstaining from all of that which He has prohibited, without caring whether or not he pleased others and without paying heed to their insults and oppression, will achieve Allah's Pleasure and He will place love for that person in the hearts of mankind; but as for him who tried to please the people at the expense of his Religion, he will incur the Wrath of Allah (swt), Most Glorified, Most High, and He (swt) will place hate of that person in the hearts of the people as a punishment for him because of his bad intentions - one only has to look at the present situation in the Muslim world to see the truth of this.

Benefits Derived From This Hadith

1. Confirmation of Allah's Divine Attribute of Pleasure.

2. That adhering strictly to the tenets of the Religion will result in Allah's Pleasure.

3. The forbiddance of hypocrisy in religious matters.

4. Confirmation of Allah's Divine Attribute of Anger.

5. That hypocrisy in religious matters results in Allah's Anger.

6. That the love or hate in the heart is in Allah's Hands.

Relevance of This Hadith to the Subject of the Chapter

That it proves the forbiddance of abandoning obedience to Allah (swt) due to fear of others or seeking to please them.

Relevance of This Hadith to the Subject of *Tawheed*

That the Hadith proves the obligation to fear Allah (swt), Alone; this proves that fear is a form of worship and directing worship to other than Allah (swt) is *shirk*.

Top | Prev | Next

Kitaab At-Tawheed, Chapter: 32

Allah's Words: " Did They Then Feel Secure Against the Plan of Allah?"

Allah (swt), says:

> *" Did they then feel secure against the Plan of Allah? But none can feel secure against the Plan of Allah except those who are lost"* (Qur'an 7:99)

In this verse, Allah (swt), Most Glorified, Most High, rebukes the people of the towns and cities to whom Guidance was sent, and all those who behave as they did, because they did not esteem Allah (swt), as is His right, nor did they fear Him, though it was from Him that they received all blessings; rather, they increased their disobedience until Allah's Wrath descended upon them and His punishment overwhelmed them. Then Allah (swt), Most High explains that no one behaves as they did except those who are doomed and will have no success in the Hereafter.

Benefits Derived From This Verse

1. The obligation to fear Allah's Plan.

2. The permissibility of describing Allah as Planning, as a comparison.

3. That belief in security from Allah's Plan results in destruction.

Relevance of This Verse to the Subject of the Chapter

That it proves the obligation of fearing Allah's Plan.

Relevance of This Verse to the Subject of *Tawheed*

That it proves the forbiddance of believing in security from Allah's Plan, because this would necessitate a lack in Allah's Completeness and this is in contradiction with a belief in pure, Islamic monotheism.

..ooOOoo..

Allah (swt), says:

> *" And who despairs of the Mercy of his Lord except those who are astray?"* (Qur'an15:56)

Because the Mercy of Allah (swt), Most Glorified, Most High, covers all things, and because the Prophets were the most knowledgeable of people concerning Allah's Mercy and His Generosity, Ibraheem (as) said that he did not doubt the news of the impending birth of a son to him, even though he and his wife were advanced in years, for he did not despair of the Mercy and Bounty of his *Rabb*. His question to the angels, " *Do you give me glad tidings that old age has seized me?"* merely reflected his surprise that he should have a son, bearing in mind the advanced age of him and his wife. Then He (swt) asked rhetorically: " *And who despairs of the Mercy of his Lord except those who are astray?"*

Benefits Derived From This Verse

1. The forbiddance of despairing of Allah's Mercy.

2. Confirmation of Allah's Divine Attribute of Mercy, in a manner befitting His Majesty.

3. That despair of Allah's Mercy is a sign of ignorance and being astray.

Relevance of This Verse to the Subject of the Chapter

That the verse proves the forbiddance of despairing of Allah's Mercy.

Relevance of This Verse to the Subject of *Tawheed*

That it proves the forbiddance of despairing of Allah's Mercy, because this suggests a lack in Allah's most perfect Generosity and this is in contradiction with a belief in pure, Islamic monotheism.

..ooOOoo..

It is reported on the authority Ibn `Abbas (ra) that the Messenger of Allah (saas) was asked about the major sins; He (saas) replied: "Associating partners with Allah (swt) (*shirk*), despairing of Allah's Mercy and believing that one is safe from Allah's Plan."

Because obedience to Allah and His Messenger (saas) was of the utmost importance to the Companions of the Prophet (saas) and the overriding goal of their lives, they asked the Messenger of Allah (saas) about the major sins in order that they might refrain from them and so He (saas) informed them about some of the worst of them: The first which he mentioned, and the worst of all, was *shirk*, or associating partners with Allah (swt), because no deeds are accepted where *shirk* is involved, no matter what they may be and no matter how praiseworthy they may be. Then He, Most High, mentioned both despair of Allah's Mercy and believing that one is safe from Allah's Plan, for the Muslim should be in a state between hope and fear: He does not despair of Allah's Mercy and Compassion, which are without limit, for to do so would be to think ill of the Most Generous of all; nor does he depend totally on Allah's Mercy to the extent that he abandons those righteous deeds [i.e worship of Allah (swt)] for which he was created.

Benefits Derived From This Verse

1. That sins are categorized as major or minor.

2. The forbiddance of all manner of *shirk*, of despair of Allah's Mercy and Compassion and of believing oneself safe from Allah's Plan, and that all of these are major sins.

3. The obligation of both fear of Allah and hope of His Mercy.

4. Confirmation of Allah's Divine Attribute of Mercy, in a manner befitting His Majesty.

5. The permissibility of describing Allah's plan in comparison with the plans of His creatures.

6. The obligation to think well of Allah, All-Mighty , All-powerful.

Relevance of This Hadith to the Subject of the Chapter

That the Hadith proves the obligation of fearing Allah (swt), while hoping for His Mercy.

Relevance of This Hadith to the Subject of *Tawheed*

That it proves the obligation of fearing Allah (swt) and hoping for His Mercy, because this is confirmation of Allah's Completeness and Perfection, a belief which is a necessary requisite for correct *tawheed*.

Important Note

Scholars have said that it is incumbent upon every Muslim that he comes to Allah (swt) in a state of fear and hope, like a bird between its wings, but that hope should predominate at the time when death approaches.

..ooOOoo..

It is reported on the authority of Ibn Mas'ood (ra) that he said: "The most heinous of all the major sins are: *shirk*, believing that one is safe from Allah's Plan, despairing of Allah's Mercy and losing hope of Allah's Relief.

Ibn Mas'ood (ra) informs us in this narration that sins are major and minor, and of the major sins, some are more serious than others and that the worst of all major sins is *shirk*, or associating partners with Allah (swt), for no deed will be accepted if it is accompanied by *shirk*. After mentioning *shirk*, he goes on to inform us of another of the worst major sins, which is believing that one is safe from Allah's Plan, i.e. that Allah (swt) will not punish the disobedient; this erroneous belief springs from complete dependence on Allah's Mercy, without fearing His punishment, hence that leads to abandoning the righteous deeds for which we were all created. Then Ibn Mas'ood (swt) mentions another of the worst major sins which is despairing of Allah's Mercy and Compassion and losing all hope of His Relief; this is because such a belief entails thinking ill of Allah (swt), All-Mighty , All-powerful.

Benefits Derived From This Narration

1. The prohibition of all forms of *shirk*, of believing oneself safe from Allah's Plan, of despairing of Allah's Mercy and Compassion and of losing all hope of His Relief, that all of these are major sins.

2. That sins are categorized as minor, major and worst major sins.

3. The permissibility of describing Allah's Plan in comparison with those of His creatures.

4. Confirmation of Allah's Divine Attribute of Mercy in a manner befitting His Majesty.

5. The obligation to be fair and just in all matters.

Relevance of This Narration to the Subject of the Chapter

That it proves the obligation of fearing Allah's punishment while hoping for His Mercy.

Relevance of This Narration to the Subject of *Tawheed*

That it proves the obligation of both fear and hope of Allah (swt), for such is necessary in order for one's *tawheed* to be complete.

Top | Prev | Next

Kitaab At-Tawheed, Chapter: 34

What Has Been Said About Ar-Riyaa`

Allah (swt), says:

> " *Say: "I am but a man like you, [but] it has been revealed to me that your God is One God: So whoever desires to meet his Lord, let him do righteous deeds and let him not associate any partners with his Lord in his worship"* (Qur'an 18:11)

In this verse, Allah (swt) commands His Prophet, Muhammad (saas) to tell the people the plain truth about himself: That he is a mere mortal, like them, without any Divine Attributes or angelic characteristics, but that Allah has distinguished him from them by inspiring him with Revelation; and from that Revelation is the Command to worship Allah (swt), Alone, without ascribing partners to him, and that whoever feared the meeting with his *Rabb* on the Day of Resurrection, and hoped for His reward, he should make his deeds purely and solely for Allah (swt),and they should be in conformity with that which the Prophet (saas) taught.

Benefits Derived From This Hadith

1. Confirmation of the Messengership of Muhammad (saas) and the denial of his possessing any Divine Attributes or angelic characteristics.

2. In this verse is proof of the *shahadataan* (i.e. None is worthy of worship but Allah (swt) and Muhammad is the Messenger of Allah (saas).

3. That the *tawheed* which our Prophet, Muhammad (saas) brought is that of worship, for even the disbeliever in Islam accepts the truth of *tawheed* of Rabbship.

4. That the acceptance of deeds is conditional upon their being performed purely and solely for Allah (swt), without *Shirk* - and *riyaa`* is a kind of *Shirk*.

Relevance of This Hadith to the Subject of the Chapter and to the Subject of *Tawheed*

That the Hadith proves the invalidity of deeds which contain elements of *Shirk* - and *riyaa`* is a form of *Shirk*.

The Meaning of *Ar-Riyaa`*

Riyaa`* is defined as the performance of a deed with the intention of pleasing other than Allah (swt ). The difference between *riyaa` and *sum'ah* (sometimes confused in the minds of some), is that while *riyaa`* is done in order to show off in front of people (such as ostentatiously giving charity or praying), the latter involves the performance of good deeds in order to be heard (such as mentioning Allah (swt) or reciting the Qur'an in a loud voice etc.) - both with the same intention: To favourably impress people.

..ooOOoo..

Muslim reports, on the authority of Abu Hurairah (ra) in a *marfoo'* form, the following *Qudsi* narration:

"I am Independent of all the partners (ascribed to me). Whoever performs a deed while associating partners with Me, I will leave him and his *Shirk*."

Allah (swt), Most High informs us in this *Qudsi* narration that He is Free and Independent of all those false partners which are associated with Him; and therefore, He does not accept any deed which includes *Shirk* and *riyaa`* is a form of *Shirk*, because it contradicts the belief that Allah (swt) is Independent and is not befitting His Nobility: In this is the clearest warning to all those who allow themselves to be seduced (by the devil) into performing actions with the intention of impressing people, rather than with the sole intention of pleasing Allah (swt), so that when they come forth on the Day of Resurrection, they will find no good deeds credited to them; instead they will find Allah (swt) and His Reckoning - and Allah (swt) is Swift in Reckoning!

Benefits Derived From This Hadith

1. Confirmation of Allah's Divine Attribute of Complete Independence from all partners.

2. That Allah (swt) does not accept deeds except those which are performed purely and solely for His sake.

3. The invalidity of *riyaa`* in deeds.

4. Confirmatiuon of Allah's Divine Attribute of Speech, in a manner befitting His Majesty.

Relevance of This Hadith to the Subject of the Chapter and to the Subject of *Tawheed*

That it proves the invalidity of deeds which contain *Shirk* - and *riyaa`* is a form of *Shirk*.

Important Note

(a) When the intention behind a deed is other than Allah's Pleasure, then the deed is in vain.

(b) When the intention behind a deed is to please Allah (swt), but after making this intention a person was guilty of *riyaa`*, but he then rejected this, his deed would be acceptable; but if he continued to be guilty of *riyaa`* until he had completed the deed, then according to some scholars, his deed would be in vain, while others said that his deed would still be accepted because of his original intention and this is the most correct saying - and Allah (swt) knows best.

..ooOOoo..

On the authority of Abu Sa'eed Al-Khudri (ra), in a *marfoo'* form, it is reported: "Shall I not tell you what I fear for you more than *Al-Maseeh Ad-Dajjaal*?" [1] They replied: "Yes." He (saas) said:

"It is hidden Shirk such as when a person stands in prayer and he improves his prayer when he knows that others are watching." (Narrated by Imam Ahmad)

Allah's Messenger (saas) informs us in this Hadith that he worries for his *Ummah* and fears for them *Al-Maseeh Ad-Dajjaal*, but that more than this, he fears for them hidden *Shirk*, which is *riyaa`*; this is because the danger of *Al-Maseeh Ad-Dajjaal* is confined to a specific time, while the danger of *riyaa`* is present at all times and in all places and because *riyaa`* is hidden and its power of seduction is great [2] and it is difficult to free oneself from its grip. In addition, it leads to showy, ostentatious behaviour, self-glorification, self-promotion, all of which appeal to the weaknesses in man.

Benefits Derived From This Hadith

1. That asking questions is an Islamic style of teaching.

2. The care and compasssion of the Prophet (saas) for his *Ummah*.

3. The great danger of *riyaa`*, which lies in its being hidden, its strength of appeal to most people and the difficulty of abstaining from it.

4. Evidence of the danger of *Al-Maseeh Ad-Dajjaal* to this *Ummah*.

Relevance of This Hadith to the Subject of the Chapter and to the Subject of *Tawheed*

That the Prophet (saas) feared more than anything else for this *Ummah*, that they would be seduced by *ar-riyaa`*; therefore it is incumbent upon us to be very careful, do our utmost to abstain from it and warn others of it.

Footnotes

1. Al-Maseeh Ad-Dajjaal: The false Messiah, who will deceive many people by performing apparent miracles, such as giving life to the dead. There are many authentic Ahadith concerning him.

2. It is a common human weakness to enjoy being praised and hearing good about oneself.

Top | Prev | Next

Kitaab At-Tawheed, Chapter: 33

Part of Belief in Allah Consists of Patience in the
Face of All That Allah Has Ordained for Us

Allah (swt), says:

> " *No kind of calamity occurs except by Allah's leave: And whoever believes in Allah, Allah*
> *will guide his heart [aright]: For Allah knows all things"* (Qur'an 64:11)

Allah (swt), Most High, informs us in this verse that no calamity, whether loss of wealth, bereavement,
or other, occurs unless Allah (swt) has written it and ordained it, and that whoever truly believes this,
will most assuredly be guided by Allah (swt), so that he accepts and bears with equanimity the trials
and tribulations of life and acknowledges Allah's Wisdom, for Allah (swt) knows what is best for His
slaves, and He (swt) is Most Kind, Most Merciful.

Benefits Derived From This Verse

1. That evil, like good, is ordained by Allah.

2. Evidence of the blessing of faith, and that it results in right guidance of the heart and an
upright character.

3. Evidence of the all-encompassing nature of Allah's Knowledge.

4. That the reward of goodness is goodness.

5. That the guidance of success comes only from Allah, Most High.

Relevance of This Verse to the Subject of the Chapter and to the Subject of *Tawheed*

That it proves that patience and equanimity, in the face of Allah's Ordainments are signs of faith in Allah
(swt).

Important Note

(a) The Arabic word, *sabr* means, linguistically speaking, prevention, while in religious
parlance, it means preventing or restraining oneself from succumbing to depression or
anxiety and guarding the tongue from complaint and angry words, and guarding the limbs
from forbidden deeds, such as slapping the cheeks, tugging at the hair and tearing the
clothes.

(b) *Sabr* may be divided into three categories: (i) Patiently persevering in obedience to
Allah (swt); (ii) refraining from what Allah (swt) has forbidden; (iii) patiently forbearing
in the face of calamities which Allah (swt) may ordain for us.

..ooOOoo..

`Alqamah said: "He (i.e. the person referred to in the verse) is the one who, when calamity strikes him, knows that it is from his *Rabb* and accepts it with equanimity and submits (himself to Allah's Will.")

Relevance of This Narration to the Subject of the Chapter

That it shows that `Alqamah considered that *sabr* in the face of calamity and calm acceptance are signs of faith.

..ooOOoo..

In Muslim's *Saheeh*, it is reported on the authority of Abu Hurairah (ra) that Allah's Messenger (saas) said: "Two traits found in people are signs of disbelief: Defaming a person's lineage and bewailing the deceased."

Because Islam came to abolish all of the vile customs of the *Jahiliyyah*, which are incompatible with the lofty principles of Islam, the Prophet (saas) informed the Companions that defaming another's ancestors and excessive mourning of the dead are traits of disbelief from the days of ignorance which will remain in this *Ummah* and this is a warning to us, for these two traits cause evil to the individual and to the community: Slandering another's ancestors is bound to cause hurt to and unjustified distress to that person. As for bewailing the deceased, this provokes renewed grief and fear on the part of the bereaved and shows lack of acceptance of Allah's *Qadr* and it is often accompanied by lying, as they indulge in exaggerated eulogies of the deceased and raise him above his true status.

Benefits Derived From This Hadith

1. The forbiddance of slandering another's ancestors and of bewailing the dead.

2. That these two traits will remain in this *Ummah*.

3. That a person may possess some of these traits of disbelief without being a disbeliever.

4. That Islam has prohibited everything that might lead to division in society.

Relevance of This Hadith to the Subject of the Chapter and to the Subject of *Tawheed*

That the Hadith proves the forbiddance of bewailing the dead, for this connotes a lack of forbearance and acceptance of Allah's *Qadr* which is a necessary requisite of the true Believer.

..ooOOoo..

It is narrated by Bukhari and Muslim, on the authority of Ibn Mas'ood (ra) in a *marfoo'* form: "He who slaps his cheeks and tears his clothes and makes supplications of the *Jahiliyyah* is not one of us."

Because Islam preaches the noblest of ideals and because it ennobles the soul, it has forbidden all manner of excessive mourning of the dead such as slapping the cheeks, tearing the clothes and making the supplications of the days of ignorance; [1] and it is made clear to us that such actions are completely un-Islamic, because they cause unnecessary and prolonged grief to the bereaved, reflect a lack of acceptance of Allah's *Qadr* and keep alive the evil customs of the *Jahiliyyah* which Islam came to destroy.

Benefits Derived From This Hadith

1. The forbiddance of slapping one's cheeks and tearing one's clothes in anguish over the death of a loved one.

2. The falseness and futility of the customs of the *Jahiliyyah* except those which are in conformity with Islaamic Law and are confirmed by the Qur'an or the *Sunnah*, such as hospitality to the guest and the like.

Relevance of This Hadith to the Subject of the Chapter and to the Subject of *Tawheed*

That it proves the forbiddance of slapping one's cheeks, tearing one's clothes and making the supplications of the *Jahiliyyah*.

Important Note

It is permissible to weep for the dead if it is due to genuine feelings of sadness and compassion, free from all traces of anger and hysteria.

..ooOOoo..

On the authority of Anas it is reported that the Prophet (saas) said: "When Allah (swt) wills good for His slave, He hastens to punish him in this life and when He wills evil for His slave, He withholds punishing him for his sins until he comes before Him on the Day of Resurrection." [2]

Allah's Messenger informs us in this Hadith that sometimes Allah (swt) afflicts a person with calamity in order to purify him of his sins, which otherwise, might cause him to be punished in the Hereafter, in order that he might on that Day receive the record of his deeds in his right hand and be among the successful. Alternatively, Allah (swt) may withhold punishment from a person, not because He loves him or honours him, but when he is called forth on the Day of Reckoning, he will bear a heavy burden of sins and he will receive the full punishment of those sins; and Allah (swt) grants His Favour to whom He Wills and punishes whom He Wills with justice; and He Will not be asked about what He does, but they will be asked about what they did.

Benefits Derived From This Hadith

1. Confirmation of Allah's Divine Attribute of Will, in a manner befitting His Majesty.

2. That good and evil are from Allah's *Qadr*.

3. That the trials and tribulations to which the Believer is subjected are signs of goodness, so long as they are borne with patience and without resorting to forbidden acts or abandoning one's obligations.

4. It is incumbent upon the Muslim to fear the continuation of blessings and good health, lest they betoken that his sins will not be wiped out by trials in this life.

5. The obligation to think well of Allah (swt) concerning the calamities which He might ordain for us.

6. It does not necessarily follow that when Allah (swt) gives us something good, that He is pleased with us.

Relevance of This Hadith to the Subject of the Chapter and to the Subject of *Tawheed*

That it proves that whoever truly believes in Allah (swt), will bear the trials and tribulations which Allah (swt) ordains for him with patience and equanimity for he believes that they bode goodness for him.

..ooOOoo..

The Prophet (saas) said: "Verily, the greatness of the reward is tied to the greatness of the trial: When Allah (swt) loves a people, he puts them to trial. Whoever accepted it, will enjoy Allah's Pleasure and whoever is displeased with it, will incur Allah's Displeasure." [3]

The Prophet (saas) informs us in this Hadith that the Believer may be afflicted by calamity in this world, such as loss of wealth, bereavement etc., but that Allah (swt) will reward him for these calamities if he bears them patiently, and He (saas) tells us also that the more a person's trials and tribulations increase, the more his reward with Allah (swt) increases and that trials are a sign of Allah's Love for the Believer, not His Anger and that Allah's Ordainment and His *Qadr* will be implemented and that whoever patiently perseveres in the face of adversity and accepts it, will incur Allah's Pleasure and His Reward, while whoever is angry at what Allah (swt) has ordained for him and dislikes it, will incur Allah's Displeasure and His punishment which will be more than suffice him.

Benefits Derived From This Hadith

1. That afflictions wipe out sins, so long as the afflicted does not abandon his obligations or commit forbidden acts.

2. Confirmation of Allah's Divine Attribute of Love, in a manner befitting His Majesty.

3. That the trials to which the Believer is subjected are signs of faith.

4. Confirmation of Allah's Divine Attribute of Pleasure, in a manner befitting His Majesty.

5. The virtue of accepting Allah's *Qadr* and His Ordainments with patience and equanimity.

6. The forbiddance of anger at Allah's *Qadr* and His Ordainments.

Relevance of This Hadith to the Subject of the Chapter and to the Subject of *Tawheed*

That the Hadith forbids anger and despair in the face of Allah's Ordainments, and this shows that patient perseverance in the face of trials and tribulations is a part of faith.

Footnotes

1. Such as: "Woe to me!" or "May I be destroyed!" etc.

2. Something very similar to this was narrated by Imam Ahmad, on the authority of 'Abdullah Ibn Mughaffal.

3. Narrated by At-Tirmizi.

Top | Prev | Next

Kitaab At-Tawheed, Chapter: 31

Allah's Words: [And Depend Upon Allah if You Truly Believe]

> " *Two men from among the God-fearing, upon whom Allah had bestowed His Grace said:
> "Assault them [the enemy] from the [proper] gate. Once you are in, victory will be yours.
> And depend upon Allah, if you truly believe"* (Qur'an 5:23)

Allah (swt), Most Glorified, Most High, informs us in this verse that two believing men from *Bani Israa`eel* [1] advised their people and requested that they enter the city of Jerusalem, promising them that they would receive Allah's Help if they did so, because they believed in Allah's Promise which they had heard from the mouth of their Prophet, Moosa (as), and they asked them to depend upon Allah (swt) and trust in [2] Him that He would fulfill His Promise and not to be intimidated by the strength of the enemy forces, for victory is in Allah's Hands - He grants it to whom He (swt) wills and He withholds it from whom He wills, and He has promised the Believers victory and He never breaks His Promise.

Benefits Derived From This Verse

1. The obligation of mutual advice and encouragement by the members of the army.

2. That faith and trust in Allah (swt) are the most important factors in attaining victory.

3. That trust in Allah (swt) is a condition of the acceptance of faith.

4. The obligation to trust in Allah (swt) and no other.

Relevance of This Verse to the Subject of the Chapter

That the verse proves the obligation of sincere dependence on Allah (swt) and trust in Him, Alone.

Relevance of This Verse to the Subject of *Tawheed*

That the verse proves that depending on Allah (swt) and trusting in Him is a form of worship, and directing an act of worship to other than Allah (swt) is *shirk*.

..ooOOoo..

Allah (swt), says:

> " *For Believers are those who, when Allah is mentioned, feel a tremor in their hearts and
> when His verses are recited to them, they [the verses] increase their faith and they put their
> trust in their Rabb, Alone"* (Qur'an 8:2)

Allah (swt), Most Glorified, Most High, informs us in this verse that the true Believers are those who, when they fear Allah (swt), fear His punishment, and as a result, obey all of His Commands and abstain from all that He has forbidden; and when verses from the Noble Qur'an are recited to them, their faith and belief are increased and they depend upon Allah (swt) and trust in Him, Alone; and they entrust all matters to Him, doing all that is beneficial to them and abandoning that which is harmful to them.

Benefits Derived From This Verse

    1. That fear of Allah (swt) and trust in Him are characteristics of the Believers.

    2. That faith increases and decreases.

    3. The obligation to depend upon Allah (swt) and trust in Him, Alone.

Relevance of This Verse to the Subject of the Chapter

That the verse proves the obligation to trust in Allah (swt) and depend upon Him, Alone.

Relevance of This Verse to the Subject of *Tawheed*

That it proves that trust and dependence are acts of worship and directing worship to other than Allah (swt) is *shirk*.

..ooOOoo..

Allah (swt), says:

> " *Oh, Prophet! Sufficient for you is Allah, and for those who follow you among the Believers"* (Qur'an 8:64)

In this verse, Allah (swt) gives glad tidings to His Prophet, Muhammad (saas) and his believing followers and promises them victory over their enemies and He commands them implicitly to trust in Him, Alone, for He (saas) is sufficient for them against their enemies.

Benefits Derived From This Verse

    1. That Allah is Sufficient for those who trust in Him and depend upon Him, Alone.

    2. That faith is an essential element in achieving victory.

    3. The obligation of faith, by loving Allah, Alone.

Relevance of This Verse to the Subject of the Chapter

That it proves the obligation of faith, by loving Allah (swt), which includes trust in Allah (swt) and no other.

Relevance of This Verse to the Subject of *Tawheed*

That the verse proves that trust and dependence are forms of worship and directing worship to other than Allah (swt) is *shirk*.

Important Note

We have said that love includes trust and dependence because whoever has faith in Allah (swt), Alone, must, of a necessity, depend upon and trust in Him Alone.

..ooOOoo..

Allah (swt), says:

" *And whoever places his trust in Allah, Sufficient is He for him, for Allah will surely accomplish His Purpose: For verily, Allah has appointed for all things a due proportion"* (Qur'an 65:3)

Allah (swt), Most Glorified, Most High, informs us in this verse that whoever trusted in Him and depended upon Him to fulfill his needs and wants, Allah (swt) will suffice him in every matter, whether worldly or religious, for Allah (swt) will surely accomplish His Purpose and nothing escapes Him and no request is difficult for Him; and in order that those who ask him be not impatient, He informs us that He has appointed for everything a time and a place, which none can delay nor bring forward.

Benefits Derived From This Verse

1. Evidence of the virtue of trust in Allah and dependence upon Him, Alone.

2. That trust and dependence are among the most important factors in achieving that which is beneficial and avoiding that which is harmful.

3. The obligation to believe in Allah's Ordainment and His Decree.

4. The Completeness and Perfection of Allah's Decree and His Wisdom.

Relevance of This Verse to the Subject of the Chapter

That the verse proves the obligation of dependence upon Allah (swt) and trust in Him, for Allah (swt) protects His slave and is Sufficient for him, when he depends upon his *Rabb*.

Relevance of This Verse to the Subject of *Tawheed*

That the verse proves that trust and dependence are forms of worship and directing worship to other than Allah (swt) is an act of *shirk*.

..ooOOoo..

Allah (swt), says:

" *[There were] those to whom people said: "The people are gathering against you, so fear them." But it only increased their faith; they said: "For us Allah is Sufficient and He is the best Disposer of affairs"* (Qur'an 3:173)

When Abu Sufyaan and his disbelieving people returned from the Battle of Uhud, they began to gather an army from among them for another attack on the Muslims. On the road, they passed by a group of riders from Bani `Abdul Qais and Abu Sufyaan advised them to inform Prophet Muhammad (saas) and his Companions that Quraish were preparing to assault them with an overwhelming force, but this threat did not discourage them; rather, they were strengthened in their faith and they trusted in Allah (swt), and He was Sufficient for them against their enemies, for He is the One Who is trusted above all others and He never fails the Believers.

Benefits Derived From This Verse

1. That one of the signs of true faith is steadfastness in the face of adversity.

2. That psychological warfare cannot harm the Believers.

3. That faith increases and decreases.

4. The preferability of of the Believer's saying: "*Hasbunallaahu wa N'imal wakeel,*" [i.e. Allah (swt) is Sufficient for us and He is the best Disposer of affairs].

5. That taking whatever measures are required in order to achieve one's objectives is not in contradiction with trust in Allah (swt) and dependence upon Him, rather it is a requirement for that trust and dependence to be correct.

Relevance of This Verse to the Subject of the Chapter

That the verse proves the obligation to trust in Allah (swt), to depend upon Him, Alone, and to suffice oneself with Him.

Relevance of This Verse to the Subject of *Tawheed*

That it proves that trust and dependence are forms of worship and directing worship to other than Allah (swt) is *shirk*.

Final Words on this Subject

It is reported on the authority of Ibn `Abbas (ra) that he said:

" Allah is Sufficient for us and He is the best Disposer of affairs" (Qur'an 3:173)

Ibraheem (as) said it when he was thrown in the fire; and Muhammad (saas) said it when it was said to him:

" The people are gathering against you, so fear them." But it only increased their faith; they said: "For us Allah is Sufficient and He is the best Disposer of affairs" (Qur'an 3:173)

Important Note

Tawakkul means dependence of the heart on Allah (swt), believing Him to be Sufficient against all others for His slaves. *Tawakkul* (dependence) upon Allah (swt) is of three kinds: (i) Depending upon one of Allah's creatures to do something which none is able to do except the Creator: This is major *shirk*; (ii) depending upon one of Allah's creatures to do something which is within his capabilities but in the belief that he is able to do so independent of Allah's Will: This is minor *shirk*; depending upon one of Allah's creatures to do something in the knowledge that it will only happen if Allah (swt) wills it: This is permissible, such as depending upon someone in business transactions to fulfill his side of the bargain etc.

Tawakkul is half of the Religion and the other half of it is turning in repentance to Allah (swt). And *tawakkul* does not negate taking precautions; instead, it is a requirement in order for the *tawakkul* to be accepted and for one's faith to be complete.

Footnotes

1. **Bani Israa`eel: The People of Israel.**

2. **Dependence upon and trust in Allah (swt), known as tawakkul in Arabic.**

Top | Prev | Next

Kitaab At-Tawheed, Chapter: 35

It is a Form of Shirk to Perform a (Good) Deed for Worldly Reasons

Allah (swt), says:

> " *To whomsever desires the life of this world and its glitter, We shall pay [the price of] their deeds therein - without decrease. They are those for whom there is nothing in the Hereafter except the Fire: Vain are their deeds therein"* (Qur'an 11:15-16)

Allah (swt), Most High, informs us in these verses that whoever performed a righteous deed in order to obtain some worldly benefit from it, such as one who fights in Allah's cause with the intention of acquiring a share of the spoils of war, Allah (swt) will reward him in this world with long life, good health and wealth etc, in accordance with his deeds and his desires; they will not suffer any loss, at least, in this world. However, in the Hereafter, they will be entitled to nothing, because they have already been rewarded in this life. And their deeds are without merit or value, since they did not perform them for Allah's sake.

Benefits Derived From This Verse

1. That Allah, Most High, may reward even the disbeliever for his deeds in this world, as He might reward the one who acts for worldly gain, but none of them will have anything in the Hereafter.

2. That *shirk* invalidates good deeds.

3. That seeking the life of this world invalidates one's good deeds in the Hereafter.

That every deed performed without the intention of pleasing Allah (swt) is invalid.

Relevance of These Verses to the Subject of the Chapter and to the Subject of *Tawheed*

That they prove that seeking the life of this world through righteous deeds invalidates their reward in the Hereafter.

Important Note

Seeking the life of this world through righteous deeds may be divided into three categories: (i) To perform deeds purely for Allah's sake, but with the hope that Allah (swt) will reward one for them in this life, such as the person who gives charity, hoping that Allah (swt) will protect him from loss - and this is prohibited; (ii) to perform deeds in order to be seen by the people (i.e. *riyaa`*) or to be heard by them (i.e. *sum'ah*) - and this is a form of *shirk*; (iii) To do good deeds in order to attain some material benefit from people, such as the one who accompanies the pilgrims to Hajj in order to receive payment for so doing, not for Allah's sake, or the one who seeks a reputaion for being pious and religious in order to make a living, or to obtain employment. As for the one who intends by his deeds only to achieve Allah's pleasure, but is granted some worldly reward by Allah (swt), he is not guilty of any sin, but he will be considered to have received the reward of that deed in this world and his recompense in the Hereafter will be adjusted accordingly, as is the case with the one who fights in the way of Allah (swt), and receives a share of the spoils.

..ooOOoo..

It is authentically reported on the authority of Abu Hurairah (ra) that he said: "Allah's Messenger (saas) said:

"Perish the slave of the deenaar, the dirham, the khameesah[1] and the khameelah.[2] If he is given these things, he is pleased and if he is not, he is displeased. May such a person perish and be of the losers and if he is pierced with a thorn, may he not find anyone to remove it. Felicity (or, according to some scholars, a tree in Paradise) is for the one who holds the reins of his horse to strive in Allah's cause, with his hair unkempt and his feet covered with dust: If he is placed in the vanguard, he will be found in the vanguard and if he is placed in the rearguard, he will be found in the rearguard. If he asks for permission, it is not granted and if he intercedes, it is not accepted."[3]

In this Hadith, the Messenger (saas) informs us that there are some people to whom the life of this world is all-important: It is all they know about and all they care about. Their first and last goals are wealth, luxury and ease. Such people will be destroyed and lost. The sign of these people is their absorption with all things material: When they are given something, they are pleased, but when they are not given it, they are angry. But there are other people who have no goal except Allah's Pleasure and the life of the Hereafter: Such people do not covet fame or glory; their only goal in life is obedience to Allah (swt) and His Messenger (saas). The sign of such people as these is their simplicity and humility and their lowly position in society, so that whenever they request something from their leaders, they are refused, and whenever they intercede on behalf of another, their intercession is not accepted, but their final destination is Paradise and the best of rewards.

Benefits Derived From This Hadith

1. The general permissibility of supplicating against the disobedient people.

2. The censure of absorption with the life of this world.

3. That whoever makes material gain his sole objective in life will be among the losers.

4. The virtue of preparing oneself for *jihaad* in Allah's cause.

5. The virtue of *jihaad* in Allah's cause.

6. That military discipline is a form of Islamic training.

7. The virtue of being in the vanguard of the army.

8. That a person is judged by his actions, not by appearances.

9. It does not necessarily follow that a person whom Allah (swt) esteems will be held in high esteem by the people and vice versa.

Relevance of This Hadith to the Subject of the Chapter and to the Subject of *Tawheed*

That the Hadith proves that whoever made material gain his main goal and purpose in life is considered a worshiper of those things, for he has taken them as partners beside Allah (swt).

Footnotes

1. Khameesah: Expensive, luxurious clothing.

2. Khameelah: Richly embroidered garments.

3. Narrated by Bukhari, At-Tirmizi and Ibn Maajah.

Top | Prev | Next

Kitaab At-Tawheed, Chapter: 36

Whoever Obeys a Scholar or a Ruler by Prohibiting What Allah Has Permitted or Permitting What Allah Has Prohibited Has Taken Them as Partners Beside Allah

Ibn `Abbas (ra ) said: "Stones are about to rain down upon you from the sky: I say to you: "Allah's Messenger (saas ) said..." and you reply: "But Abu Bakr and `Umar said...?" [1]

Because obedience is a form of worship, it is not allowed to obey anyone - be he man or jinn - unless it conforms with obedience to Allah (swt) and His Messenger (saas). This is why Ibn `Abbas (ra ) repudiated those who, when they were informed that the Prophet (saas ) had pronounced upon a matter, objected that Abu Bakr As-Siddeeq and `Umar Ibn Al-Khattab (may Allah be pleased with them both) [2] had said something different, thus, in effect, preferring the opinions of these two pious Companions over the Revelation of Allah (swt). This incident allegedly occurred during a discussion about Hajj in which Ibn `Abbas (ra ) mentioned something which he had heard from Muhammad, the Messenger of Allah (saas ). Ibn `Abbas (ra) warned them of Allah's approaching punishment and His Anger for those who preferred the opinions of Abu Bakr and `Umar (may Allah be pleased with them) to the guidance of Allah's Messenger (saas). - In view of this, what may be said of those who prefer the opinions of lesser men over the Book of Allah (swt) and the *Sunnah* of His Prophet (saas). [3]

Benefits Derived From This Narration

    1. Evidence of the virtue of Ibn `Abbas and his excellent understanding of religious matters.

    2. That no opinion which contradicts the Qur'an and *Sunnah* is to be given heed, no matter from whom it emanated.

    3. The obligation to be angry for Allah and His Messenger's sake.

Relevance of This Narration to the Subject of the Chapter and to the Subject of *Tawheed*

That the narration proves that Ibn `Abbas (ra) held that it is forbidden to prefer the opinion of any of Allah's creatures over the *Sunnah* of the Messenger of Allah (saas) and this is because to do so is an act of *Shirk* since it constitutes obedience to other than Allah (swt).

..ooOOoo..

Imam Ahmad Ibn Hanbal said: "I am amazed at those people who know that a *sanad* is authentic and yet, in spite of this, they follow the opinion of Sufyan, for Allah (ra), says:

> " *Let those who oppose his [the Messenger's] commandment beware, lest some fitnah befall them or a painful torment be inflicted on them"* (Qur'an 24:63)

Do you know what that *fitnah* is? That *fitnah* is *Shirk*. Maybe the rejection of some of his words would cause one to doubt and deviate in his heart and thereby be destroyed."

In this narration, Imam Ahmad Ibn Hanbal rejects those who abandon the *Sunnah* of the Prophet (saas), after it has been made clear to them its authenticity and the meaning has been explained to them, in favour of the opinion of Sufyaan Ath-Thawri[4] and other scholars, in spite of their fallibility. And he warns them against deviating, by rejecting Allah's Book or the *Sunnah* of His Prophet (saas); this is because the blind followers of the *mazahib*[5] frequently change the meanings of Qur'anic verses and Ahadith or quote them out of context, or claim that they have been abrogated in order to make them conform with their particular *mazhab*. Then the Imam supports his contention by mentioning the Words of Allah (swt), Most High; let the Qur'an be sufficient proof for us all.

Benefits Derived From This Narration

1. That in the opinion of Imam Ahmad it is forbidden to abandon the *Sunnah* of Allah's Messenger in favour of the saying of any person, no matter how knowledgeable and pious he may be.

2. That every commandment of the Prophet is considered obligatory, unless there is some proof to indicate its preferability.

3. That rejecting the Law of Allah leads to destruction in this world and in the Hereafter.

Relevance of This Narration to the Subject of the Chapter and to the Subject of *Tawheed*

That it proves that Imam Ahmad considered that deviating from the *Sunnah* of the Messenger of Allah (saas) in favour of the sayings of others is *Shirk*, because it involves obedience to other than Allah (swt) and His Messenger (saas); and he quotes from the Qur'an to prove his contention.

..ooOOoo..

On the authority of `Adi Ibn Hatim (ra), it is reported that he heard the Messenger of Allah (saas) reciting this Qur'anic verse:

> " *They have taken their rabbis and their monks as lords beside Allah and [they take as a lord] Al-Maseeh, `Eesaa, the son of Maryam, yet they were not commanded but to worship One God: None has the right to be worshipped but He - Praise and Glory to Him: [Far is He] from having the partners they associate [withHim]*" (Qur'an 9:31)

> "*...and I said to him (swt): "We don't worship them." He (saas) said: "Do they not forbid what Allah (swt) has permitted and do you not then forbid it (to yourselves), and do they not make permissible for you what Allah (swt) has forbidden, and do you not then make it permissible (to yourselves)?" I replied: "Certainly!" He (saas) said: "That is worshipping them."* (Narrated by At-Tirmizi, who graded it as *Hasan*)

`Adi Ibn Hatim (swt) informs us in this Hadith, that when he heard the Prophet (saas) reciting Allah's Words:

> " *They have taken their rabbis and their monks as lords beside Allah. And [they take as their lord] Al-Maseeh, `Eesaa, the son of Maryam*" (Qur'an 9:31)

He contradicted the Prophet (saas), saying that they do not worship them; for to his mind, what was meant by worship was bowing, prostration, supplication, sacrifice etc. But the Prophet (saas) informed him that their obedience to the rabbbis and monks in forbidding the permissible and permitting the forbidden was a form of worship, because they have thus made their rabbis and monks partners to Allah (swt) in obedience and in ordaining the Law.

Benefits Derived From This Hadith

1. Evidence that the rabbis and monks are astray.

2. Confirmation of the Jews' and Christians' *Shirk*.

3. That the original Message of all the Messengers and Prophets was *tawheed*.

4. That obedience to any of Allah's creatures, if it entails disobedience to Allah (swt), constitutes an act of worship.

5. The obligation to inquire from the people of knowledge about matters which one does not understand.

6. The rejection of blind obedience to Allah's creatures, for all except the Prophets are fallible.

Relevance of This Hadith to the Subject of the Chapter and to the Subject of *Tawheed*

That it proves that whoever obeyed a religious scholar by making the permissible forbidden, or vice versa has committed an act of *Shirk*.

Footnotes

1. While according to a number of scholars of Hadith, this is a weak narration, its meaning is correct.

2. Abu Bakr As-Siddeeq and 'Umar Ibn Al-Khattab: Two close friends of the Prophet (saas) and the first and second Khaleefah (Caliph) respectively, after his death. They were among the most knowledgeable and pious of the Companions.

3. Such as those who, when confronted with a Prophetic Hadith say: "Yes, but our Shaikh says..." or: "Yes, but in our mazhab (i.e. school of Islamic jurisprudence)..."

4. Sufyaan Ibn Sa'eed Ibn Masrooq Ath-Thawri: A great scholar of Hadith and fiqh, who lived in the first century after the hijrah. He died in the year 61 A.H., aged 64 years.

5. Mazahib: Plural of mazhab.

Top | Prev | Next

Kitaab At-Tawheed, Chapter: 37

Allah's Words: " Do You Not See Those Who Claim That They Believe in What Was Revealed to You and to Those Before You? They Wish to Resort to At-Taaghoot for Judgement..."

" *Do you not see those who claim that they believe in what was revealed to you and to those before you? They wish to resort to At-Taaghoot for judgement"* (Qur'an 4:60)

In this verse, Allah (swt), Most High, rebukes those hypocrites who pretend to believe in the Revelations sent down to the Messengers, but then make their hypocrisy clear by referring their disputes for judgement to other than Allah (swt) and His Messenger (saas), contradicting their claims of faith, for they were ordered in the Last Revelation to reject the judgement of all, save Allah (swt) and His Messenger (saas); but Satan - may Allah (swt) curse him - makes their deviation from the Law of Allah (swt) in favour of the opinions of men who seem attractive to them, in order to lure them to that which is false and to lead them far astray from the Straight Path, and then he abandons them to their fate.

Benefits Derived From This Verse

1. That the Books of Allah are revealed, not created.

2. The forbiddance of seeking judgement from other than the Book of Allah and the *Sunnah* of His Messenger.

3. That seeking judgement from other than the Law of Allah is a sign of hypocrisy in belief.

4. That whoever judged by other than what Allah has revealed, is a *Taaghoot* - This includes all those who judge by man-made laws in contradiction to the Qur'an and *Sunnah*.

5. That the cause of the Muslims' problems and hardships in this day and age is their shunning Allah's Law.

6. The forbiddance of separating the Religion from all matters of life, including politics and law.

Relevance of This Verse to the Subject of the Chapter

That it proves the hypocrisy of those who seek judgement from other than Allah (swt) and His Messenger (saas).

Relevance of This Verse to the Subject of *Tawheed*

That the verse rejects those who do not fulfill the obligations of the *shahaadatain*: *Laa ilaaha illallaah, Muhammadur-Rasoolullaah*, which include faith in the judgement of Allah's Messenger (saas) and action in accordance with it.

..ooOOoo..

Allah, says:

*" And do no mischief on the earth after it has been set in order, but call on Him with fear
and longing for the Mercy of Allah is [always] near to those who do righteous
deeds"* (Qur'an 7:56)

Islam came to set the world and Allah's slaves to rights; for this reason, Allah (swt), Most Glorified,
Most High, forbids in this verse all manner of corruption on the earth and wanton destruction, such as
cutting down trees, vandalising private property etc. or violating the rights of others, such as murder,
theft, rape etc. after Allah (swt) has set it in order by sending Messengers with Revealed Books full of
wisdom, knowledge and guidance for mankind and the jinn. Then Allah (swt) commands us to turn to
Him in supplication in fear of His punishment, but in hope of His Mercy; so that the worshiper might
not lose hope if his prayer is not immediately answered, He (swt), Most High, informs us that His
Mercy is near to the Believers, who do righteous deeds in the best way, in the knowledge that though
they do not see Allah (swt), He is always watching them.

Benefits Derived From This Verse

1. The forbiddance of spreading all manner of corruption on the earth, by any means
whatsoever.

2. That every kind of righteousness and goodness in the earth is the result of obedience to
Allah and His Messenger.

Relevance of This Verse to the Subject of the Chapter

That the verse forbids spreading corruption on the earth, which includes seeking the judgement of other
than Allah (swt) and His Messenger (saas).

Relevance of This Verse to the Subject of *Tawheed*

That it includes a prohibition of seeking judgement from other than Allah (swt) and His Messenger
(saas), because this conflicts with the testimony of the Muslim: *Laa ilaaha illallaah, Muhammadur-
Rasoolullaah* (i.e. none is worthy of worship except Allah (swt) and Muhammad is the Messenger of
Allah saas).

..ooOOoo..

Allah (swt), says:

*" And when it is said to them: "Do not make mischief in the earth," they say: "We are only
peace-makers." Of a surety, they are the mischief-makers, but their [hearts] understand
not"* (Qur'an 2:11-12)

Allah (swt), Most Glorified, Most High, makes clear in these verses, the depth of wickedness and
foolishness of the hypocrites, and that when it is requested of them that they cease their disobedience
and their attempts to divide the Muslims, they reply that they want only to achieve peace between the
Muslims and the People of the Book by their actions. But Allah (swt) makes plain to us in the second
verse, that they, themselves are the cause of the corruption and mischief and that the reason for their
willful deception and misguidance is their ignorance of the fact that Allah (swt) will send down
revelation to His Prophet *(saas)*, exposing them and revealing their hypocrisy.

Benefits Derived From These Verses

1. That disobedience causes corruption in the earth.

2. The danger of the hypocrites who dwell among the Muslims.

3. The prohibition of acting upon opinion when it contradicts with the Qur'an and the *Sunnah*.

4. That attempting to justify acts of disobedience is an attribute of the hypocrites.

Relevance of These Verses to the Subject of the Chapter

That they prove the forbiddance of spreading corruption in the earth, which includes seeking judgement of other than Allah's Revelation.

Relevance of These Verses to the Subject of *Tawheed*

That they prove the forbiddance of abandoning the Judgement of Allah (swt) and accepting the judgement of others.

..ooOOoo..

> " *Do they then seek a judgement from the [days of the] Jahiliyyah? But who, for a people who have firm faith, can give better judgement than Allah?"* (Qur'an 5:50)

In this verse, Allah (swt), Most High, rebukes those who abandon the Judgement of Allah (swt), whose wisdom, justice and mercy are complete and incomparable, in favour of the flawed, ignorant, unjust, vain judgements of His creatures. Then He (swt), Most Glorified, Most High, confirms, a second time, that His Judgement is better and wiser than all other judgements, for He (swt) is the Creator of mankind and therefore, knows best what is beneficial for them and what is harmful to them; and there is general agreement amongst Muslim scholars that the Muslims will never be free from the serious problems which beset them unless and until they return to the teachings of Islam. The truth of this is apparent when one compares the situation of Islam's enemies to that of the Muslims.

Benefits Derived From This Verse

1. That every judgement which does not come from the Book of Allah or the *Sunnah* of His Messenger is of the *Jahiliyyah*.

2. The falseness of every judgement which does not come from Allah's Law.

3. The forbiddance of divorcing the Religion from the affairs of government.

Relevance of This Verse to the Subject of the Chapter

That the verse proves the prohibition of abandoning the Judgement of Allah (swt) in favour of the judgement of others.

Relevance of This Verse to the Subject of *Tawheed*

That it proves the forbiddance of abandoning the Judgement of Allah (swt) in favour of that of others, for this constitutes a negation of the *shahaadah*: *Laa ilaaha illallaah*.

..ooOOoo..

It is reported on the authority of `Abdullaah Ibn `Amr (ra) that the Messenger of Allah (saas) said:

"None of you (truly) believes until his desires are in accordance with that which I have brought." (Narrated by An-Nawawi, who graded it as Ha*san* in his book, *Al-Hujjah*)

Allah's Messenger (saas) informs us in this Hadith that none will achieve the necessary complete faith unless and until his words and deeds and his beliefs are in accordance with the Prophetic *Sunnah*.

Benefits Derived From This Hadith

1. The incompleteness of faith of those, whose desires conflict with that, which Allah (swt) and His Messenger (saas) love.

2. The forbiddance of judging by other than that, which Allah (swt) has revealed.

3. The invalidity of every religious deed, which does not conform to Islamic Law.

4. That complete obedience is a part of complete faith.

Relevance of This Hadith to the Subject of the Chapter

That the Hadith proves the forbiddance of judging by other than Allah's Law.

Relevance of This Hadith to the Subject of *Tawheed*

That it proves the prohibition of judging by other than that which Allah's Messenger (saas) has brought, because this invalidates the *shahaadataan*: *Laa ilaaha illallaah, Muhammadur-Rasoolullaah*.

..ooOOoo..

Ash-Sha'abi said: "A dispute took place between a man from among the hypocrites and a man from among the Jews; and so the Jew said: "Let us seek judgement from Muhammad," for he knew that He (saas) did not accept bribes. But the hypocrite said: "Let us seek judgement from the Jews," for he knew that they accepted bribes. And so both of them agreed to take their case to a fortune-teller in Juhainah and seek his judgement; then Allah (swt) revealed:

" Do you not see [oh, Muhammad,] those who claim to have faith in what was revealed to you and to those before you? They desire to resort for judgement to At-Taaghoot" (Qur'an 4:60)

Ash-Sha'abi (ra) informs us in this narration that a dispute took place between a man from among the hypocrites (i.e. those who outwardly affected to have embraced Islam, while retaining disbelief in their hearts) and a man from among the Jews of Madinah; and so the Jew, knowing of the Messenger of Allah's impartiality, justice, honesty and even-handedness, suggested that they refer their dispute to him (saas). The hypocrite, also knowing this, and fearing it, suggested that instead, they refer their matter to the Jews, whom he knew could be bribed. In the end, they both agreed to refer their case to a fortune-teller from the village of Juhainah, at which Allah (swt) revealed to His Messenger (saas) the above verse which exposed their wickedness, disgrace and baseless to the world until the Day of Resurrection.

Benefits Derived From This Narration

1. The miracle of the Prophet, that even his enemies testified to his honesty and justice.

2. The forbiddance of giving or accepting bribes.

3. That one of the signs of hypocrisy is seeking judgement from other than Allah's Law.

4. That one of the characteristics of the Jews is their acceptance of bribery.

Relevance of This Narration to the Subject of the Chapter

That it proves the forbiddance of seeking judgement from other than Allah (swt) and His Messenger (saas).

Relevance of This Narration to the Subject of *Tawheed*

That it proves the hypocrisy of those who claim to believe in Allah (swt) and His Messenger (saas), yet seek judgement from others, for this is a negation of the *shahadataan*.

..ooOOoo..

It was also said that this verse was revealed with respect to two men who became involved in a dispute; one of them said: "Let us raise the matter with the Prophet (saas)," while the other said: "(let us go) to Ka'ab Ibn Al-Ashraf." Then they went to `Umar (ra ) and one of them informed him of what had happened. He (ra ) then said to the one who had refused the judgement of the Messenger of Allah (saas ): "Is it so?" He replied: "Yes," upon which, `Umar (swt) struck him with his sword and killed him.

The narrator informs us in this account that the Words of Allah (swt), Most High:

> " *Do you not see [oh, Muhammad] those who claim to have faith in what was revealed to you and to those before you? They desire to resort for judgement to At-Taaghoot"* (Qur'an 4:60)

Were revealed concerning two men, one of them a Jew and the other a hypocrite, who fell into a dispute. The Jew suggested that they refer their dispute to the Messenger of Allah (saas) because of his well-known sense of justice and fair play and his honesty; but the hypocrite suggested that they go instead to Ka'ab Ibn Al-Ashraf, the Jew, because he knew that the Jews accepted bribes. In the end, they agreed to seek judgement from `Umar Ibn Al-Khattab (ra ), but when `Umar heard that the hypocrite had rejected the judgement of Allah's Messenger (saas), he slew him with his sword.

Benefits Derived From This Narration

1. The miracle of the Prophet, about whose honesty and fairness, even his enemies testified.

2. That calling for judgement from other than the Book of Allah and the *Sunnah* of His Messenger is a sign of hypocrisy.

3. The obligation to kill whoever cast aspersions upon the judgement of the Prophet or his Religion.

4. The obligation to feel anger for Allah (swt), over one who profanes Him, His Religion or His Prophets.

5. The obligation to rebuke those who profane Islam. [1]

Relevance of This Narration to the Subject of the Chapter

That it proves the prohibition of seeking judgement from other than the Messenger of Allah (saas).

Relevance of This Narration to the Subject of *Tawheed*

That the narration forbids seeking judgement from other than Allah's Messenger (saas) because doing so invalidates the *shahadataan*.

Footnotes

1. It must not be understood from this narration that it is the right of every Muslim in an Islamic State to punish the sinner or the disbeliever. The position of 'Umar (ra) due to his status as one of the foremost Companions and his great knowledge and wisdom is not to be compared to that of any Muslim today. Were it to be permitted for every Muslim to take the law into his own hands, the situation in Muslim societies would rapidly descend into chaos.

Top | Prev | Next

Kitaab At-Tawheed, Chapter: 38

Whoever Denies Any of the Names and Attributes of Allah

Allah (swt), says:

> " *Thus We have sent you among a people [before whom] other peoples have passed away,*
> *in order that you might recite to them what We have revealed to you. But they reject*
> *[Allah,] the Most Gracious! Say: "He is my Rabb: There is none worthy of worship save*
> *He; in Him I have placed my trust and to Him I shall return"* (Qur'an 13:30)

In this verse, Allah (swt), Most Glorified, Most High, informs us that He has sent His Messenger, Muhammad (saas) to this *Ummah* to lead them from the darkness of ignorance and despair, into the light of guidance and certainty, just as He sent to the previous nations, Messengers with Revelation, and that it is the responsibility of the Messenger (saas) to impart to his people the Message that was revealed to him, even though the disbelievers may reject it and deny Allah's Divine Names Attributes. In addition, He (saas) must remain steadfast in broadcasting the message of *Tawheed*, firm in his dependence upon Allah (swt) in all matters, and that he must turn to his *Rabb* in repentance and for guidance in every important affair.

Benefits Derived From This Verse

1. That rejection of any confirmed Name or Attribute of Allah is *kufr*.

2. Confirmation of Allah's Name: *Ar-Rahman* (the Most Merciful to all His creatures in the life of this world).

3. The obligation to place one's trust and dependence in Allah, Most High, and no other.

4. The obligation of turning to Allah (swt) in repentance.

Relevance of This Verse to the Subject of the Chapter and to the Subject of *Tawheed*

That it proves that rejecting any of Allah's Names or His Divine Attributes is *kufr* because it invalidates the belief in *Tawheed Al-Asmaa`i Was-Sifaat* (i.e. the Oneness of Allah (swt) in His Names and Attributes.

..ooOOoo..

In Saheeh Bukhari, it is reported that `Ali (ra) said: "Speak to the people in a way they will understand. Would you like that Allah (swt) and His Messenger (saas) be denied?"

In this narration, the fourth *Khaleefah*, `Ali Ibn Abi Talib (ra) commands the people of knowledge to guide the people by speaking to them in a manner suited to their intellects in order that they may understand, and not to engage them in speech which is above their level of comprehension. This would include lengthy and involved explanations of Allah's Name and Attributes, for that might lead to misunderstanding, causing them to deny something from Allah's Book or the *Sunnah* of His Prophet (saas), causing them to be destroyed without even knowing the reason.

Benefits Derived From This Narration

    1. #9; That whatever leads to the prohibited is itself prohibited.

    2. That it is not permissible to talk to people in a manner which they cannot understand, particularly in religious matters.

Relevance of This Narration to the Subject of the Chapter and to the Subject of *Tawheed*

That the narration proves that it is forbidden to talk to people in a manner which they do not understand; this includes long and complex explanations of Allah's Names and Attributes for that might lead to their rejecting something of His Names and Attributes which would amount to *kufr* because it entails negation of *Tawheed Al-Asmaa Was-Sifaat.*

..ooOOoo..

'Abdul-Razzaq report, on the authority of Ma'amar Ibn Tawoos, on the authority of his father, on the authority of Ibn 'Abbas (ra) that he saw a man springing to his feet in disapproval when he heard a Hadith from the Prophet (saas) About the Divine Attributes. Then he (Ibn 'Abbas ra) said: "What kind of fear is it that these people have? They find in the completely clear verses which admit of no ambiguity that, which they fear but they are brought to ruin by those verses which are not entirely clear."

Abdullah Ibn 'Abbas (ra) informs us in this narration that he saw a man rise to his feet in anger and disbelief when he heard a Hadith of the Prophet (saas) concerning Allah's Divine Attributes and that he (Ibn 'Abbas ra) rejected that man's action, asking what do such people fear and why is it that they fear the clear, unambiguous Qur'anic verses, yet fear not and reject those which are not entirely clear to them due to their limited knowledge.

Benefits Derived From This Narration

    1. The obligation to reject the detestable.

    2. The obligation to believe in all of Allah's Name and Attributes.

    3. The obligation to believe in the clear and the unclear verses.

    4. The permissibility of mentioning what relates to Allah's Names and Attributes from the Qur'an and *Sunnah* before the general populace.

Relevance of This Narration to the Subject of the Chapter and to the Subject of *Tawheed*

That it proves the obligation of belief in all of Allah's Names and Attributes from the Qur'an and *Sunnah* which is a necessary part of correct *Tawheed Al-Asmaa` Was-Sifaat.*

When Quraish heard Allah's Messenger mention *Ar-Rahman*, they rejected it, at which Allah (swt) revealed:

" *And they reject Ar-Rahmaan"* (Qur'an 13:30)

We are informed in this narration that when the Prophet (saas) wished to include Allah's Name: *Ar-*

Rahmaan in the Treaty of Al-Hudaibiyyah, the pagans of Quraish rejected it, saying that they did not know this Name, and that after this Allah (swt) revealed:

" *And they reject Ar-Rahman"* (Qur'an 13:30)

Benefits Derived From This Narration

1. Confirmation of Allah's Name: *Ar-Rahman*, which connotes the Divine Attribute of Mercy and Beneficence.

2. That whoever denied anything relating to Allah's Names and Divine Attributes is a disbeliever and is destroyed.

Relevance of This Narration to the Subject of the Chapter and to the Subject of *Tawheed*

That it proves the *kufr* of one who denies anything of Allah's Names and Attributes, because this is a negation of *Tawheed Al-Asmaa Was-Sifaat.*

Top | Prev | Next

Kitaab At-Tawheed, Chapter: 39

Allah's Words: " They Know the Favours of Allah, Then They Deny Them"

> " *They know the favours of Allah, then they deny them: And most of them are disbelievers*" (Qur'an 16:83)

In this verse, Allah (swt), Most Glorified, Most High, rejects all those who recognize in their hearts that all blessings are from Allah (swt), and yet in spite of this, they deny them by their evil deeds, worshipping other than Him and by their words, saying: "We achieved these blessings from Allah (swt), through the intercession of our idols," or they say: "It is our inheritance from our fathers and our grandfathers." And Allah (swt), Most High, informs us also that all those who do so are disbelievers in Allah (swt) and deniers of His Blessings.

Benefits Derived From This Verse

1. That even the pagans believed in *Tawheed Ar-Ruboobiyyah* (i.e. that Allah is the One *Rabb*, Creator and Sustainer of the Universe).

2. That gratitude to Allah is not complete unless it is expressed in belief, word and deed.

3. That using the blessings of Allah for the purpose of disobedience to Him is to deny them.

Relevance of This Verse to the Subject of the Chapter

That the verse proves that whoever attributed Allah's Blessings to other than Him has denied them.

Relevance of This Verse to the Subject of *Tawheed*

That the verse charges those who attribute Allah's Blessings to other than Him with disbelief, because in so doing, they set up partners with Allah (swt) in the bestowal of blessings.

..ooOOoo..

Mujahid said: "He (the one referred to in the above verse) is the man who says: "They (Allah's Blessings) are mine, an inheritance from my fathers and my forefathers."

Relevance of This Narration to the Subject of the Chapter

That the narration proves that Mujahid considered that whoever attributes Allah's Blessings to other than Him is a denier of those Blessings.

Relevance of This Narration to the Subject of *Tawheed*

That Mujahid considered any person who attributed Allah's Blessings to other than Him to be a disbeliever, because to do so is an act of *Shirk*.

..ooOOoo..

`Aoun Ibn `Abdillaah said: "They say: "If it were not for so-and-so, such-and-such an event would not have occurred.

`Aoun Ibn `Abdillah considered that attributing events to any of Allah's creatures is *kufr*, because this entails attributing benefit or harm to other than Allah (swt), while in fact they possess no power to harm or benefit except by Allah's Will.

Relevance of This Narration to the Subject of the Chapter

That it proves that `Aoun Ibn `Abdillah considered that believing that benefit or harm may occur due to the actions of other than Allah (swt), independent of Allah's *Qadr*, is *kufr*.

..ooOOoo..

Ibn Qutaibah said: "They say: "This is due to the intercession of our gods."

Ibn Qutaibah informs us in this narration that the polytheists attribute the blessings which they receive to be achieved through the power of intercession of their idols; in doing so, they combine the sin of associating partners with Allah (swt) by worshipping others, with the sin of *kufr*, by attributing blessings to other than Him, the true granter of blessings.

Relevance of This Narration to the Subject of the Chapter

That the narration proves that Ibn Qutaibah considered that attributing Allah's Blessings to the intercession of idols is *kufr*.

..ooOOoo..

After the Hadith of Zaid Ibn Khalid (page 151) in which Allah (swt), Most High, said: "*Some of My slaves this morning are true Believers in Me and others are disbelievers...*" Abul `Abbas (i.e. Ibn Taymiyah) said: "Such commandments occur frequently in the Qur'an and *Sunnah*. Allah (swt) condemns those who attribute His Blessings to others whom they associate with Him. Some of the *Salaf* have said that it is like the saying of some: "The wind was favourable," or: "the sailor was skillful," etc. and the statements of many of the people are like this."

The meaning of the above-mentioned narration is that when a ship is driven by a fair wind by Allah's Command, they attribute this to the goodness of the wind or the skill of the sailor in sailing the ship, forgetting their *Rabb*, Who drove the ship on the sea as a mercy to them; and attributing a speedy or safe voyage to the favour of the wind or the skill of the sailor is a kin to crediting the rain to the movements of the stars and planets. Even if a person does not intend by his words to suggest that the wind is the creator or instigator of these events along with Allah (swt), that it is only the means by which the objective was achieved, it is still not fitting to include it beside Allah (swt), the One, for it does not befit Allah's Favour that anyone should forget that it is He (swt) Alone, Who deserves gratitude and thanks, for all good is in His Hands and He (swt) is able to do all things and it is He (swt) Who grants all blessings in this world and in the Hereafter - He is One and He has no partners.

Benefits Derived From This Narration

1. That attributing blessings to any of Allah's creatures is *Shirk*. In Rabbship if it is believed that he is the provider and instigator of those blessings. If it is believed that he is the means by which the blessings were attained, then this is at the very least, bad manners towards Allah (swt), the true Provider of all blessings.

Relevance of This Narration to the Subject of the Chapter and to the Subject of *Tawheed*

That it proves that Ibn Taymiyah considered that whoever attributed blessings to other than Allah (swt) has denied them and is guilty of *Shirk*.

Top | Prev | Next

Kitaab At-Tawheed, Chapter: 40

Allah's Words: " And Do Not Ascribe Partners to Allah When You Know [the Truth]"

> *" Oh, you people! Worship your Lord, Who created you all and those before you that you may become righteous, Who has made the earth a couch for you and the heavens a canopy and sent down rain from the heavens; and brought forth therewith fruits for your subsistence; so do not set up Andaad with Allah"* (Qur'an Al-Baqarah 2:21-22)

Allah (swt), Most High, commands the people to worship Him Alone, in sincerity, because He is the One Who created them and those before them from nothing and then bestowed upon them innumerable blessings, such as the earth which He flattened and fixed, that they may dwell upon it and the rain which He sends down in abundance, and from which they derive countless blessings, such as food to eat, water to drink and trees for shade. Then Allah (swt), Most Glorified, Most High, says that in spite of this, they set up partners and equals with Him, though in reality, they know that He is their Creator and Provider; and this is mere willfulness on their part to commit *kufr*, *Shirk* and acts of disobedience.

Benefits Derived From This Verse

1. Evidence of a number of Allah's Blessings bestowed upon His creatures.

2. Evidence of *Tawheed Al-Uloohiyyah* (*Tawheed* of Worship) through *Tawheed Ar-Ruboobiyyah*.

3. The obligation to worship Allah, Alone, without partners.

Relevance of This Verse to the Subject of the Chapter and to the Subject of *Tawheed*

That it proves the obligation to abstain from obvious *Shirk* and from hidden *Shirk*, the latter including the saying of a person, for example: "Had it not been for the guard, the burglars would have come to us.

..ooOOoo..

Ibn `Abbas (ra) said, concerning this verse: "*Al-Andaad* means *Shirk* which is less conspicuous than a black ant crawling on a black stone in the darkness of the night, such as the saying: "By Allah and by your life, oh so-and-so!" or: "By your life," or: "If it had not been for this little dog, the burglars would have come to us," or "Had it not been for the duck in the house, the burglars would have come," or like a man's saying to his companion: "By Allah's and your will..." or: "As Allah (swt) and you will," or the saying of a man: "Had it not been for Allah (swt) and so-and-so..." - Do not mention anyone with Allah (swt), because all of this is *Shirk*." (Narrated by Ibn Abi Hatim)

Relevance of This Narration to the Subject of the Chapter and to the Subject of *Tawheed*

That the narration proves that Ibn `Abbas (ra), one of the best and wisest of the Companions in understanding the Religion, held the view that hidden *Shirk* includes swearing by other than Allah (swt), such as the saying of a person: "By your life!"; and that like wise, it includes attributing benefit to the deeds of one of Allah's creatures, such as the saying: "Had it not been for the guard, the burglars would have stolen from us;" and it also includes the attribution of benefit to the deeds of another alongside Allah (swt), such as the saying of a man: "Had it not been for Allah (swt) and so-and-so, the house would have burnt down.

..ooOOoo..

On the authority of `Umar Ibn Al-Khattab, it is reported that the Messenger of Allah (ra) said:

> *"Whoever swears by other than Allah (swt) has committed an act of kufr or Shirk."* (Narrated by At-Tirmizi, who graded it as *Hasan* and by Al-Hakim, who graded it as *Saheeh*)

The Messenger of Allah (saas) informs us in this Hadith that swearing by other than Allah (swt), Most Glorified, Most High, is tantamount to a denial of Allah (swt), the One True God and equivalent to associating partners with Him. This is because the essence of swearing is glorification and it is not fitting that we should glorify any save Allah (swt), the One True God and *Rabb*, for to do so is *Shirk*.

Benefits Derived From This Hadith

1. That swearing by other than Allah (swt) is an act of major *Shirk* - according to some scholars, it takes one out of the fold of Islam, while according to others, it is a sinful act of *Shirk* which however does not necessitate one's becoming a disbeliever. It has also been said that it is an act of minor *Shirk* - and Allah (swt) knows best.

2. That there is no recompense for swearing by other than Allah (swt), since it is an act of *Shirk*; the culprit must instead turn in repentance to Allah (swt) and seek His Forgiveness.

Important Note

(a) There is no contradiction between this Hadith and the words of the Prophet (saas): "By his father! he has succeeded," and other similar Hadith, for it has been explained by scholars that this and other similar Ahadith have been abrogated by the above Hadith.

(b) There is no recompense for swearing by other than Allah (swt) nor is it binding upon anyone to fulfill a promise made by swearing by other than Him. What is incumbent upon him is to declare: "*Laa ilaaha illallaahu Wahdahu Laa Shareeka Lahu,*" (None is worthy of worship except Allah (swt), Alone, without partners) then he should spit over his left shoulder three times and seek refuge with Allah (swt) and he should never repeat this act of *Shirk*.

..ooOOoo..

Ibn Mas'ood (ra) said: "That I should swear by Allah upon a lie is more preferable to me than that I should swear by another upon the truth."

Ibn Mas'ood (ra) informs us in this narration that every lie upon which Allah's Name is invoked and every truthful statement upon which the name of another is invoked is a sin, but that the sin of swearing by Allah (swt) upon a lie is lighter than the sin of swearing by another upon the truth, because to swear by Allah (swt) upon a lie is a major sin, while to swear by another is an act of *Shirk*.

Benefits Derived From This Narration

1. The forbiddance of swearing by Allah upon a lie.

2. The permissibility of swearing by Allah upon the truth.

3. The forbiddance of swearing by other than Allah, whether to the truth or to a lie.

4. That if one is forced by circumstances to choose one of two courses of action, against one's will, he should do that which is less harmful.

5. The precise understanding of Ibn Mas'ood.

6. That swearing by other than Allah is a greater sin than swearing by Allah upon a lie.

Relevance of This Narration to the Subject of the Chapter and to the Subject of *Tawheed*

That it proves that Ibn Mas'ood (ra) considered that swearing by other than Allah (swt) is forbidden, because swearing by one of Allah's creation entails glorification of that person or thing and glorification is a form of worship and directing an act of worship to other than Allah (swt) is *Shirk*.

..ooOOoo..

On the authority of Huzaifah (ra), it is reported that the Prophet (saas) said:

> *"Do not say: "As Allah (swt) wills and so-and-so wills," but (instead) say: "As Allah (swt) wills and then as so-and-so wills."* (Narrated by Abu Dawood with an authentic *sanad*)

Huzaifah (ra) informs us in this Hadith that the Prophet (saas) ordered his Companions not to equate the will of man with the Will of Allah (swt), but to mention Allah's Will first, then the will of others, as this makes it clear that the will of man is subservient to the Will of Allah (swt); and it is clear that if man wills something but Allah (swt) wills it not, it can never happen, while if Allah (swt) wills something, even if the whole of mankind united to oppose it, it will, without any shadow of doubt, take place.

Benefits Derived From This Hadith

1. The forbiddance of equating the will of Allah's creatures with the Will of Allah (swt).

2. The permissibility of mentioning the will of man after the Will of Allah (swt) by saying then as opposed to end.

3. Confirmation of Allah's Divine Attribute of Will.

Relevance of This Hadith to the Subject of the Chapter and to the Subject of *Tawheed*

That the Hadith proves the prohibition of equating the will of man with the Will of Allah (swt) by saying: "As Allah (swt) wills and so-and-so wills," because using the word and suggests parity between the Will of Allah (swt) and the will of man, which amounts to *Shirk* in matters of Rabbship.

..ooOOoo..

It is reported on the authority of Ibraheem An-Nakha'i that he hated for anyone to say: "I seek refuge in Allah (swt) and in you," but he considered it permissible to say: "I seek refuge in Allah (swt) and then in you." Then he added: "A person should say: "If not for Allah (swt), then so-and-so..." and he should not say: "If not for Allah (swt) and so-and-so."

Relevance of This Narration to the Subject of the Chapter and to the Subject of *Tawheed*

That the narration proves that Ibraheem An-Nakha'i held that it is forbidden to link seeking refuge in Allah (swt) with seeking refuge in one of His creatures. Likewise he considered it forbidden to link the Actions of Allah (swt) with those of His creation, for do so is to set up a partner with Allah (swt).

Top | Prev | Next

Kitaab At-Tawheed, Chapter: 41

What Has Been Said Concerning One Who is Not Satisfied With an Oath Sworn in Allah's Name

It is reported on the authority of Ibn `Umar (ra) that the Messenger of Allah (saas) said:

"Do not swear by your fathers: Whoever swears by Allah (swt), let him speak the truth and the one for whom the oath is taken in the Name of Allah (swt) should be satisfied with it; and whoever is not satisfied with it, is not (one of the slaves) of Allah (swt)." (Narrated by Ibn Majah, with a good *Sanad*)

In this Hadith, the Messenger of Allah (saas) forbids the swearing of oaths in other than Allah's Name, because this entails glorifying Allah's creatures and humility towards them and Islam does not permit humility towards other than Allah (swt). Then He (saas) commands those who swear in Allah's Name to speak the truth, because truth is a virtue at all times, even in ordinary speech, so what may be said of speech reinforced by an oath in Allah's Name?. Then He (saas) orders the one to whom an oath in Allah's Name is made, to believe his Muslim brother, unless it is proved that he has not spoken the truth, for it is incumbent upon the Muslim to think well of his brother and whoever does not do so, Allah (swt) has nothing to do with him.

Benefits Derived From This Hadith

    1. The forbiddance of swearing by other than Allah.

    2. The permissibility of swearing by Allah, so long as one is truthful.

    3. The prohibition of swaering by Allah upon a lie.

    4. The obligation to accept the word of one who swears by Allah (swt), unless it is proved that he has lied.

Relevance of This Hadith to the Subject of the Chapter

That the Hadith proves the obligation to accept the word of one who swears by Allah (swt).

Relevance of This Hadeeth to the Subject of *Tawheed*

That it proves the obligation to accept the word of one who swears by Allah (swt), because by doing so, one is glorifying Allah (swt) and that is part of the completeness of *Tawheed*.

Kitaab At-Tawheed, Chapter: 42

Saying: "As Allah Wills and You Will."

It is reported on the authority of Qatelah (ra) that a Jewish man came to the Prophet (saas) and said to him: "Verily, you (Muslims) commit *Shirk*, for you say: "As Allah (swt) Wills and as you will;" and you say: "By the *Ka'abah*!" And so the Prophet (saas) ordered whoever wanted to swear, to say: "By the *Rabb* of the *Ka'abah*!" and to say: "As Allah (swt) Wills, then as you will." (Narrated by An-Nasaa`i, who said that it is authentic)

Qatelah (ra) informs us in this Hadith that a man from among the Jews of Madinah came to the Prophet (saas) intending to malign Islam and the Muslims; he told the Prophet (saas) that he and all the other Muslims were guilty of *Shirk*, as if he wished to say: "You and your Qur'an say that we, the Jews commit *Shirk*, then what about you, when you swear by the *Ka'abah* and when you say: "As Allah (swt) and you will," - is this not also *Shirk*?" Thenceforth, the Messenger of Allah (saas) forbade the Muslims from doing so, in order that, their *Tawheed* might be pure and so that there might not be even the slightest blemish upon the Muslims' Religion which their enemies might exploit; and He (saas) guided them to the correct manner of swearing an oath, which is to swear by the *Rabb* of the *Ka'abah*, not by the *Ka'abah* itself, for it is a created thing; and He (saas) told them that if they wish to mention Allah's Will along with the will of others, they should say: " As Allah (swt) Wills, then as you will," because the use of the word `then' does not imply parity between the Will of Allah (swt) and the will of others, as does the use of the word "and".

Benefits Derived From This Hadith

1. That the Jews know what minor *Shirk* is.

2. That a person knowing of the truth does not necessitate his believing in it.

3. That linking Allah's Will with the will of others by saying: "...and..." is minor *Shirk*.

4. That swearing by other than Allah (swt) is *Shirk*, no matter how elevated the status of the object upon which the oath is taken.

5. The obligation to accept the truth, no matter what its source.

6. Confirmation of Allah's Divine Attribute of Will.

7. Confirmation of the Will of Allah's creatures, but in the knowledge that it is subordinate to the Will of Allah (swt).

8. The permissibility of linking Allah's Will with that of His creatures by using the word then, as opposed to "and".

Relevance of This Hadith to the Subject of the Chapter and to the Subject of *Tawheed*

That the Hadith proves that saying: "As Allah (swt) Wills and you will," is an act of minor *Shirk*.

An-Nasaa`i also narrate, on the authority of Ibn `Abbas (ra) that a man came to the Prophet (saas) and he said: "As Allah (swt) and you, will," at which, the Prophet (saas) said: "Would you set me up as a partner beside Allah (swt)? (Say:) "As Allah (swt), Alone Wills."

Ibn `Abbas (ra) informs us that a man came to Allah's Messenger (saas) and consulted him about a certain matter; after hearing the Prophet's advice, he said: "As Allah (swt) and you will, oh, Messenger of Allah (saas)!" The Prophet (saas) rebuked him for this statement and explained to him that placing his will on a par with the Will of Allah (swt) was tantamount to ascribing him as a partner to Allah (swt), which is prohibited to the Muslim. Then He (saas) guided the man to the correct manner, which is to say: "As Allah (swt), Alone Wills."

Benefits Derived From This Hadith

1. The obligation to reject that which is detestable.

2. That the ignorant man is excused due to his ignorance (until such time as he becomes aware of his mistake).

3. That linking the Will of Allah (swt) with that of His Creatures, using the word and, is an act of minor *Shirk*.

4. Confirmation of Allah's Divine Attribute of Will.

Relevance of This Hadith to the Subject of the Chapter and to the Subject of *Tawheed*

That the Hadith proves that saying: "As Allah (swt) and you will," is an act of minor *Shirk*.

Important Note

There is no contradiction between this Hadith and the saying of the Prophet (saas): "Say: "As Allah (swt) Wills, then as you will," because to do so is permissible, while to say: "As Allah (swt), Alone wills," is preferred.

On the authority of At-Tufail, the half brother of `A`ishah (may Allah be pleased with them both), it is reported that he said: "I saw in a dream that I came upon a number of Jews and I said to them: "You are indeed a good people were it not that you claim that `Uzair (as) is the son of Allah (swt)." They replied: "You too are good, were it not that you say: "As Allah (swt) Wills and as Muhammad wills." Then, I came upon a number of Christians and I said to them: "You are indeed a good people were it not that you claim that the Messiah (Eisa as) is the son of Allah (swt)." They replied: "You are also good, were it not that you say: "As Allah (swt) Wills and as Muhammad wills." When I awoke, I told someone about this, then I went to the Prophet (saas) and repeated it to him. He asked me: "Have you told anyone about this?" I said: "Yes." Then he went to the pulpit and, after praising Allah (swt), he said: "At-Tufail had a dream which he has already communicated to some of you. You used to say something which I was prevented from forbidding to you until now. Henceforth, do not say: "As Allah (swt) Wills and as Muhammad wills," but say: " What Allah (swt), Alone Wills." (Narrated by Ibn Majah)

At-Tufail (ra) informs us that he had a dream in which he saw the Jews and Christians and that he praised them both, except that he pointed out to them their shameful behaviour in elevating their Prophets to the status of deities, claiming them to be sons of Allah (swt). They replied by praising the Muslims, except that they pointed out a blot on the Muslims' character, in that they used to link the Will of Allah (swt) with that of Muhammad (saas). When At-Tufail awoke, he informed a number of people about what he had dreamt, and then he went to the Prophet (saas) and told him about it. The Prophet (saas) then rose and addressed the Muslims in the mosque: After praising Allah (swt), Most High, he ordered them to be strict in their implementation of *Tawheed*, particularly in what concerns His Will. Then he (saas) told them that he had previously hated this saying, but that he had not been ordered to forbid it until now. Thenceforth, he forbade the Muslims from saying this, without fear of the truth, and regardless of its source.

Benefits Derived From This Hadith

1. The virtue of At-Tufail (ra).

2. Confirmation of Allah's Divine Attribute of Will.

3. The prohibition of linking Allah's Will with that of His creatures, using the word `and', because to do so is to commit minor *Shirk*.

4. That in the time of the Prophet (saas) a dream might form the basis for a legal judgement.

5. The good character of the Prophet (saas) who did not hide anything from the people.

6. The lawfulness of beginning a speech by praising and thanking Allah (swt).

7. The lawfulness of addressing the people on important matters.

8. The lawfulness of saying, after praising Allah (swt): "*Ammaa ba'adu...*" [1]

9. The lawfulness of making sure of the truth of a matter and not making hasty decisions.

10. The command to practise *Tawheed* in the matter of Allah's Will.

Relevance of This Hadith to the Subject of the Chapter and to the Subject of *Tawheed*

That it proves the prohibition of linking the Will of Allah's creatures with that of Him, Most High, using the word `and', for this suggests parity between the two and this leads to *Shirk*.

Footnotes

1. Ammaa ba'adu: As for what follows...

Top | Prev | Next

Kitaab At-Tawheed, Chapter: 43

Whoever Curses Time Wrongs Allah

Allah (swt), says:

> " *And they say: "There is nothing but our life in this world: We die and we live and nothing destroys us except time." And they have no knowledge of it, they only conjecture"* (Qur'an 45:24)

Allah (swt), Most Glorified, Most High, informs us in this verse about the disbelieving *dahris*[1] from among the Arabs and others, who do not believe in any life, save the life of this world, nor in the *Rabb* and Creator, Allah (swt), Most High. They believe that nothing causes death except the passage of time. Then Allah (swt), Most Glorified, Most High, refutes their claims, saying that they have absolutely no evidence for what they claim, but instead, depend upon surmise and their own vain opinions.

Benefits Derived From This Verse

1. That attributing good or evil to the passage of time is a sign of atheism.

2. Confirmation of a life after death for mankind.

3. That *ad-dahr* (time) is not one of Allah's Names.

Relevance of This Verse to the Subject of the Chapter

That the verse rejects those who attribute events to time, for they commit a great wrong against Allah (swt).

Relevance of This Verse to the Subject of *Tawheed*

That it rejects those who attribute events to time, because in so doing, they are ascribing a partner to Allah (swt), for it is He, Alone Who decrees what will be and what will not be.

..ooOOoo..

It is authentically reported on the authority of Abu Hurairah (ra) that the Prophet (saas) said: "Allah (swt), Most Blessed, Most High, says: "The son of Adam wrongs Me: He curses time, though I am time: In My Hands are all things and I cause the night to follow the day." [2] In another narration, He (saas) says: "Do not curse time, for verily, time is Allah (swt)."

Allah (swt), Most Glorified, Most High informs us in this Hadith *Qudsi*, that man commits a great wrong against Allah (swt) when he curses time and attributes the occurrence of events to it, for Allah (swt) is the *Rabb* of time and the Disposer of affairs and it is by His *Qadr* that events take place. Therefore to curse time is to curse the Owner of time.

In the second narration, the Prophet (saas) forbids us from cursing time, saying that Allah (swt) is the

Owner of time and the Disposer of it and all events and affairs, and this is confirmation of what was reported in the preceding Hadith *Qudsi*.

Benefits Derived From This Hadith

1. The forbiddance of cursing time.

2. That no actions may be attributed to time.

Relevance of This Hadith to the Subject of the Chapter

That it proves that to curse time is to commit a great wrong against Allah (swt).

Relevance of This Hadith to the Subject of *Tawheed*

That the Hadith proves that cursing time is a great wrong against Allah (swt), because those who do so believe that it is time which causes events to take place and this is *shirk* in *Tawheed Ar-Ruboobiyyah*, for it is Allah (swt), Alone Who determines events.

Footnotes

1. Dahris: An atheistic sect among the Arabs, their views are widely held in the West today: There is no God, no Resurrection, no punishment, no reward etc., etc.

2. Narrated by Bukhari.

Top | Prev | Next

Kitaab At-Tawheed, Chapter: 44

To Be Called Judge of Judges and the Like

It is authentically reported on the authority of Abu Hurairah (ra) that the Prophet (saas) said: "Verily, the lowest name to Allah is that of a man who calls himself "King of kings," for there is no king except Allah (swt)."[1] Sufyaan added: "Like the title *Shaahinshaah*." In another narration, it was said: "The man who angers Allah most on the Day of Ressurrection and the vilest..."

Allah's Messenger (saas) informs us in this Hadith that the vilest, most contemptible, most wretched human being in the sight of Allah (swt) is, the one who calls himself "King of kings" or the like, or is so called by others and is pleased with that, because in so doing, he has elevated himself to the position of *Rabb*, comparing himself to Allah (swt), the true King of kings. Then He (saas) makes clear that there is no king of the universe, except Allah (swt), the Almighty, the All-powerful. And here is a warning to all those who take such names and titles for themselves or attribute them to others, without perhaps, fully understanding the meaning or being aware of the great sin which they commit in so doing.

Benefits Derived From This Hadith

1. The forbiddance of naming oneself King of kings or any other name which carries the same meaning such as Emperor of all mankind, Judge of judges etc.

2. The obligation to abstain from using reprehensible expressions.

Relevance of This Hadith to the Subject of the Chapter

That it proves the forbiddance of taking the name King of kings.

Relevance of This Hadith to the Subject of *Tawheed*

That the Hadith forbids taking or giving such names as King of kings or Judge of judges because this is *Shirk* in Rabbship.

Footnotes

1. Narrated by Bukhari.

Kitaab At-Tawheed, Chapter: 45

Honouring the Names of Allah and Changing One's Name Because of That

It is reported on the authority of Abu Shuraih (ra) that he used to be known as Abul Hakam, until the Prophet (saas) said to him: "Allah is Al-Hakam and His Judgement will prevail." Abu Shuraih (ra) replied: "When my people dispute in any matter, they come to me for adjudication; and when I judge between them, both parties are pleased with my judgement." The Prophet (saas) said: "How excellent is this! Do you have any children?" He said: "Yes, Shuraih, Muslim and `Abdullah." Then the Prophet (saas) asked: "Who is the eldest?" He answered: "Shuraih." Then the Prophet (saas) said: "Then (from now on,) you will be known as Abu Shuraih." (Narrated by Abu Dawood and others)

Abu Shuraih (saas), whose real name was Haani Ibn Yazeed Al-Kindi, came to the Prophet (saas) in a delegation from his tribe; and his nickname at that time was Abul Hakam (Father of Judgement) *1* but when the Prophet (saas) heard his people addressing him thus, he rejected it, informing him that Al-Hakam is one of Allah's Names, for His is the final Judgement, from which there is no appeal. Abu Shuraih then explained to him that his people had given him this name because of his skill in adjudication and arbitration which in most cases, satisfied both parties. The Prophet (saas) was pleased with what Abu Shuraih (ra) told him and he praised him for his wisdom and good judgement. Then He (saas) asked him if he had any children. Abu Shuraih (ra) replied in the affirmative, stating that he had three sons, the eldest of whom was named Shuraih. At this, the Prophet (saas) informed him that thenceforth, he would be known as Abu Shuraih.

Benefits Derived From This Hadith

1. That Islam erases what came before it.

2. That the ignorant man is excused his faults until such time as he is made aware of them.

3. The obligation to reject that which is detestable.

4. Confirmation of one of Allah's Names: Al-Hakam.

5. The permissibility of referring disputes to those who are capable of wise and fair judgement, even though he may not be an appointed judge and the obligation upon both parties to accept his judgement.

6. The virtue of accepting a Muslim's excuse when it is sound.

7. The permissibility of naming a person after his first-born daughter.

8. The lawfulness of naming onself after one's eldest child.

Relevance of This Hadith to the Subject of the Chapter

That the Hadith proves the obligation to change one's name if there is any similarity with the Names of Allah (swt).

Relevance of This Hadith to the Subject of *Tawheed*

That the Hadith rejects similarity in men's names to the Names of Allah (swt) because to describe oneself by one of Allah's Names or a name with the same meaning is *shirk*, for it is a negation of *Tawheed Al-Asmaa Was-Sifaat*.

Footnotes

1. It was, and continues to be a practice among the Arabs, when they notice a certain trait in someone to name him (literally) father of that trait; thus Abu Hurairah (ra) - Father of Kittens, because he was so fond of kittens etc.

Top | Prev | Next

Kitaab At-Tawheed, Chapter: 46

Whoever Made Fun of Anything in Which
Allah, the Qur'an or His Messenger (saas) Are Mentioned

Allah (swt), says:

> " *And if you question them, they declare emphatically: "We were only talking idly and joking." Say: "Was it at Allah, His Aayat and His Messenger you were mocking?" Make no excuses! You have rejected faith after you had accepted it, if We pardon some of you, We will punish others amongst you because they were sinners"* (Qur'an 9:65-66)

In these two verses, Allah (swt), Most Glorified, Most High, refers to an incident in which the hypocrites, having taken part in the Battle of Tabuk with the Muslims, began to discredit and insult them and their Religion: He (swt), Most High, informs His Prophet, Muhammad (saas) about the reply of those hypocrites, when they are questioned about their lack of faith, that they will put forward untruthful and invalid excuses for their behaviour, claiming that the slanders which issued from their mouths were spoken only as a jest. Then He (swt), Most High, tells the Prophet (saas) to reply to them that their excuses are not acceptable, for they are guilty of mocking Allah (swt), His Revelation, His Proofs, His Signs and His Messenger (saas); but in spite of this, He (swt), Most Merciful does not close the door completely on the hope of forgiveness and mercy for those of them who cease their hypocrisy and turn sincerely in repentance to Allah (swt). Finally, He (swt), Most Blessed, Most High, confirms the severe chastisement which awaits them because of their hypocrisy and disbelief.

Benefits Derived From These Verses

1. That making fun of Islam and the Muslims is, an act of disbelief.

2. According to some scholars of the Hanbali school of *fiqh*, repentance is not accepted from anyone who makes fun of Islam and the Muslims, while others held the view that there is repentance for him. [1]

Relevance of These Verses to the Subject of the Chapter

That they prove the disbelief of one who mocks Allah (swt), His *Aayat* or His Messenger (saas).

..ooOOoo..

It is reported on the authority of Ibn `Umar (ra), Muhammad ibn Ka'ab, Zaid Ibn Aslam and Qatadah that in the course of the Battle of Tabuk, a man came up and declared: "We have seen none greedier, none so untruthful and none so cowardly as these (Qur'anic) reciters of ours (i.e. Allah's Messenger (saas) and the Companions). `Awf Ibn Malik replied: "(In fact) you are the liar and a hypocrite; I shall inform the Messenger of Allah (saas) (about what you have said)." And so `Awf went to Allah's Messenger (saas) in order to inform him of what had occurred, but he found that Revelation had already preceded him. Then that man came to the Messenger of Allah (saas) when he was just starting out on a journey on his camel. The man pleaded: "We were only joking and indulging in travellers' talk to pass the time." Ibn `Umar (ra) said: "It is as if I see him before me now, clinging to the saddle-belt of the Allah's Messenger's camel and the rough stones were battering his legs as he ran and he was saying:

"We were only talking idly and joking." But the Messenger of Allah (saas) replied: "" *Was it at Allah, His Aayat and His Messenger you were mocking? Make no excuses! You have rejected faith after you had accepted it.*"" ." He (saas) did not look towards him, nor did he say anything further."

`Abdullah Ibn `Umar (ra) and the other above-mentioned narrators inform us in this Hadith, that during the Tabuk Campaign, a man from among the hypocrites began to malign the Messenger of Allah (saas) and the Companions and to mock them, claiming that they ate too much food and that they were liars and cowards in battle. When `Awf Ibn Malik (ra) heard these words, he became angry for Allah (swt) and His Messenger's sake and he refuted these words, branding him a liar and a hypocrite and warning him that he would inform the Prophet (saas) about what he had said; but when he came to him, he found that he already knew of the incident, because Allah (swt) had informed him through Revelation: The Qur'an had uncovered the baseness and deceit of the hypocrites for all to see and cursed their disbelief. After this, the hypocrite came to the Messenger of Allah (saas) to try to explain his behaviour with patently false excuses, but Allah's Messenger refused even to look in his direction; he merely replied quoting the verse which Allah (swt) had revealed to him concerning this man and all those like him.

Benefits Derived From This Verse

1. The danger of the hypocrites to Islam and the Muslims.

2. That maligning Islam is a sign of hypocrisy.

3. That hatred for the Muslims and disparaging them is an act of *kufr*.

4. The obligation to refute immediately that which is evil.

5. The true faith of `Awf Ibn Malik.

6. The permissibility of branding a person a hypocrite if he exhibits unmistakable signs of hypocrisy.

7. Confirmation of the miracle of the Prophet in that he was informed by Revelation of the incident before `Awf came to him.

8. The non-acceptance of vain excuses.

9. The obligation to be severe with those who mock the Religion.

Relevance of This Hadith to the Subject of the Chapter and to the Subject of *Tawheed*

That the Hadith and the verse contained there in, prove the disbelief of one who makes fun of Allah (swt), His Book or His Messenger (saas).

Footnotes

1. Those scholars of the mazhab of the great scholar of fiqh, Ahmad Ibn Hanbal who held that there is no repentance for the one who mocks the Religion doubtless drew for evidence upon the Words of Allah (swt): (Qur'an 9:66). According to these scholars, the only alternative for such a person would be to embrace Islam anew, by testifying that none is worthy of worship except Allah (swt) and that Muhammad (saas) is the Messenger of Allah.

Kitaab At-Tawheed, Chapter: 47

Allah's Words: " And Truly, If We Give Him a Taste of Mercy From Us, After Some Adversity Has Touched Him... "

Allah (swt), says:

> " *And truly, if We give him a taste of mercy from Us, after some adversity has touched him, he is sure to say: "This is for me; I think not that the Hour will be established, but if I am brought back to my Lord, surely, there will be for me the best with Him." Then, We verily, will show to the disbelievers what they have done and We shall make them taste a severe torment"* (Qur'an 41:50)

In this verse, Allah (swt), Most Glorified, Most High, informs us when He blesses the disbelieving man or the doubter with health, well-being and wealth, after being afflicted with sickness, poverty or loss, he will not be thankful to his *Rabb*, but instead will boast that it is his right upon Allah (swt). Then He (swt), Most High, makes clear that the reason for this is his doubt in the reality of the Day of Judgement and all that it entails, including the Resurrection and the Gathering and that in his ignorance and stupidity, he exceeds even this, for he believes that should it prove that the Hereafter is a reality, he will find great blessings with his *Rabb*.

Then Allah (swt) warns him that he will be shown his deeds and that he will be held to account for them on that Day and he will receive a terrible punishment.

Benefits Derived From This Verse

1. That good and evil are by Allah's Decree.

2. The obligation to be thankful for Allah's Blessings.

3. Confirmation of the establishment of the Hour.

4. That doubt concerning the truth of the Resurrection is *kufr*.

5. That belief in Allah is not sufficient without belief in the Resurrection.

6. Confirmation of the reward and punishment.

Relevance of This Verse to the Subject of the Chapter

That it proves that attributing blessings to other than Allah (swt) is *kufr*.

Relevance of This Verse to the Subject of *Tawheed*

That it forbids attributing blessings to other than Allah (swt), because to do so is to set up partners with Him, Most High, in Rabbship.

..ooOOoo..

It is reported on the authority of Abu Hurairah (ra) that he heard the Messenger of Allah (saas) say: "Verily, three men from Bani Israel, a leper, a bald-headed man and a blind man were tested by Allah (swt): He (swt) sent to them an angel, who came (first) to the leper and said to him: "What thing would you like most?" He replied: "A good complexion and a good skin and that that which causes the people to be averse to me (i.e. the leprosy) should depart from me." The angel touched him and his disease was cured and he was given a fair complexion and a good skin. The angel then asked him: "What kind of property do you prefer?" The man replied: "Camels," or "Cows." (Ishaq, the narrator is not sure which). So he was given a pregnant female camel, and the angel said to him: "May Allah (swt) bless you in it." Then the angel came to the bald man and said to him: "What is the thing most loved to you?" The man replied: "Good hair and that which causes the people to be averse to me (baldness) should depart from me." And so the angel touched him and his affliction was gone and he was given fine hair. Then the angel asked him: "What kind of property would you like best?" He replied: "Cows," or "Camels." The angel gave him a pregnant cow and said: "May Allah (swt) bless you in it." Then the angel went to the blind man and said to him: "What thing would you like best of All?" He said: "I would like that Allah (swt) restore my sight to me so that I might see the people." And so the angel touched him and Allah (swt) restored his sight to him. Then the angel asked him: "What kind of property do you most prefer?" He replied: "Sheep." So the angel gave him a pregnant sheep. Later, all three of the pregnant animals gave birth to young and multiplied until one of them had a valley full of camels, while another had a valley full of cows and the third had a valley full of sheep. Then the angel disguised as a leper, went to the leper and said: "I am a poor man who has lost all his means while on a journey, and so there is none who can satisfy my needs today except Allah (swt) and then you. I ask you by the One Who gave you your fair complexion and your fine skin and granted you so much wealth in livestock to give me a camel so that I may reach my destination." The man replied: "I have many obligations (so I cannot give you one)." The angel said: "I think I know you; were you not a leper to whom the people had a strong aversion? Were you not a poor man and then Allah (swt) gave you (all of this)?" The man replied: "(No,) I got this property by way of inheritance from my forefathers." The angel said: "If you are lying, May Allah (swt) make you as you were before." Then the angel went to the bald man, in the shape of a bald man and said to him the same as he had said to the first man, but he too answered as the first one had. The angel said to him: "If you are lying, May Allah make you as you were before." Then the angel, disguised as a blind man, went to the blind man and said: "I am a poor man and a traveller whose livelihood has been cut off during the journey. I have no one to help me except Allah and then you. I ask you by Him Who has given you back your sight to give me a sheep that I may, with its help, complete my journey." The man said: "Without doubt, I was blind and Allah (swt) gave me back my sight, so take what you wish from my property. By Allah (swt)! I will not prevent you from taking anything of my property, which you may have for Allah's sake." The angel replied: "Keep your property with you. You have (all) been tested and Allah (swt) is pleased with you and is angry with your two companions." (Narrated by Bukhari)

The Prophet (saas) informs us in this Hadith about the true story of three poor men from the tribe of Bani Israel: A leper, a bald man and a blind man, whose faith Allah (swt) wished to test. He (swt) sent to them an angel who cured them of their afflictions, by Allah's Will and gave them wealth in livestock. Later, he came back to them and asked each of them for material help, assuming in each case, the form of the man prior to his cure and reminding each of them of Allah's Mercy and Beneficence to him when he was in need. As for the leper and the bald man, they were ungrateful to Allah (swt) and refused, while as for the blind man, he acceded gladly to the angel's request; as a result, the former two earned Allah's Anger, while the third earned His Pleasure and Allah (swt) allowed him to retain his wealth.

Benefits Derived From This Verse

1. Confirmation of the Prophetic miracle, in that Allah had granted him something of the knowledge of former peoples.

2. That attributing blessings to other than Allah is *kufr* and the cause of their loss.

3. That attributing blessings to Allah is to express gratitude to Him and causes them said blessings to continue.

4. Confirmation of the human attribute of will, but that it is subordinate to the Will of Allah.

5. Confirmation of Allah Divine Attribute of Pleasure.

6. Conformation of Allah's Divine Attribute of Anger.

Relevance of This Hadith to the Subject of the Chapter

That it proves that attributing blessings to other than Allah (swt) is an act of disbelief in Allah (swt).

Relevance of This Hadith to the Subject of *Tawheed*

That the Hadith prohibits attributing blessings to other than Allah (swt), because this is *Shirk* in Rabbship.

Top | Prev | Next

Kitaab At-Tawheed, Chapter: 48

Allah's Words: " But When He Gives to Them A Righteous Child, They Ascribe to Him Partners in That Which He Has Given Them"

Allah (swt), says:

> " *It is He Who created you from a single being and made from it its mate, in order that he might dwell with her. When he united with her [in intercourse], she bore [i.e. becomes pregnant with] a light burden and she continued to carry it. When she grew heavy, they both prayed to Allah, their Lord: "If You give us a righteous child, good in every respect, we vow we shall be of the grateful ones." But when He gave them a righteous child, they ascribed to others a share in that which He had given them: But Allah is Exalted High above the partners they ascribe to Him"* (Qur'an 7:189-190)

Allah (swt), Most Glorified, Most High, informs us in these verses that He (swt) created mankind from a single human being, Adam (as) and that He created from him a wife, Hawwa`,[1] in order that they might live together in peace and harmony and that He created in them the desire for sexual intercourse and made it permissible to them, in order that they might enjoy complete stability and repose and that their progeny might continue to multiply. And when she became pregnant, they both called upon Allah (swt), asking Him to give them a healthy, strong, righteous child and swearing that if He did so, they would be eternally be grateful to Him. But when Allah (swt) answered their supplications and gave them that which they had requested, they named him `Abdul Harith,[2] thus ascribing others as partners with Allah (swt); and Allah (swt) is far above that which they attributed to Him.

Benefits Derived From These Verses

1. The superiority of man over woman in that he was created before her.

2. The preferability of marriage over bachelorhood.

3. The obligation to abstain from naming one's children with detestable names.

4. Evidence of the virtue of motherhood and of what a mother endures during pregnancy and childbirth.

5. The lawfulness of supplication and confirmation of its benefits.

6. That ascribing partners to Allah invalidates one's gratitude to Him.

7. The obligation to abstain from anthropomorphic concepts and ideas regarding Allah.

Relevance of These Verses to the Subject of the Chapter and to the Subject of *Tawheed*

That the verses prove the correctness of the saying of Ibn `Abbas (ra), who said that submission to other than Allah (swt) by naming one's children as slaves of other than Allah (swt) is *Shirk*.

On the authority of Ibn `Abbas (ra) it is reported that he said: "When Adam (as) joined with her, she became pregnant and then *Iblees* came to her and said: "I am your companion, who caused you to be expelled from Paradise. Obey me, or I will cause your child to grow two horns like a deer by which he will puncture your belly when he comes out! So do it! Do it! Thus he tried to frightened them into naming their child `Abdul Harith, but they did not obey him and a dead child was born to them. When Hawwa` became pregnant a second time, *Iblees* again approached them and repeated the same demand but again they refused and the child was born dead. She became pregnant a third time and *Iblees* came to them and made the same demand, reminding them of what had happened before. At this point, they were overcome by love for their (unborn) child and named him `Abdul Harith and this is why Allah (swt), the Almighty, the All-powerful said:

" *They ascribed to others a share in that which He had given them"* (Qur'an 7:190)

..ooOOoo..

Ibn `Abbas (ra ) informs us in this narration that when Hawwa` became pregnant by Adam (swt), Allah (swt) wished to test them and so He allowed *Iblees* to come to them and demand from them that they obey him by naming their child `Abdul Harith and he kept on repeating this demand with threats to the unborn foetus' life, until eventually they gave in out of fear for their child and acceded to his ultimatum and Allah (swt) then saved the child from death as a trial to them, in order to see whether they attributed its safety to Allah (swt) or another.[3]

Benefits Derived From This Narration

1. Confirmation of *Iblees'* enmity towards Adam (as).

2. The obligation to avoid Satan and his evil whispering.

3. *Iblees'* persistence in seducing mankind.

4. That Allah (swt) may test a righteous person by afflicting him with calamities.

5. The weakness of man's resolve.

6. That love of one's children is a natural instinct with which Allah (swt) has endowed us.

7. The prohibition of naming anyone as slave of other than Allah (swt).

Relevance of This Narration to the Subject of the Chapter and to the Subject of *Tawheed*

That it proves that naming one's child as slave of other than Allah (swt) is an act of *Shirk*.

..ooOOoo..

Also narrated by Ibn Abi Hatim, with an authentic *sanad*, [4] on the authority of Qatadah is the following: "They attributed partners to Him by obeying other than Him, not by worshiping him (*Iblees*)."

Relevance of This Narration to the Subject of the Chapter and to the Subject of *Tawheed*

That it proves that naming one's children as slaves of other than Allah (swt) is an act of *Shirk*.

It is also authentically narrated by Ibn Abi Hatim, on the authority of Mujahid, that he said concerning Allah's Words:" *If You give us a righteous child, good in every respect"* : "They were afraid that the child would not be human." The same thing was said by Al-Hasan, Sa'eed and others.

Mujahid informs us concerning the above mentioned Qur'anic verse that the reason for Adam and his wife's calling their son `Abdul Harith was out of fear that he would be born in a non-human form after *Iblees* had deceived them into believing that he had the power to do as he had threatened - May Allah's curse be upon him.

Footnotes

1. Hawwaa`: Eve.

2. 'Abdul Harith: Slave, or worshipper of the cultivator.

3. Not because Allah (swt) did not know what they would do, for He knows all things, but in order that their action should be a proof either for or against them on the Day of Judgement.

4. In fact, this narration has been graded as weak by Ibn Katheer amongst others.

Top | Prev | Next

Kitaab At-Tawheed, Chapter: 49

Allah's Words: " The Most Beautiful Names Are For Allah, So Call on Him by Them"

Allah, Most High says:

" *The most beautiful Names are for Allah, so call on Him by them, but shun those who deny His Names"* (Qur'an 7:180)

Allah (swt), Most Glorified, Most High, informs us in this verse that His Names are of the utmost beauty and that He (swt) is Most Perfect and Complete in all of His Divine Attributes, then He (swt) tells us that we should supplicate Him using these Names, in order that our prayers be answered and that they be answered quickly. Then He (swt), Most High, commands us to avoid those who reject His Names or knowingly alter their meanings in order to suit their deviated understanding of *Tawheed*. Then He (swt), Almighty, All-powerful, warns them of the condign punishment which awaits those who deny His Names and Attributes on the Day of Resurrection.

Relevance of This Verse to the Subject of the Chapter

That it proves the forbiddance of denying Allah's Divine Names and Attributes.

Relevance of This Verse to the Subject of *Tawheed*

That it forbids the denial of Allah's Divine Names and Attributes; such denial includes bestowing His Names upon His creatures or bestowing His creatures' names upon Him, for this is *Shirk* in the matter of His Names and Attributes.

Important Note

(a) Mentioning the Divine Names by which the Believer may enter Paradise may be described as being on three levels: (i) Pronouncing the words; (ii) understanding their meanings and (iii) calling upon Allah (swt) by them.

(b) Some of Allah's Names may be pronounced alone, such as Al-Hakeem (the Judge), while others may be pronounced together, such as *As-Samee'* (the All-hearing) and *Al-Baseer* (the All-seeing), while others must never be pronounced except together, such as *An-Naafi'* (the Benevolent) and *Adh-Dhaarr* (the Harmer), because Allah's Complete-ness is not made clear except by this combination, for were one to pronounce the Name *Adh-Dhaarr* alone, it would not be a word of praise unless the Name *An-Naafi'* was mentioned along with it.

(c) The rule regarding Allah's Names and Attributes is that we do not ascribe to Him any name or attribute which is not found in the Qur'an or the authentic Ahadith of the Prophet (saas), and we reject all names and attributes which He (swt) and His Messenger (saas) have rejected, and we remain silent concerning matters connected with His Names and Attributes about which we have no knowledge.

(d) It is not permissible to derive names for Allah (swt) from the verbs used in the Qur'an to describe His Actions: Thus, we may not refer to Him as Al-Mun'im (the Provider of Blessings), even though the Qur'an speaks of His *Ni'am* (Blessings), nor is it allowed for us to call Him *As-Sattaar* (the Veiler) even though He has been described as *As-Satteer* (derived from the same verb) in an authentic Hadith; and whoever does so is in error.

(e) Denial of Allah's Divine Names and Attributes is of five types: (i) Bestowing Allah's Names or names derived from them upon idols, as the pagan Quraish did, when they named one of their gods Al-Laat, which is derived from the same root as Allah (swt); (ii) ascribing to Allah (swt) names which do not befit His Majesty, as the Christians do when they refer to Him as the Father, or as the philosophers do when they refer to him as the Active Cause, or the Power etc.; (iii) ascribing to Him attributes which He is far above, such as the Jews' obnoxious claim that He rested on the seventh day (i.e. Saturday); (iv) changing the meaning of Allah's Divine Names and Attributes and rejecting the true meanings as did the *Jahmiyyah*[1] who claimed that Allah (swt) is the All-hearing, but He does not hear and that He is the Living, but He does not live;[2] (v) Comparing the Attributes of Allah (swt) with those of His creatures, when in truth, we should affirm only that which does not suggest any comparison between Allah (swt) and His creation.

..ooOOoo..

Ibn Abi Hatim reported on the authority of Ibn `Abbas (ra) that he said: "Those who belie or deny His Names are guilty of *Shirk*."

Relevance of This Narration to the Subject of the Chapter and to the Subject of *Tawheed*

That the narration proves that Ibn `Abbas (ra) held that ascribing Allah's Names to idols is an act of denial of those Names and it is confirmed that those who do so are guilty of *Shirk*.

..ooOOoo..

It is reported on the authority of Al-A'amash that he said that they used to ascribe names to Allah which were not His.

Relevance of This Narration to the Subject of the Chapter and to the Subject of *Tawheed*

That the narration is evidence that Al-A'amash was of the view that calling Allah (swt) by names which are not His is a denial of those Names and it has been confirmed that denial of Allah's Names is *Shirk*.

Footnotes

1. The Jahmiyyah: A deviant sect which perverted Islamic beliefs. Although, as a group, they are no longer present, many of their distorted beliefs have been adopted by others.

2. That is, these are just names, without meaning.

Top | Prev | Next

Kitaab At-Tawheed, Chapter: 50

One Should Not Say: Peace Be Upon Allah

It is authentically reported on the authority of Ibn Mas'ood (ra) that he said: "Whenever we prayed behind the Prophet (saas), we used to recite: "*As-Salaam* (Peace) be upon Allah (swt) from His slaves and *As-Salaam* be upon so-and-so and so-and-so, until the Prophet (saas) told us: "Do not say: "*As-Salaam* be upon Allah (swt)," for verily, He is *As-Salaam*." [1]

Ibn Mas'ood (ra) informs us that when he and the other Companions prayed with the Messenger of Allah (saas), they used to invoke Allah's Peace and Blessings upon Allah (swt) and then upon a number of people during *tashahhud* (sitting). But then he forbade them from doing so, informing them that *As-Salaam* is one of Allah's Names, therefore it is not acceptable that they should invoke Allah's Peace and Blessings upon Himself, for He is not in need of peace or blessings rather He is the Owner and Source of all peace and blessings.

Benefits Derived From This Hadith

1. The forbiddance of invoking peace upon Allah (swt).

2. That when Islam forbids a thing, it guides us to that which is better.

3. That *As-Salaam* is one of the Names of Allah (swt).

4. The permissibility of supplicating Allah (swt) on behalf of His slaves in prayer.

Relevance of This Hadith to the Subject of the Chapter

That it proves that it is forbidden to invoke peace and blessings upon Allah (swt).

Relevance of This Hadith to the Subject of *Tawheed*

That it proves that invoking peace and blessings upon Allah (swt) is contrary to *Tawheed*, because *As-Salaam* is a form of supplication on behalf of the weak, and those in need and Allah (swt) is neither of these things.

Footnotes

1. Narrated by Bukhari and Muslim.

Kitaab At-Tawheed, Chapter: 51

Saying: "Oh, Allah! Forgive Me if You Will."

It is authentically reported on the authority of Abu Hurairah(swt) that the Messenger of Allah (saas) said: "None of you should say: "Oh, Allah (swt), Forgive me if You will," or: "Oh, Allah (swt), Have mercy upon me if You Will." Rather he should always appeal to Allah (swt) firmly, for nobody can force Allah (swt) to do something against His Will."[1] According to Muslim's report, He (saas) said: "One should appeal to Allah (swt) with firm determination for nothing is too much or too great for Allah (swt) to give it."

Because all of us are wretched and humble before Allah (swt), Most High, and He is Self-sufficient, Most Praiseworthy, Allah's Messenger (saas) forbade anyone who supplicates Allah (swt) from adding to his request: "...if You will," as this suggests a lack of interest on Allah's part in the needs of His slaves, nor is it befitting the true spirit of humility in which the Muslim is supposed to approach his *Rabb*. Nor is it fitting to suggest that Allah (swt) treats His slaves in such a fickle manner, acceding to some requests, while rejecting others on a whim – Allah (swt), Most High, is far above that. In fact He has informed us that he answers the supplication of everyone who asks Him:

> " *And when My slaves ask you about Me, I am indeed near: I answer the supplication of the suppliant when he asks Me"* (Qur'an 2:185).

Then He (swt), Most Glorified, Most High, commands us that when we ask Him, we should do so imploringly, beseechingly, whether the request is big or small since no request is difficult for Him, Most High, to grant, for He (swt) is the Owner of all things in the heavens and the earth, the absolute Disposer of all affairs therein and He (swt) is Able to do all things.

Benefits Derived From This Hadith

1. The prohibition of saying: "...if You will," when supplicating Allah (swt).

2. The lawfulness of supplication and confirmation of its effectiveness.

3. Confirmation of Allah's Completeness and Perfection.

4. That imploring Allah (swt) firmly, rather than timidly and apologetically, is to think well of Him, Most Glorified, Most High.

5. Allah's freedom from all imperfection.

Relevance of This Hadith to the Subject of the Chapter

That the Hadith proves the prohibition of saying: "...if You will," when making supplication to Allah (swt).

Relevance of This Hadith to the Subject of *Tawheed*

That it proves that it is forbidden to say: "...if You will," when supplicating Allah (swt), as this suggests some lack or imperfection in Allah (swt), as if He might answer us or not according to His whim, and such an idea is incompatible with correct *Tawheed*.

Footnotes

1. Narrated by Bukhari.

Top | Prev | Next

Kitaab At-Tawheed, Chapter: 52

One Should Not Say: "My Slave," or: "My Slave-girl)

It is authentically reported on the authority of Abu Hurairah (ra) that the Messenger of Allah (saas)
said: "None of you should say: "Feed your *Rabb*," or: "Help your *Rabb* in performing ablution," but
instead he should say: "My master," or: "My guardian," and none should say: "My slave," or: "My slave-
girl," but instead he should say: "My lad," or: "My lass," or: "My boy." [1]

Because Rabbship and worship necessitate glorification - and none should be glorified but Allah (swt),
Almighty All-powerful - the Messenger of Allah (saas) forbade referring to a slave-owner as *Rabb* or to
a bonded slave as *`abd*, [2] since this suggests some kind of partnership with Allah (swt), when in fact,
we are all His slaves and He is the only *Rabb*. Then the Prophet (saas) guided us to that which is better
and does not connote Rabbship of the slave-owner or worship on behalf of the slave, which is to say:
"My lad," or: "My lass," or: "My boy." This is better and safer for those whom Allah (swt) has tested
with the responsibility of slave-ownership or the burden of being a slave.

Benefits Derived From This Hadith

1. The obligation to block all roads to *Shirk*.

2. That *Ar-Rabb* is one of Allah's Names which it is forbidden to ascribe to any other unless
it is linked with something without sense, such as: *Rabbul Bait* (Owner of the House) or
Rabbud-Daabbah (Owner of the beast).

3. The forbiddance of calling the slave *`abd* or the slave-girl *amah*.

4. The permissibility of referring to the slave-owner as master or protector.

Relevance of This Hadith to the Subject of the Chapter

That it prohibits calling the slave *`abd* and the slave-girl *amah*.

Relevance of This Hadith to the Subject of *Tawheed*

That the Hadith forbids calling the slave *`abd* and the slave-girl *amah*, because this is *Shirk* in matters of
worship.

Important Note

(a) There are those who have claimed that it is permissible to call the slave-owner *Rabb* and
that there is no restriction on this; as proof, they have cited the Words of Allah (swt), Most
High:

" *Mention me to your lord"* (Qur'an 12:42)

And the words of the Messenger of Allah (swt): "...and the *amah* will give birth to her *rabbah*." The answer to these claims is that in the Qur'anic verse, the reference is to a time before the Messengership of Muhammad (saas), when such terminology had not been forbidden. As for the above-mentioned Hadith, what is mentioned here is *rabbah*, which is the feminine form of the word *rabb*, and as such, does not connote Rabbship; rather, the word would mean mistress or lady.

(b) In this Hadith, the Prophet (saas) has permitted reference to a slave-owner as *mawlaa*, while in another Hadith, he has forbidden it. It may be that the way to understand both of these Hadith without refering any contradiction, is to say that, while it is permissible to do so, it is preferable not to; this would be particularly so in the case of those people who refer to their scholars or sheikhs as *Mawlaanaa* (our Protector) - for Allah has so described Himself in Qur'an *Al-Baqarah*, where He tells us to address Him thus:

" *You are Mawlaanaa [our Protector] so give us victory over the disbelievers"* (Qur'an 2:285)

Footnotes

1. Narrated by Muslim.

2. While it is true that the word 'abd means slave, it also connotes worship and submission, thus it is not permissible to say, e.g.: "'Abd Ahmad," meaning the bonded slave of Ahmad. Thus, Allah (swt) refers to His slaves in the Qur'an as 'Ibadullah (the slaves of Allah swt).

Top | Prev | Next

Kitaab At-Tawheed, Chapter: 53

Whoever Asks in the Name of Allah Should Not Be Refused

It is reported on the authority of Ibn `Umar (ra) that he said: "Allah's Messenger (saas) said:

> *"Whoever asks for something in Allah's Name, give it to him; if anyone seeks refuge in Allah's Name, give him refuge; if anyone gives you an invitation, accept it; and if anyone does you a kindness, recompense him; but if you have not the wherewithal to do so, pray for him until you feel that you have recompensed him."* (Narrated by Abu Dawood and An-Nasaa`i, who graded it as authentic)

The Prophet (saas) commands us in this Hadith to help whoever asks for assistance in Allah's Name in all that does not entail disobedience to Allah (swt) and His Messenger (saas); and to protect from evil whoever seeks protection in Allah's Name; and to accept an invitation when one is invited, so long as it does not entail anything forbidden;[1] and to respond in kind to those who do favours for us; He (saas) also said that, if we are unable to respond in kind, then we should supplicate Allah (swt) on their behalf until we feel that we have repaid them in full. If we do all of these things, the result will be to foster brotherly love, compassion, generosity and unity amongst the Muslim community and put an end to enmity, division, strife, miserliness and disunity.

Benefits Derived From This Hadith

1. The obligation to give to the one who asks in Allah's Name.

2. The obligation to defend from evil the one who seeks shelter in Allah's Name.

3. The obligation to accept a brother Muslim's invitation to a meal, a wedding celebration, birth celebration etc. so long as doing so does not involve anything forbidden.

4. The obligation to recompense those who do good to us.

Relevance of This Hadith to the Subject of the Chapter

That it proves the obligation to give to whomsoever what is asked in Allah's Name.

Relevance of This Hadith to the Subject of *Tawheed*

That it proves that it is forbidden to refuse a person in need when he asks in Allah's Name because to do so is to fail to glorify Allah (swt), as is His right upon us, and this conflicts with correct *Tawheed*.

Footnotes

1. For example, were one to be invited to a gathering where, drinking of alcoholic beverages, playing of music, smoking, playing of games of chance etc. were taking place, it would not be obligatory to attend; rather, it would be obligatory to decline the invitation.

Kitaab At-Tawheed, Chapter: 54

Nothing But Paradise Should Be Asked For by Allah's Countenance

Allah (swt), says:

> " *After distress, He sent down calm on a group of you overcome with slumber, while another group was stirred to anxiety by their own feelings, moved by wrong thoughts about Allah - thoughts which belonged to the Jahiliyyah: They said: "Is this matter anything to do with us?" Say to them: "Verily, the matter is for Allah." They hide within themselves what they would never reveal to you: They say: "If the matter had been left to us, none of us would have been killed here." Say: "Even if you had remained in your homes, those for whom death was written would have gone forth to their deaths." But [all this was] that Allah might test what is in your hearts and purge what is in your hearts, for Allah knows well the secrets of your hearts"* (Qur'an 3:154)

Allah (swt), Most Glorified, Most High, informs us in this verse about the Believers upon whom He (swt) sent the blessing of slumber after they had been distressed and worried, in order that they might be invigorated and refreshed. Then He (swt), Most High, tells us that among them were a number of hypocrites who did not share their faith and whose sole concern was for their own safety. This is why they asked of the Prophet (saas) in tones of criticism and rebuke why they should risk their lives in that battle. But Allah (swt) commanded the Prophet (saas) to inform them that the matter was for Allah (swt) to decide, not for him, but that Allah (swt) aids whom He wills.

Finally, Allah (swt) reveals their hypocrisy, saying that their faith in His Promise and that of His Messenger (saas) was not genuine, for were it so, they would not have feared to go out and fight and they would have realized that if death is written for someone, he cannot avoid it, no matter whether he go forth in battle or stay at home, and that all of this was no more than a test of their faith and sincerity to reveal their true nature.

Benefits Derived From This Verse

1. That good and evil are ordained by Allah, Almighty, All-powerful.

2. That adversity often reveals a person's true nature.

3. That rejection of Allah's *Qadr* is a sign of hypocrisy in belief.

4. That taking precautions against any eventuality will not prevent what Allah has decreed from taking place.

5. Confirmation of Allah's Divine Attribute of possessing a Face.

Relevance of This Verse to the Subject of the Chapter

That it proves that it is forbidden to reject Allah's *Qadr*.

Relevance of This Verse to the Subject of *Tawheed*

That the verse proves the obligation to submit to Allah's *Qadr*, because this is true *Tawheed*.

..ooOOoo..

Allah (swt), says:

> " *Those who said about their brethren, while they, themselves sat at home: "If only they had obeyed us, they would not have been killed." Say: "Avert death from your ownselves, if you speak the truth!""* (Qur'an 3:168)

Allah (swt), Most High, informs us in this verse about what took place in a heated debate between the Believers who had fought valiantly in Allah's cause, and the hypocrites, who had stayed away from the battle and sat at home: The hypocrites belittled the sacrifice made by the Believers who had died on the battlefield of Uhud due to the express command of the Prophet (saas) being ignored, saying that if only they had followed the example of the hypocrites and stayed at home, they would now be alive. But Allah (swt), Most High, in response, challenged them that if they spoke the truth, then let them save themselves from death, for no warning can avert what Allah (swt) has ordained.

Benefits Derived From This Verse

1. The lawfulness of struggle (*jihaad*) in Allah's cause.

2. The danger of the hypocrites to the Muslim *Ummah*.

3. That warnings can not avert Allah's *Qadr*.

Relevance of This Verse to the Subject of the Chapter

That the verse proves the prohibition of rejecting Allah's *Qadr*.

Relevance of This Verse to the Subject of *Tawheed*

That it proves the obligation to accept Allah's *Qadr*, for this is an essential part of *Tawheed*.

..ooOOoo..

It is authentically reported on the authority of Abu Hurairah (swt) that the Messenger of Allah (saas) said: "Seek what benefits you, and seek help only from Allah (swt) and do not lose heart. If any adversity comes to you, do not say: "If I had only acted in such-and-such a way, it would have been such-and-such;" but instead, say: "Allah (swt) has decreed (it) and what He willed, He has done," for verily, (the word) (if) opens the way for the work of Satan." [1]

Because Islam calls mankind to that which leads to success, prosperity and betterment of society, Allah's Messenger (saas) commanded the Muslims to take part in *jihad* in Allah's cause; and in order that they might attain the aforementioned blessings - in this life and the Hereafter – he ordered them to accept calamities - which are all from Allah's *Qadr* - with equanimity, and not to become depressed or open the door to regret or blame by saying: "If only I had done such-and-such a thing, I might have avoided this outcome;" for to do so will lead to anger and despair, and these are the works of the devil. Instead he guided them to that which is better and more worthy, which is to say: "Allah (swt) has decreed (it) and what He willed He (swt) has done."

Benefits Derived From This Hadith

1. That undertaking the necessary precautions in order to achieve one's objectives does not conflict with *Tawheed*.

2. That man has a measure of free will and is not driven helplessly by events.

3. That despair conflicts with seeking help from Allah (swt).

4. The forbiddance of seeking help from other than Allah (swt) in those matters over which they have no control.

5. That Islam encourages the Muslim to work and be productive.

6. The prohibition of rejecting Allah's *Qadr*.

7. That good and evil are ordained by Allah (swt).

8. Confirmation of Allah's Divine Attribute of Will in a manner befitting His Majesty.

9. Confirmation of Allah's Divine Attribute of Action.

10. That belief in Allah's *Qadr* is a cure for what ails the heart and leads to mental peace and stability.

Relevance of This Hadith to the Subject of the Chapter

That the Hadith proves the forbiddance of rejecting Allah's *Qadr*.

Relevance of This Hadith to the Subject of *Tawheed*

That the Hadith proves the obligation to accept and submit to Allah's *Qadr* because this is an essential part of *Tawheed*.

Footnotes

1. Narrated by Muslim.

Top | Prev | Next

Kitaab At-Tawheed, Chapter: 55

The Prohibition of Maligning the Wind

On the authority of Ubayy Ibn Ka'ab (ra) it is reported that Allah's Messenger (saas) said:

> *"Do not malign the wind; if you see that which displeases you, say: "Oh, Allah (swt)! We ask of You the good of this wind and the good that it is commanded to bring with it; and we seek refuge with You from the evil of this wind and the evil that it is commanded to bring with it."* (Narrated by At-Tirmizi, who graded it authentic)

Because Islam has ordered us to be of good character and good manners, the Messenger of Allah (saas) forbade the Muslims from maligning or cursing the wind; this is because the wind is one of Allah's creations: It does not blow or remain still, or harm or benefit except by Allah's Command therefore vilifying it amounts to vilifying Him Who sent it. Then Allah's Messenger (saas) informs us that the wind may bear good or ill and that it is incumbent upon the Believer to ask Allah (swt), Most High, for the good and to seek protection with Him from the evil.

Benefits Derived From This Hadith

1. The prohibition of maligning the wind.

2. The virtue of using the above-mentioned supplication when one sees anything disliked brought by the wind.

3. The lawfulness of supplication and its benefit.

Relevance of This Hadith to the Subject of the Chapter

That it proves the forbiddance of maligning the wind.

Relevance of This Hadith to the Subject of *Tawheed*

That it proves that it is prohibited to curse or vilify the wind because doing so amounts to maligning Him Who sent it and this conflicts with correct *Tawheed*.

Kitaab At-Tawheed, Chapter: 56

Allah's Words: " [They Were] Moved by Wrong Thoughts About Allah - Thoughts Which Belonged to the Jahiliyyah"

Allah (swt), says:

> " *[They were] moved by wrong thoughts about Allah - thoughts which belonged to the Jahiliyyah: They said: "Is the matter anything to do with us?" Say to them: "Verily, the matter is for Allah." They hide within themselves what they would never reveal to you: They say: "If the matter had been left with us, none of us would have been killed here." Say: "Even if you had remained in your homes, those for whom death was written would have gone forth to their deaths." But [all this was] that Allah might test what is in your hearts and purge what is in your hearts, for Allah knows well the secrets of your hearts"* (Qur'an 3:154)

Relevance of This Verse to the Subject of the Chapter

That the verse proves the forbiddance of thinking ill of Allah (swt).

Relevance of This Verse to the Subject of *Tawheed*

That it proves the obligation to think well of Allah (swt) for this is an essential aspect of *Tawheed*.

..ooOOoo..

Allah (swt), says:

> " *And that He may punish the hypocrites, men and women, and the polytheists, men and women, who think evil of Allah: On them is a round of evil: The Wrath of Allah is on them: He has cursed them and prepared for them the Hell-fire: And an evil destination is it"* (Qur'an 48:6)

In this verse, Allah (swt), Most High, informs us that the disbelievers from among the hypocrites and the polytheists hold false beliefs concerning Allah (swt), and they wish for the Believers defeat and destruction, but Allah (swt) will defeat their nefarious plotting and He promises them two punishments: One in this world, when their hearts will be crushed at the ultimate success of the Muslims over the disbelievers, and another in the Hereafter, when Allah's mighty Wrath will overtake them: They will receive no mercy from Him and they will be plunged into the Hell-fire to dwell therein for eternity.

Benefits Derived From This Verse

1. That the hypocrites are the greatest danger to the Muslim *Ummah*.

2. The forbiddance of thinking ill of Allah.

3. That the Qur'an customarily mentions males before females.

4. That thinking ill of Allah is a sign of hypocrisy.

5. Confirmation of Allah's Divine Attribute of Anger in a manner befitting His Majesty.

6. The general permissibility of cursing the disbelievers.

7. Confirmation of the existence of the Hell-fire.

Relevance of This Verse to the Subject of the Chapter

That it proves the forbiddance of thinking ill of Allah (swt).

Relevance of This Verse to the Subject of *Tawheed*

That the verse proves the obligation to think well of Allah (swt), because this is an essential aspect of *tawheed*.

Ibn Al-Qayyim said, concerning the first verse: "The explanation of this thought (of the unbelievers) is that they believed that Allah (swt) would not help His Messenger (saas) and that his affair (i.e. *Islam*) will be forgotten. It is also explained as meaning that the afflictions which befell him were not from Allah's *Qadr* and His Wisdom. It is therefore explained as a denial of Allah's *Qadr* and His Wisdom and denial that the matter (i.e. Message) of His Messenger (saas) would be completed and that it would prevail over all religions. These were the evil thoughts of the hypocrites and the polytheists as mentioned in Qur'an *Al-Fath* - and they are only that: evil thoughts. Any person who believes that falsehood will prevail over Truth (i.e. Islamic Monotheism) continuously, and that it will cause Truth to disappear, or who denies that things occur in accordance with Allah's *Qadr* and His Decision, or denies the overriding wisdom behind His *Qadr*, which is deserving of all praise, and thinks that it is due to an aimless, purposeless will: These are the thoughts of those who disbelieve. Woe to those who disbelieve in the Hell-fire - and most of them think ill of Allah (swt), when it concerns that which affects them in particular and what He does to others, and none is saved from such evil thoughts except those who truly know Allah (swt) and His Divine Names and Attributes and understand the necessity of His Wisdom and of praising Him. Let the wise recipient of good counsel look at himself closely in this matter and repent to Allah (swt) and ask His Forgiveness for having thought ill of his *Rabb*. And if you were to examine such individuals, you would see each of them in distress and anger with what Allah (swt) has decreed, blaming and finding fault in it and thinking that it should have been such-and-such. In this, some are more guilty than others. Examine yourself: Are you free from such thoughts? If you are saved from it, you have been saved from a great calamity, but if you are not, I cannot regard you as saved."

Top | Prev | Next

Kitaab At-Tawheed, Chapter: 57

What Has Been Said About Those Who Deny Allah's Qadr

Ibn `Umar (ra ) said: "By Him in Whose Hand is the soul of Ibn `Umar, if anyone possessed gold as much as the mountain of Uhud and spent it in Allah's cause, Allah (swt) would not accept it from him unless he believed in Allah's *Qadr*." Then he (saas) cited as evidence the words of the Prophet (saas): "*Eemaan* (faith) is to believe in (i) Allah (swt), (ii) His angels, (iii) His revealed Books, (iv) His Messengers, (v) the Day of Resurrection and (vi) *Al-Qadr*, both the good and bad of it."

In this narration, `Abdullah Ibn `Umar (ra) swears by Allah, that no matter how much wealth a person may spend in Allah's cause, no matter how many righteous deeds he may perform, it will benefit him nothing and Allah (swt) will not accept it from him if he does not believe in Allah's *Qadr*; this is because belief in, it is one of the six pillars of faith as expounded by the Messenger of Allah (saas) in a well known authentic Hadith, known as the Hadith of Jibreel (as) in which he visited the Prophet (saas) in human form in front of a number of the Companions and questioned him about *Islam* in order to teach the Muslims their faith. This Hadith, Ibn `Umar (ra) cited as proof for what he had said concerning the obligation of belief in Allah's *Qadr*.

Benefits Derived From This Narration

1. That faith consists of six pillars without all of which, faith is invalid.

2. That good and evil are by Allah's Decree (*Qadr*) and His Decision (*Qadhaa`*).

3. The permissibility of swearing to something which is beneficial to the community.

4. The virtue of confirming the truth of important juristic rulings by swearing to them.

Relevance of This Narration to the Subject of the Chapter

That it proves that those who reject Allah's *Qadr* are disbelievers.

Relevance of This Narration to the Subject of *Tawheed*

That it proves that whoever rejects Allah's *Qadr* is a disbeliever, because denial of *Al-Qadr* is a form of *Shirk* in Rabbship.

Important Note

(a) *Al-Qadr* consists of four levels: (i) Allah's Knowledge of events before they take place; (ii) His having written them before the creation of all things; (iii) His irresistable Will, which none in creation can evade, nor can they evade His Deeds (iv) His creation of all things, in which He has no partners - and all besides Him is created.

(b) The Prophet (saas) said, in the above-mentioned Hadith that faith is to believe in His *Qadr*, both the good and the bad of it, while in another Hadith, he said: "...and evil is not from You." There is no contradiction here, for what is meant by the latter Hadith is that, while Allah (swt) created evil and ordained it, He does not do evil. It may be said that when Allah (swt) ordains evil for a person, it is only evil from the point of view of that person, for it is an affliction sent to him because of some sins he has committed; however, in Allah's Sight, it is not an evil, for it represents Allah's Wisdom, Justice and Knowledge.

..ooOOoo..

It is reported on the authority of `Ubadah Ibn As-Samit (ra) that he said to his son: "Oh, son! You will never taste true faith until you know that whatever afflicts you would not have missed you, and whatever has missed you would never have come to you. I heard the Messenger of Allah (saas) say: "The first thing Allah (swt) created was the pen; He commanded it to write. It said: "My *Rabb*! What shall I write?" He said: "Write down what has been ordained for all things until the establishment of the Hour." Oh, my son! I heard Allah's Messenger (saas) say: "Whoever dies believing something other than this does not belong to me." In another narration by Imam Ahmad, it was reported: "Verily, the first thing which Allah (swt), Most High, created was the pen, and He said to it: "Write;" and in that very hour all what was to occur (was written) up to the Day of Resurrection." In another version from Ibn Wahab, it was said: "Allah's Messenger (saas) said: "Whoever disbelieved in *Al-Qadr*, the good and the bad of it, will be burnt in the Hell-fire."

In this Hadith, `Ubadah Ibn As-Samit (ra ) advised his son that faith has a taste and that none shall savour it except one who believes in Allah's *Qadhaa`* (Decision) and His *Qadr*, the good and the bad of it. As proof, he cited the Hadith of the Prophet (saas) in which he informed us that Allah commanded the pen to write the destiny of all things up to the Day of Resurrection and that whoever died without believing in Allah's *Qadaa`* and His *Qadr* would be outside the fold of *Islam* and that his eternal abode would be the Hell-fire where he would burn forever - a wretched end.

Benefits Derived From This Hadith

1. The lawfulness of a father advising and teaching his sons.

2. The precise understanding of the Companions of matters pertaining to Allah's *Qadr* and their faith in it.

3. That the first of all created things was the pen.

4. Confirmation of Allah's Divine Attribute of Speech, in a manner befitting His Majesty.

5. That whoever rejected Allah's *Qadr* is a disbeliever.

6. That it is the last acts in a person's life which are important.

7. Confirmation of Allah's Promise of punishment for those who deny His *Qadr*.

Relevance of This Hadith to the Subject of the Chapter

That the Hadith proves that whoever rejected Allah's *Qadr* is a disbeliever.

Relevance of This Hadith to the Subject of *Tawheed*

That the Hadith proves that whoever denied Allah's Qadr is a disbeliever because this is *Shirk* in

Rabbship.

Important Note

Which was created first, the Throne or the pen? It has been said that it was the Throne by some and by others it was said the pen. Those who said the pen cited as proof the above Hadith, understanding the word `pen' to be the object of the verb `created,' while those who said that the Throne was created first cited as evidence a number of authentic Ahadith which support this view. The latter group would therefore understand the first Hadith to say: "Verily, directly after creating the pen, Allah (swt) commanded it to write..."

..ooOOoo..

In Imam Ahmad's *Musnad* and in the *Sunan* of Abu Dawood, it is reported that Ibn Ad-Dailami said: "I went to Ubayy Ibn Ka'ab and said to him: "There is some doubt within me concerning *Al-Qadr*; please tell me of something by which Allah (swt) might take it (the doubt) from my heart." He said: "Even were you to spend gold equivalent in weight to the mountain of Uhud, Allah (swt) would not accept it from you until you believe in *Al-Qadr*. And know that what has afflicted you could not be avoided and what did not come to you could never be attained; and if you die believing other than this, then you are one of the people of the Hell-fire."

I then went to `Abdullah Ibn Mas'ood, Huzaifah Ibn Al-Yaman, Zaid Ibn Thaabit (ra) and all of them told me something similar from the Prophet (saas)." (Narrated by Al-Hakim, who graded it authentic)

Ibn Ad-Dailami informs us in this narration that he was afflicted by doubts concerning Allah's *Qadr*, and so he went to Ubayy Ibn Ka'ab (ra) to seek counsel and guidance from him in the hope that he might teach him something which would assuage his doubts. Ubayy (ra) then narrated to him a Hadith of the Prophet (saas) which explained in simple terms what belief in Allah's *Qadr* entails: That whatever was written for us will happen and whatever was not written will never happen and that whoever disbelieves in *Al-Qadr* is a disbeliever in Allah (swt) who will never taste the fruits of success, even if he were to perform innumerable good deeds. Then, in order to make assurance doubly sure, Ibn Ad-Dailami went to a number of other Companions and asked them the same question, only to receive a similar answer from all of them.

Benefits Derived From This Narration

1. The obligation to seek guidance from the people of knowledge in matters of which one is ignorant.

2. The breadth of the Companions' knowledge and understanding of Islamic beliefs and jurisprudence.

3. That those who deny *Al-Qadr* are disbelievers.

4. That the most important deeds are those performed before a person dies.

Relevance of This Narration to the Subject of the Chapter

That it proves that whoever denied *Al-Qadr* is a disbeliever.

Relevance of This Narration to the Subject of *Tawheed*

That it proves that whoever rejected Allah's *Qadr* is guilty of disbelief because this constitutes *Shirk* in Rabbship.

Top | Prev | Next

Kitaab At-Tawheed, Chapter: 58

What Has Been Said About Those Who Make
Pictures (of Living Things)

On the authority of Abu Hurairah (ra) it is reported that the Messenger of Allah (saas) said:

"Allah (swt), Most High said: "And who is more unjust than those who try to create the
likeness of My creation? Let them create an atom, or let them create a wheat grain, or let
them create a barley grain." (Narrated by Bukhari and Muslim)

Allah (swt), Most High, informs us in this Hadith *Qudsi*, through the mouth of His Prophet, Muhammad
(saas), that there is none more unjust than those people who make pictures of living things, wishing to
resemble Allah (swt) in His act of Creation. Then He (swt), Almighty, All-powerful, challenges such
people to create even the smallest and most insignificant of His visible, living creations, which is an
atom, or to create the simplest of plant materials, such as a grain of wheat or a grain of barley; this He
(swt), Most High, does, in order to expose their weakness and inability.

Benefits Derived From This Hadith

1. The forbiddance of making drawings, paintings or carvings of any living things.

2. The lack of proper regard and respect for Allah (swt) of those who depict living things.

3. *The Power of Allah (swt) and His Ability to create what He Wills.*

4. The weakness and incapacity of those other than Him to create even the simplest of
things from nothing.

Relevance of This Hadith to the Subject of the Chapter

That it proves that depicting living things is forbidden.

Relevance of This Hadith to the Subject of *Tawheed*

That the Hadith forbids making pictures of living things because this is an attempt to imitate Allah (swt)
in His act of Creation, which is *Shirk* in Rabbship.

..ooOOoo..

On the authority of `A`ishah (may Allah be pleased with her) it is reported that the Messenger of Allah
(saas) said:

"The most severely punished of people on the Day of Resurrection will be those who try to
make the like of Allah's creation." (Narrated by Bukhari and Muslim)

The Prophet (saas) informs us in this Hadith that those who depict living creatures in their drawings,
paintings and carvings, attempting to imitate Allah (swt) in His act of Creation, will face the most

severe chastisement on the Day of Judgement for they are the worst of people in respect to Allah (swt) and the most wicked in committing evil - this is why they are most deserving of Allah's Wrath and His punishment.

Benefits Derived From This Hadith

1. The strictness of the forbiddance of making pictures of living creatures.

2. Evidence of the reason for the prohibition of depicting living things.

3. That punishment on the Day of Resurrection is in proportion to one's sins.

Relevance of This Hadith to the Subject of the Chapter

That the Hadith proves the forbiddance of making pictures of living things.

Relevance of This Hadith to the Subject of *Tawheed*

That it forbids the depiction of living creatures because this is an attempt to imitate Allah (swt) in His act of Creation and this is *Shirk* in Rabbship.

Important Note

He who makes pictures of living creatures will receive the severest punishment on the Day of Judgement if he did so in order to have that image worshipped because in so doing, he is guilty of *kufr*, while if he intends by it to imitate Allah (swt), he is also guilty of disbelief.

..ooOOoo..

On the authority of Ibn `Abbas (ra) it is reported that he heard the Messenger of Allah (saas) say:

"Every picture maker is in the Fire. A soul will be placed in every picture made by him and it will punish him in the Hell-fire." (Narrated by Bukhari and Muslim)

Because the picture makers are the wickedest of people in respect to Allah (swt), and the worst of them in performing deeds which Allah (swt) forbidden, the Prophet (saas) informed us in this Hadith that whoever made a picture of a living creature in this life, Allah (swt) will breathe life into it on the Day of Resurrection after which that image will punish him in the Fire and this is the recompense for his evil deeds. Therefore, it behoves every picture maker to fear Allah (swt), the Almighty, the All-powerful and to abandon his evil employment; and if he does that, Allah (swt) will reward him, for whoever abandoned something for Allah's sake will be rewarded with something better by Him, Most High.

Benefits Derived From This Hadith

1. The forbiddance of making pictures of living creatures.

2. The permissibility of making pictures of things which do not possess a soul.

3. That reward is in accordance with one's deeds.

4. That the remuneration which the picture maker receives for his work is forbidden because when an action is prohibited, so too is profiting from it.

Relevance of This Hadith to the Subject of the Chapter

That the Hadith proves that it is forbidden to make pictures of living creatures.

Relevance of This Hadith to the Subject of *Tawheed*

That it prohibits making pictures of living things, because doing so constitutes an attempt to imitate Allah (swt) in His action of Creation and this is *Shirk* in Rabbship.

..ooOOoo..

It is reported in a *marfoo'* form, on the authority of Ibn `Abbas (ra): "Whoever made pictures in this life, will be charged with breathing life into it and he will not be able to do so." (Narrated by Bukhari and Muslim)

The Prophet (saas) informs us in this Hadith that whoever made pictures of creatures possessing a soul in this life, will be charged on the Day of Judgement with breathing life into them; and Allah (swt) knows that he will not be able to do so, but He will charge him thus in order to make clear to him his own powerlessness and weakness and to reproach him for his sin.

1. The forbiddance of depicting living creatures.

2. The permissibility of making pictures of things without a soul.

3. That reward is in accordance with one's deeds.

Relevance of This Hadith to the Subject of the Chapter

That it proves that it is forbidden to make pictures of living creatures.

Relevance of This Hadith to the Subject of *Tawheed*

That it prohibits making pictures of living things because doing so is an attempt to imitate Allah (swt) in His action of Creation and this is *Shirk* in Rabbship.

..ooOOoo..

On the authority of Abul Hayaaj Al-Asadi, it is reported that `Ali (ra) said to him: "Shall I not send you on a mission on which I was sent by Allah's Messenger (saas)?

> *"Do not leave any image without erasing it, nor any elevated grave without leveling it to the ground."* (Narrated by Muslim)

Because *Islam* is careful to block all roads to *Shirk*, whether apparent or hidden, `Ali Ibn Abi Talib (ra) informs us that the Messenger of Allah (saas) charged him with the task of effacing all of the pictures of living things which he might find and with leveling all of those graves which had edifices or grave stones over them. This he did in order to protect the Muslims' beliefs from the evils of worship of graven images and adoration of graves, because making pictures of living creatures and building over graves leads to their glorification and reverence and attributing to them that, which they do not deserve - that which is for Allah (swt), Alone; and anyone who has travelled throughout the Muslim world will have found such things in profusion - things which make one with correct beliefs shudder and sadden his heart: Circumambulation of graves in the manner in which the pilgrims circumambulate the Ka'abah, in Makkah; animals sacrificed to the graves' inhabitants instead of their being slaughtered in Allah's Name, supplication of the graves' inhabitants and many other acts of *Shirk* and innovation unknown to the Messenger of Allah (saas), his Companions or the pious generations who came after them.

Benefits Derived From This Narration

1. The obligation to reject that which is detestable.

2. That making images of living creatures is forbidden.

3. That building over graves is forbidden.

Relevance of This Narration to the Subject of the Chapter

That it proves that making pictures of living things is prohibited.

Relevance of This Narration to the Subject of *Tawheed*

That it prohibits the making of images of living creatures because doing so amounts to attempting to imitate Allah (swt) in His action of Creation and this is *Shirk* in Rabbship.

Important Note

This forbiddance of making pictures includes all living creatures which possess a soul. It is pure fancy to imagine that by putting a line across the neck of the image, or obliterating its features, it becomes permissible.

Top | Prev | Next

Kitaab At-Tawheed, Chapter: 59

What Has Been Said About Frequent Swearing

Allah (swt), says:

> " *Allah will not call you to account for what is futile in your oaths, but He will call you to account for your deliberate oaths: For expiation feed ten indigent persons what would be average food for your families; or clothe them; or give a slave his freedom. And whoever did not find [the means for that, let him] fast for three days. That is the expiation for the oaths you have sworn. But keep to your oaths. Thus does Allah make clear to you His Signs, that you may be grateful"* (Qur'an 5:89)

Allah (swt), Most High, informs us in this verse that He (swt) Will not hold accountable those who make unthinking oaths, only those who swear positively, knowingly. He also tells us that the atonement for one who swears falsely, which is to feed ten poor persons, without extravagance and without niggardliness, or to clothe them, or to free a believing slave, but that whoever does not find himself able to do any of these things must fast for three consecutive days. Allah (swt) has made this expiation as a solution for us, should we fall into error by making a false oath. Then Allah (swt), Most High, commands the Muslims to keep to their oaths and not to make them excessively in order that they not swear falsely and be thus disgraced before their *Rabb.* Then Allah (swt) informs us that what He has made plain of His Judgements are Blessings from Him, Almighty, All-powerful, for which we should be grateful. Thus does Islam, by Allah's Grace and Mercy make things easy for us and provide a way out for us from the problems which we sometimes make for ourselves. And Allah (swt) called us and encouraged us to free the slaves more than fourteen centuries ago - long before the West awoke from its ignorance and claimed the initiative for the abolition of slavery for themselves.

Benefits Derived From This Verse

1. Evidence of the tolerance and forebearance of Islam.

2. That there is no sin and no expiation for unmindful oaths.

3. The forbiddance of deliberately making vain, false oaths.

4. The obligation to make expiation for swearing a false oath.

5. That Islam had taken the initiative in the abolition of slavery before any other nation.

6. The forbiddance of excessive swearing.

7. The obligation to preserve one's oaths from lying.

Relevance of This Verse to the Subject of the Chapter

That it proves the prohibition of excessive swearing.

Relevance of This Verse to the Subject of *Tawheed*

That the verse proves the forbiddance of excessive swearing because doing so diminishes the glorification which is Allah's right and is an imperfection in *Tawheed*.

..ooOOoo..

It is reported on the authority of Abu Hurairah (ra) that he said: "I heard Allah's Messenger (saas) saying:

> *"Swearing may benefit (the sale of) commodities, but it will erase the reward (in the Hereafter)."* (Narrated by Bukhari and Muslim)

The Prophet (saas) informs us in this Hadith that when a seller swears falsely as to the worth of his goods, he may attain some temporary benefit from it, but in the long term he will not gain by it, for he will lose the reward of it in the Hereafter and loss will come to him from other directions: He might lose his capital and his profits might dwindle to nothing, for Allah (swt) does not allow people to profit from disobedience to Him although He may delay their recompense. And in the end there awaits the disobedient ones loss and punishment in the Hereafter.

Benefits Derived From This Hadith

    1. The forbiddance of excessive swearing.

    2. The forbiddance of selling goods by means of swearing.

    3. That lying in order to achieve a sale will result in loss in the Hereafter.

Relevance of This Hadith to the Subject of the Chapter

That the Hadith proves the forbiddance of excessive swearing without adequate reason.

Relevance of This Hadith to the Subject of *Tawheed*

That it forbids excessive swearing because doing so diminishes the glorification which is Allah's right and is an imperfection in *Tawheed*.

..ooOOoo..

On the authority of Salman (ra), it is reported that the Messenger of Allah (saas) said:

> *"There are three types of people to whom Allah (swt) will not speak and neither will he bless them and for them is a severe torment. They are: (i) The white-haired old adulterer; (ii) the arrogant beggar; and (iii) the one who makes Allah (swt) as his merchandise: He does not purchase except by swearing (by Allah swt) and he does not sell except by swearing (by Allah swt)."* (Narrated by At-Tabarani, with an authentic *Sanad*)

The Prophet (saas) informs us in this Hadith that there are three categories of people to whom Allah (swt) will not speak on the Day of Resurrection nor will He cleanse them of their sins with forgiveness - this is because they committed sins without any excuse or justification; and the first of these three is the fornicator and adulterer who continues to sin in spite of his advanced years and consequent lessening of sexual urge, and his knowledge that the end of his life is near. The second is the man who behaves arrogantly towards people, though he possesses none of the wealth, rank or privilege which often leads men to behave thus. The third is one who treats Allah's Name with impropriety, frequently swearing by Him, Most High, without cause or valid excuse.[1]

Benefits Derived From This Hadith

1. Confirmation of Allah's Divine Attribute of *Kalaam* (Speaking) in a manner befitting His Majesty.

2. Evidence that Allah will speak to the obedient ones.

3. The forbiddance of adultery, pride and excessive swearing of oaths.

Relevance of This Hadith to the Subject of the Chapter

That it proves the forbiddance of excessive swearing without reason.

Relevance of This Hadith to the Subject of *Tawheed*

That the Hadith prohibits frequent swearing because doing so is demeaning to Allah (swt) and this conflicts with correct *Tawheed*.

..ooOOoo..

It is authentically reported on the authority of `Umran Ibn Husain (ra), that he said: "Allah's Messenger (saas) said:

> *"The best of my Ummah is my generation, then those who follow them, then those who follow them." `Umran (ra) said: "I don't know if he mentioned two generations after his, or three." "Then after you," continued the Prophet (saas), "there will come a generation who will testify without being called upon to do so and they will be treacherous and untrustworthy. They will swear oaths, but they will not fulfill them and obesity will be seen in them."* (Narrated by Muslim)

The Messenger of Allah (saas) informs us in this Hadith that the best of this community of Muslims are his Companions and the two or three generations who succeeded them due to their adherence to Islam and their correct beliefs and practices and their freedom from hypocrisy, deviation and innovation. After them, the good will decrease in this *Ummah* and evil will increase with each succeeding generation until there will be seen people who will belittle the importance of giving testimony so that they will offer it even before it is requested from them and they will betray those who place trust in them and when they swear oaths, they will not keep them and they will become so immersed in the life of this world that obesity will become common amongst them due to their excessive eating of rich foods and lack of work or exercise.

Benefits Derived From This Hadith

1. The virtue of the first three or four generations of Muslims over their descendants.

2. The forbiddance of treachery.

3. The obligation of keeping one's oaths.

4. The prohibition of becoming obsessed with the life of this world and its pleasures at the expense of the Hereafter.

Relevance of This Hadith to the Subject of the Chapter

That the Hadith proves the forbiddance of not keeping one's oaths.

Relevance of This Hadith to the Subject of *Tawheed*

That it prohibits not keeping oaths because to do so is to demean Allah (swt), in Whose Name the oath was taken and this is in conflict with correct *Tawheed*.

Important Note

There is no contradiction between this Hadith and the words of the Prophet (saas): "The best of witnesses is the one who comes forward with his testimony before he is asked about it," because this means that it is preferable for him to present his testimony without being asked in cases where there is a danger that a person may lose his rights due to any delay on the witness's part. However, in cases where the evidence is known to the person concerned, the witness should not present his testimony before being asked.

..ooOOoo..

On the authority of Ibn Mas'ood (ra) it is reported that Allah's Messenger (saas) said:

> *"The best of people are those of my generation, then those who follow them, then those who follow them, after which there will come a people whose testimonies will precede their oaths and whose oaths will precede their testimonies."* (Narrated by Bukhari and Muslim)

In this Hadith, the Prophet (saas) informs us that the best and most virtuous people of this *Ummah* are the Companions, then the first two generations after them and that after them the doors of evil will be opened and much of what He (saas) has told us has already come to pass: Apostasy, atheism, materialism and following of baseless philosophies have become common and religious matters are taken lightly by many, including the swearing of oaths and giving testimony: People rush hastily into swearing oaths and bearing witness before they are requested to do so, as if these matters are of little moment.

Benefits Derived From This Hadith

1. Evidence of the superiority of the first generations over their descendants.

2. The miracle of the Prophet's predicting events which have since transpired.

3. The forbiddance of hastening to give testimony before one is asked to do so.

4. The prohibition of swearing without cause or necessity.

Relevance of This Hadith to the Subject of the Chapter

That it proves the forbiddance of hastily swearing oaths.

Relevance of This Hadith to the Subject of *Tawheed*

That the Hadith prohibits hastening to swear oaths, because this demeans Allah (swt) and belittles His Majesty and this is in conflict with correct *Tawheed*.

..ooOOoo..

Ibraheem An-Nakha'i said: "When we were children, they used to beat us concerning oaths and testimonies."

Relevance of This Narration to the Subject of the Chapter and to the Subject of *Tawheed*

That it shows that some of the *Salaf* used to forbid their children from hastily making oaths and giving testimony so as to protect them from falling into sin.

Footnotes

1. This is the case with many Arabic speaking Muslims today: The expression Wallaahi (by Allah I) is used in almost every sentence by some!

Top | Prev | Next

Kitaab At-Tawheed, Chapter: 60

What Has Been Said About Allah's Covenant and the Covenant of His Prophet (saas)

Allah (swt), says:

> " *And fulfill the Covenant of Allah when you have entered into it, and break not your oaths after you have confirmed them: Indeed you have made Allah your surety for Allah knows all that you do"* (Qur'an16:91)

In this verse, Allah (swt), Most High, commands the Muslims to keep their promises when they promise someone because breaking one's promise is despicable and contrary to the spirit of Islam. Then Allah (swt) reinforces this by forbidding us from breaking especially those promises which we have already confirmed, informing us that those who make promises have made Him their guarantor and that He is well acquainted with all that they do and He will reward good with its like and evil with its equivalent.

Benefits Derived From This Verse

1. The obligation to keep one's promises.

2. The forbiddance of breaking promises without reason or excuse.

3. The all-encompassing nature of Allah's Knowledge.

Relevance of This Verse to the Subject of the Chapter

That the verse proves the obligation to keep one's promises.

Relevance of This Verse to the Subject of *Tawheed*

That the verse proves the forbiddance of breaking one's promise because breaking promises indicates a lack of respect for Allah (swt) and this invalidates correct *Tawheed*.

Important Note

There is no contradiction between this verse and the words of the Prophet (saas): "Whoever swore an oath then saw something better than it, he should do that which is better and make expiation for not fulfilling his oath," for the verse is a general commandment, while the Hadith provides an exception to it when there is the possibility of doing something better than it; however, it is incumbent upon the Believer in this case to perform an act of atonement for breaking his promise.

..ooOOoo..

It is reported on the authority of Buraidah (ra) that he said: "Whenever Allah's Messenger (saas) charged someone with leadership in the army or sent someone on an expedition, he would admonish him to fear Allah (swt) and be good to the Muslims who were with him: He would say: "Fight in the Name of Allah (swt) and in Allah's cause and fight those who disbelieve in Allah (swt). Do not take excessive booty and do not break treaties and do not mutilate (the enemies' dead) and do not kill children. When you meet your enemies from among the polytheists, call them to three virtues - if they respond (in a positive manner), respond them in like fashion and accept it from them and cease making war upon them: (i) Invite them to Islam and if they respond positively, accept it from them and (ii) ask them to leave their land and migrate to the land of the *Muhajirun*.[1]

Inform them that after migrating, they will be entitled to everything to which the *Muhajirun* are entitled and they will be under the same obligations as the *Muhajirun*. If they refuse to migrate, then tell them that they will have the same status as the bedouin Muslims, subject to the Commands of Allah (swt), like other Muslims, but they will not receive any share of the booty or returns of war unless they fight *jihad* with the Muslims. If they refuse to embrace Islam, then impose the *jizyah* upon them and if they agree to this, then accept it from them and cease fighting them. But if they refuse, then seek Allah's Help and fight them. When you besiege a people in their fort, and they beseech you for protection in Allah's Name and His Prophet, do not grant them the Covenant of Allah (swt) and His Prophet (saas), but grant them your covenant and that of your companions, for it is a lesser sin if the covenant of you and your companions is broken than if the Covenant of Allah (swt) and His Prophet (saas) is broken. When you besiege a fort and they request you to let them out in accordance with Allah's Command, do not let them out in accordance with His Command, but do so at your own command, for you know not whether you will be able to carry out Allah's Command with regard to them." (Narrated by Muslim)

Buraidah (ra) informs us in this Hadith that whenever the Prophet entrusted anyone with the command of an army or sent anyone in charge of a punitive expedition against the disbelievers, he would order him to adhere to a number of guidelines: (i) That he be pious and God-fearing in the treatment of his troops and treat them well; (ii) that the army must refrain from excesses, such as taking too much war booty, breaking treaties, mutilating the enemies' dead or killing non-combatants; (iii) that he must call the enemy to Islam before making war on them and that if they accept Islam, he must make peace with them and request them to migrate from the land of disbelief to the city of Madinah, where they will enjoy all the rights and obligations of the *Muhajirun*. They are under no obligation to migrate, but should they not do so, they will be treated like the nomadic desert Arabs who have embraced Islam: They will receive no share of the spoils of war, unless they join the Muslims in battle; (iv) that in the event of their refusing to accept Islam, they must pay the *jizyah*; (v) that should they refuse to pay the *jizyah*, he must seek Allah's Help and declare war on them; (vi) that should he and his troops besiege the enemy in their fort, they should not grant them Allah's Covenant and that of His Prophet (saas), but instead they should grant them their own covenant because if their covenant is broken, it will be a lesser sin than if Allah (swt) and His Prophet's Covenant were broken. Likewise, he should not allow them safe passage from the fort by Allah's Command, but by his own command and that of his troops.

Benefits Derived From This Hadith

1. The lawfulness of a Commander and of guiding him towards correct behaviour.

2. The forbiddance of excessive seizure of war booty, breaking treaties, mutilating the war dead and killing no-combatants, especially children.

3. The obligation to call the enemy to Islam before declaring war on them, if the call to Islam has not previously reached them and the preferability of doing so if they have been called to Islam previously but refused the call.

4. That if the disbelievers refuse the call of the Commander of the *Mujahideen* to Islam, he must order them to pay the *jizyah* or else fight.[2]

5. The preferability of emigrating from the land of disbelief to the land of Islam and of calling the people to that.

6. That the spoils of war are only for the *Muhaajirun* and not for the nomadic Arabs, unless they participate in *Jihad*.

7. That it is not permissible to grant a covenant in Allah's Name or that of His Prophet (saas).

8. The forbiddance of breaking treaties.

9. That not everyone who resorts to *ijtihad* [3] reaches the correct conclusion; the one who does so is he who has sufficient knowledge of *fiqh*, *tafseer*, Hadith and related Islamic subjects and uses his knowledge in accordance with the Commands of Allah (swt) and His Prophet (saas) and with the rules of *usool al-fiqh*. [4]

Relevance of This Hadith to the Subject of the Chapter

That the Hadith proves the obligation to take care of Allah's Covenant and that of His Prophet (saas) and protect it from being broken.

Relevance of This Hadith to the Subject of *Tawheed*

That the Hadith proves the obligation to take care of Allah's Covenant and that of His Prophet (saas) and to protect it from being broken because to betray Allah's Covenant is to demean Him, Most High, and this conflicts with pure Islamic *Tawheed*.

Important Note

It is obligatory for the one who embraces Islam in a land of disbelievers but is unable to declare his faith due to fear of the consequences, to migrate to a Muslim land if he is able to do so and it is preferred for those who are not in fear to do so.

Footnotes

1. The Muhaajiroon: The Muslims who fled with the Prophet (saas) from the persecution of Makkah to the sanctuary of Madinah.

2. See page .

3. Ijtihad: Islamic juristic reasoning - resorted to by qualified Muslim scholars in matters where there is no clear ruling from the Qur'an and Sunnah.

4. Usool Al-Fiqh: Fundamentals of Islamic jurisprudence; it is said that Imam Ash-Shafi'i was the first Muslim scholar to write down these fundamental rules.

Kitaab At-Tawheed, Chapter: 61

What Has Been Said About Oaths Binding Upon Allah

It is reported on the authority of Jundub (ra) that he said: "Allah's Messenger (saas) said:

> *"A man said: "By Allah (swt)! Allah (swt) will not forgive such-and-such a person, at which Allah (swt), Almighty, All-powerful said: "Who is he who swears about Me that I would not forgive so-and-so? I have pardoned him and wiped out your (the swearer's) deeds."* (Narrated by Muslim)

According to another narration on the authority of Abu Hurairah (ra) it is reported that the man who said this was a believing slave; Abu Hurairah said: "He spoke one word which destroyed his life in this world and in the Hereafter."

The Prophet (saas) informs us in this Hadith that there were two men, a righteous man and a sinful man; the former condemned the latter and swore that Allah (swt) would never forgive him his sins. Allah (swt) became angry at this statement which suggests that anyone may be barred from Allah's Mercy and Forgiveness and declared that, on the contrary, He had already forgiven the sinner and He (swt), Most High, further added that He (swt) had invalidated the deeds of the righteous man. Thus due to an injudicious word, the righteous man's deeds were made to count for nothing while the sinner was forgiven.

Benefits Derived From This Hadith

1. The forbiddance of swearing on Allah's behalf.

2. The prohibition of making assumptions about Allah (swt).

3. Confirmation of Allah's Divine Attribute of Speech in a manner befitting His Majesty.

4. The obligation to be circumspect when speaking of Allah (swt).

5. Evidence of the vastness of Allah's Bounty and Mercy.

6. That the most important deeds are the last ones in a person's life.

7. That a person might be forgiven his sins because of the words or actions of another.

8. That a person's deeds might be invalidated because of an injudicious word.

9. The forbiddance of barring anyone from Allah's Bounty and Mercy.

Relevance of This Hadith to the Subject of the Chapter

That it proves the forbiddance of swearing on Allah's behalf.

Relevance of This Hadith to the Subject of *Tawheed*

That it proves the prohibition of swearing on Allah's behalf because to do so is to claim for oneself rights in Rabbship which belong solely to Allah (swt).

Important Note

There is no contradiction between this Hadith and the words of the Prophet (saas): "Verily, among Allah's slaves are those who, when they swear upon Allah (swt), He fulfills it," because what the first Hadith tells us is that swearing on Allah's behalf in what entails thinking ill of Him is forbidden and invalidates one's good deeds, while swearing to something good and beneficial which entails thinking well of Allah (swt) is permissible.

Top | Prev | Next

Kitaab At-Tawheed, Chapter: 62

Allah May Not Be Asked to Intercede With His Creatures

It is reported on the authority of Jubair Ibn Mut'im (ra) that he said: "A bedouin Arab came to the Prophet (saas) and said: "Oh, Messenger of Allah (saas)! The people are enfeebled, families are starving and wealth has perished, so ask your *Rabb* to send us some rain and we will seek Allah's intercession upon you and yours upon Allah (swt)." The Prophet (saas) said:

> *"Subhaan Allaah! Subhaan Allaah!"* [1] *He continued to do so until the effect of it was apparent in the faces of his Companions. Then he said: "Woe to you! Do you not know Who Allah (swt) is? Allah's Sublimity is far greater than that! There is no intercession of Allah (swt) upon anyone."* (Narrated by Abu Dawood)

Jubair Ibn Mut'im (ra) informs us in this Hadith that a bedouin man came to the Prophet (saas) and complained to him of the deprivation, hunger and financial loss which they were suffering due to a prolonged drought and he requested from the Prophet (saas) that he pray to Allah (swt) to lift this affliction from them and send rain; but the method used by this bedouin man constituted a great wrong upon Allah (swt) and His Messenger (saas) - may Allah (swt) forgive him - for he sought Allah's intercession upon the Prophet (saas) and that of the Prophet (saas) upon Allah (swt)! When the Messenger of Allah (saas) heard this, he became extremely angry and rejected the bedouin's words and he began to praise Allah (swt) repeatedly, proclaiming His Exaltedness and rebuking the bedouin and informing him that Allah (swt) is Greater than to be called as an intercessor for any of His creatures because He possesses all of them and they are under His complete authority – He (swt) is not asked about what He does, but they will be asked about what they do.

Benefits Derived From This Hadith

1. The permissibilty of seeking supplication from the living.

2. The forbiddance of praying for rain from other than Allah (swt).

3. The lawfulness of supplicating Allah (swt) and confirmation of its effectiveness.

4. Proof of the harmfulness of ignorance.

5. The obligation to reject that which is detestable.

6. The obligation to proclaim Allah (swt) Exaltedness above all that is not befitting to His Majesty.

7. The forbiddance of seeking intercession from Allah (swt) with any of His creatures.

Relevance of This Hadith to the Subject of the Chapter

That the Hadith proves the forbiddance of seeking Allah's intercession with any of His creatures.

Relevance of This Hadith to the Subject of *Tawheed*

That it proves the prohibition of seeking Allah's intercession with any of His creatures because to do so is to belittle His Majesty and His Greatness and this is in conflict with correct *Tawheed*.

Footnotes

1. Subhaan Allaah!: Allah (swt) is Exalted far above any of His creation, free of any imperfection and without any need.

Top | Prev | Next

Kitaab At-Tawheed, Chapter: 63

What Has Been Said About the Prophet's Safeguarding of Tawheed and His Blocking All Paths to Shirk

It is reported on the authority of `Abdullah Ibn Ash-Shikhkheer (swt ) that he said: "I went with a delegation of Banu `Amir to the Messenger of Allah (saas) and we said (to him): "You are our *Sayyid.*"[1] He (saas) replied:

> *"As-Sayyid is Allah (swt), Most Glorified, Most High." We said: "And you are the most excellent and superior of us." He (saas) answered: "Say what you have to say, or part of what you have to say and do not let Satan make you get carried away."* (Narrated by Abu Dawood with a good *Ssanad*)

The narrator informs us in this Hadith that some of the Companions wished to show their love and respect for the Messenger of Allah (saas) by praising him while in his presence; and though they spoke the truth about him, the Prophet (saas) wished to cleanse their hearts and souls and protect their beliefs from *Shirk* and so he forbade them from praising him excessively, especially in his presence in order to protect them from all paths by which the devil might lead them to the darkness of *Shirk* after they had escaped from it. Then he (saas) permitted them to praise him in a manner allowed by their Religion, befitting his position as Allah's Slave and Messenger.

Benefits Derived From This Hadith

    1. The Prophet's great influence over the hearts and minds of the Companions.

    2. The permissibility of referring to Allah as *As-Sayyid* (the Master).

    3. That excess is an invitation to Satan.

Relevance of This Hadith to the Subject of the Chapter and to the Subject of *Tawheed*

That the Hadith forbids excessive praise of the Prophet (saas) or anyone else because this is a path that leads to *Shirk*.

Important Note

There is no contradiction between this Hadith and the Hadith which says: "I am the *Sayyid* of the sons of Adam," for this indicates the permissibility of referring to other than Allah (swt) as *Sayyid*, while the former Hadith tells us that it is preferred not to do so.

..ooOOoo..

On the authority of Anas (ra) it is reported that some people said: "Oh, Messenger of Allah (saas)! Oh, the best of us and the son of the best of us! Our Master and the son of our Master!" He (saas) replied:

> *"Oh, you people! Say what you have to say and do not allow yourselves to be seduced by Satan. I am Muhammad, the slave of Allah (swt) and His Messenger (saas). I do not like*

you to raise me above the status assigned to me by Allah (swt), Almighty All-powerful. " (Narrated by An-Nasaa`i with a good *Ssanad*)

Anas (swt) informs us in this Hadith that a number of people addressed the Prophet (saas) in terms of excessive praise and eulogy and that the Prophet (saas) rejected this, informing them that such was the temptation of the devil, that he might lead them by this means into *Shirk*. Then he informed them of the correct manner of addressing him which is to say: Muhammad, the slave and Messenger of Allah (saas); and he indicated to them his dislike of being elevated above the position which Allah (swt) has designated for him.

Benefits Derived From This Hadith

1. The high esteem in which the Companions held the Prophet (saas).

2. The forbiddance of excessively praising someone and evidence that it is one of the works of Satan.

3. Evidence of the status of the Prophet (saas) that he is a slave of Allah (swt) and His Messenger (saas).

4. The prohibition of raising the Prophet (saas) above his designated status.

Relevance of This Hadith to the Subject of the Chapter and to the Subject of *Tawheed*

That the Hadith proves the forbiddance of elevating the Prophet above his assigned status because this constitutes excess and it leads to *Shirk*.

Footnotes

1. **Sayyid: Master.**

Top | Prev | Next

Kitaab At-Tawheed, Chapter: 64

What Has Been Said About Allah's Words: " They Made Not a Just Estimate of Allah"

Allah (swt), says:

> *" No just estimate have they made of Allah, such as is due to Him: On the Day of Resurrection, the whole earth will be in His Grasp and the heavens will be rolled up in His right Hand. Glory to Him! High is He above the partners they attribute to Him"* (Qur'an 39:67)

Allah (swt), Most Glorified, Most High, informs us in this verse that the polytheists do not glorify Allah (swt) as is His right, because they worship others beside Him, when He (swt) is the Owner of everything and Able to do all things: He will hold the whole world and the heavens and the earth in His right Hand on the Day of Resurrection and He (swt) is Exalted far above that which they attribute to Him.

Benefits Derived From This Verse

1. That those who worship others beside Allah do not glorify Him as is His right upon them.

2. The obligation to glorify Allah and to abstain from attributing to Him that which does not befit His Majesty.

3. Confirmation of Allah possessing Hands in a manner befitting His Majesty.

Relevance of This Verse to the Subject of the Chapter and to the Subject of *Tawheed*

That it proves the obligation to glorify Allah (swt) as is His right which means by affirming His Oneness (Islamic Monotheism) and abstaining from *Shirk*.

..ooOOoo..

It is reported on the authority of Ibn Mas'ood (ra) that he said: "Arabbi came to Allah's Messenger (saas) and said: "Oh, Muhammad (saas)! We are told that Allah (swt) will put all the heavens on one Finger and the earths on one Finger and the trees on one Finger and the water and the dust on one Finger and all the other created beings on one Finger. Then He will say: "I am the King." Thereupon, the Prophet (saas) laughed until his molar teeth were visible and this was confirmation of the rabbi's words. Then he recited: "" *No just estimate have they made of Allaah such as is due to Him: On the Day of Resurrection, the whole of the earth will be in His Grasp"* ." In another narration by Muslim, it is stated: "...and the mountains and the trees on one Finger, then He will shake them saying: "I am the King, I am Allah." In a narration of Bukhari, it is said: "Allah will put the heavens on one Finger and the rest of creation on one Finger."

Ibn Mas'ood (ra) informs us in this Hadith that a Jewish rabbi came to the Prophet (saas) and told him that they, the Jews, had found in their Scriptures that on the Day of Judgement Allah (swt) will place the heavens on one Finger, the earths on one Finger, the trees on one Finger, the water on one Finger and the dust on one Finger; and in another narration, that He will place the water on one Finger and all of the rest of creation on another Finger. Thus will He reveal something of His Might and Power and His complete control over all affairs and His sole right to be worshipped.

Benefits Derived From This Hadith

1. The agreement between the Scripture of the Jews and Islam, in that they both confirm that Allah (swt) has Fingers, though they are unlike our fingers and exactly how they are is unknown to us.

2. Evidence of Allah's Might and His Ability to do all things.

3. That laughter for a specific reason is not bad manners.

4. The obligation to accept the truth, whatever its source.

5. Confirmation of two of Allah's Divine Names: (i) Allah (swt), which constitutes proof of Allah's sole right to be worshipped and (ii) Al-Malik (the King), which proves His Divine Attribute of Ownership.

6. Confirmation of Allah's Divine Attribute of Speech in a manner befitting His Majesty.

Relevance of This Hadith to the Subject of the Chapter and to the Subject of *Tawheed*

That the Hadith proves the obligation to glorify Allah (swt) through *Tawheed* and by abstaining from every kind of *Shirk*.

..ooOOoo..

Muslim narrates, on the authority of Ibn `Umar (ra) in a *marfoo'* form: "Allah (swt) will fold up the heavens on the Day of Resurrection and then He (swt) will take them in His right Hand and say: "I am the King, where are the tyrants? Where are the arrogant ones?" Then He (swt) will fold up the seven earth and take them in His left Hand and say: "I am the King, where are the tyrants? where are the arrogant ones?"

Ibn `Umar (ra) informs us that he heard from the Prophet (saas) that on the Day of Judgement, Allah (swt), Most Glorified, Most High, will fold up the seven heavens and take them in His right Hand and He will fold up the seven earth and take them in His left Hand and as He folds each of them, He will call forth the tyrants and the arrogant people, making them realise their insignificance by His Words: "I am the King." - i.e. He is the true Owner of all things; He is Perfect in every respect and there is no weakness or defect in Him and that all those who claim kingship or sovereignty are in fact weak and feeble, powerless in His Grasp. He will not be asked about what He does, but they will be asked.

Benefits Derived From This Hadith

1. Confirmation of Allah's possessing two Hands, right and left.

2. Confirmation of Allah's Divine Attribute of Speech in a manner befitting His Majesty.

3. Confirmation of Allah's Name: Al-Malik (the King), from which is inferred His Ownership of all things.

4. Evidence that there are seven earths.

5. The forbiddance of tyranny and arrogance.

6. Evidence of Allah's Perfection and infallibility.

Relevance of This Hadith to the Subject of the Chapter and to the Subject of *Tawheed*

That the Hadith proves the obligation to glorify Allah (swt), Almighty All-powerful, by Declaring and practising *Tawheed* in all one's affairs and abstaining from all manner of *Shirk*.

..ooOOoo..

It is reported on the authority of Ibn `Abbas (ra) that he said: "The seven heavens and the seven earths are no more in Allah's Hand than a mustard seed in the hand of one of you."

Ibn `Abbas (ra) informs us in this narration that the seven heavens and the seven earths in comparison to Allah's Hand - in spite of their enormity - are as insignificant as a mustard seed in a man's hand; and this is a comparison between the heavens and the earths and a mustard seed, not a comparison between Allah's Hand and the hand of man because nothing resembles Allah (swt), either in His Attributes or in His Self.

Benefits Derived From This Narration

1. That the heavens are seven.

2. That the earths are seven.

3. That Ibn `Abbas confirms Allah's Possessing a Hand.

Relevance of This Narration to the Subject of the Chapter and to the Subject of *Tawheed*

That it proves the overwhelming Might and Power of Allah (swt) and the insignificance of His creatures and thus the obligation to glorify Him, Alone, without partners, by professing His Oneness in word and deed.

..ooOOoo..

Ibn Jareer said: " Yoonus told me that Ibn Wahb informed him that Ibn Zaid said: "My father told me: "Allah's Messenger (saas) said: "The seven heavens are no more in comparison to the *Kursi* than seven dirhams set in a shield." Abu Zarr (ra) said: "I heard Allah's Messenger (saas) say: "The *Kursi* is no more in comparison to the `Arsh (Throne) than an iron ring thrown in a vast desert."

The Prophet (saas) informs us in both of the above narration that Allah (swt) possesses a *Kursi* (Footstool) and an `Arsh (Throne) and that they are both immense, though the `Arsh is greater than the *Kursi*, for the comparison of the seven heavens to the *Kursi* is that of seven dirham coins set in a shield, while the comparison of the *Kursi* to the `Arsh is that of a ring thrown in a vast desert. And it has been reported in another Hadith on the authority of Ibn `Abbas (ra) that the *Kursi* is the resting place of the Feet of the Most Beneficent, and that none can estimate its vastness but He (swt), Most Glorified, Most High.

Benefits Derived From These Two Hadith

1. Confirmation of the existence of Allah's `Arsh and His *Kursi* and that they are both His creations.

2. That making comparisons is a valid way of teaching in Islam.

3. Evidence of Allah's Greatness and Glory.

Relevance of These Two Hadith to the Subject of the Chapter and to the Subject of *Tawheed*

That both of them prove the obligation to glorify Allah (swt) by professing His Oneness and abstaining from all manner of *Shirk*.

..ooOOoo..

On the authority of Ibn Mas'ood (ra) it is reported that he said: "Between the lowest heaven and the next is the distance of five hundred years and between each of the seven heavens is the distance of five hundred years and the distance between the seventh heaven and the *Kursi* is also five hundred years and between the *Kursi* and the water is also five hundred years and the `Arsh is above the water and Allah (swt ) is above the `Arsh and nothing is hidden from Allah (swt) of your deeds."

Benefits Derived From These Two Hadith

1. That there is a distance between each of the heavens and between the seventh heaven and the *Kursi* and between the *Kursi* and the water and between the water and the `Arsh, each equivalent to five hundred years' travel.

2. Confirmation of the existence of the *Kursi*, the water and the `Arsh, which is above them.

3. Confirmation of Allah's Divine Attribute of being above His creation.

4. Evidence that Allah's Knowledge encompasses all things.

5. Evidence of Allah's Might and Majesty.

..ooOOoo..

It is reported on the authority of Al-'Abbas (ra) that Allah's Messenger (saas) said:

"Do you know what is the distance between the heaven and the earth?" We said: "Allah (swt) and His Messenger (saas) know best." He (saas) said: "The distance between them is five hundred years and the distance between one heaven and the next is five hundred years and the dimension of each heaven would take five hundred years to travel and there is a sea between the seventh heaven and the `Arsh which has between its lowest and highest ends the distance eqvualent to that between the heavens and the earth. And Allah (swt), Most High, is above that and nothing is withheld from Him of the deeds of the sons of Adam." (Narrated by Abu Dawood and others)

Allah's Messenger (saas) informs us in this Hadith that the distance between each of the seven heavens is equivalent to five hundred years' travel and the distance between the earth and the lowest heaven is also equivalent to five hundred years' travel and between the seventh heaven and the `Arsh is a like distance and that the breadth of each heaven is likewise five hundred years and that Allah (swt ) is above His `Arsh and nothing of His creation is hidden from Him.

Benefits Derived From This Hadith

1. Proof of the distances between the heavens and the earth, between each heaven and between the seventh heaven and the `Arsh.

2. That the seven heavens are separate from each other.

3. That the heavens are masses with a defined breadth.

4. Evidence of the position of the water.

5. Evidence of the existence of the `Arsh.

6. Confirmation of Allah's Divine Attribute of being above His creation.

7. The all-encompassing nature of Allah's Knowledge.

Relevance of This Hadith to the Subject of the Chapter and to the Subject of *Tawheed*

That the Hadith proves the obligation to glorify Allah (swt) by professing and practising *Tawheed* and abstaining from all manner of *Shirk*.

Top | Prev | Next

Made in the USA
Middletown, DE
06 April 2023

28378791R00136